DEMOCRACY'S SCHOOLS

Democracy's Schools

THE RISE OF PUBLIC EDUCATION IN AMERICA

JOHANN N. NEEM

WESTERN WASHINGTON UNIVERSITY

BELLINGHAM, WASHINGTON

Johns Hopkins University Press | *Baltimore*

Johns Hopkins University Press
2715 North Charles Street
Baltimore, Maryland 21218-4363
www.press.jhu.edu

Library of Congress Cataloging-in-Publication Data

Names: Neem, Johann N.
Title: Democracy's schools : the rise of public education in America /
    Johann N. Neem.
Description: Baltimore, Maryland : John Hopkins University Press, 2017. |
    Includes bibliographical references and index.
Identifiers: LCCN 2016049255| ISBN 9781421423203 (hardcover : alk. paper) |
    ISBN 9781421423210 (pbk. : alk. paper) | ISBN 9781421423227 (electronic)
Subjects: LCSH: Public schools—United States—History—19th century. |
    Democracy and education—United States—History—19th century. |
    Education—Aims and objectives—United States—History—19th century. |
    Public schools—United States—History. | Education—United States—History.
Classification: LCC LA215 .N44 2017 | DDC 371.010973—dc23
    LC record available at https://lccn.loc.gov/2016049255

A catalog record for this book is available from the British Library.

Special discounts are available for bulk purchases of this book.
For more information, please contact Special Sales at 410-516-6936 or
specialsales@press.jhu.edu.

Johns Hopkins University Press uses environmentally friendly book materials,
including recycled text paper that is composed of at least
30 percent post-consumer waste, whenever possible.

In this country the mass of the people are distinguished by possessing means of improvement, of self-culture, possessed nowhere else. To incite them to the use of these is to render them the best service they can receive.

William Ellery Channing, "Self-Culture" (1838)

Society does not find ready-made in individual consciousnesses the bases on which it rests; it makes them for itself.

Emile Durkheim, *The Division of Labor in Society* (1893)

GEORGE: I don't see how you can sit still that long. I guess you like school.

EMILY: Well, I always feel it's something you have to go through.

Thornton Wilder, *Our Town* (1938)

CONTENTS

PREFACE

I AM AN IMMIGRANT. My parents and I migrated from Mumbai, India, to the San Francisco Bay area when I was two and a half years old. After a short stay in an apartment near the Naval Air Station in Alameda, we moved to the suburbs. My parents still live in the home where my younger sister and I grew up. I was a suburban California kid.

After preschool, I attended public schools from kindergarten through high school: Sequoia elementary and middle schools, and College Park High School. These schools were diverse, as the Bay Area was filled with recent and not-so-recent immigrant families. Despite and because of this, there was something very American in the way I grew up.

When I was in the fifth grade, we became citizens. I remember attending the swearing-in ceremony with my parents and other new Americans in a courthouse in San Francisco. When I returned to school, one of my closest friends, Mike, handed me a card signed by my fifth-grade classmates, with a pin of the American flag attached to it. I still have it.

The schools brought us all together. We went to pumpkin patches and carved jack-o-lanterns. We learned about American literature and history, and considered these inheritances to be our own. I am still in touch with my first-grade teacher, Mrs. Cooley, who taught me to love reading. In third grade, my teachers read *Where the Red Fern Grows*, and we all cried at the end. I lost the spelling bee that same year to my friend Will, who knew how to spell Wyoming. I remember in eleventh-grade English reading *The Woman Warrior*, a book by a Chinese American author. Books took us from the rural Ozarks to contemporary California. Our teachers introduced us to the American experience in all its wonderful diversity and complexity.

The schools were for all Americans, and the schools helped make us Americans. My public education prepared me for success. My teachers, and of course my family, cultivated the dispositions, developed the skills, and provided the knowledge vital for my future life. I interacted with people whom I might not otherwise have known. I learned that I was part of something larger than myself, that I belonged to a nation with a past, a present, and a future.

And that is why the common schools mattered then, and why they matter today. They are democracy's schools. As such, they reflect all the tensions and contradictions one might expect of democratic institutions. And, by democratizing access to the kind of liberal education that was once reserved for the few, the common schools prepare all young people to take part in the shared life of our democracy.

I am thankful for my public school education. This book therefore is dedicated to my teachers.

ACKNOWLEDGMENTS

AS EVERYONE KNOWS, A BOOK TAKES A VILLAGE. I have accumulated many debts. I am particularly grateful to the Spencer Foundation, the University of Virginia's Institute for Advanced Studies in Culture, and Western Washington University for their financial support. During my two years at the institute, the institute's scholars provided intellectual fellowship and personal support. I am thankful for the institute's sponsorship of a day-long workshop in Charlottesville to discuss an earlier draft of this book. Rachel Hope Cleves, Joseph E. Davis, Thomas Fallace, Jeffrey Guhin, and Reeve Huston devoted hours to dissecting my manuscript. The book would have been significantly different, and worse, without their intervention. I also benefited immensely from Joseph F. Kett's engagement with early drafts of each chapter.

My editors Elizabeth Demers, Robin Einhorn, and Richard R. John collectively read several drafts and offered thoughtful criticism and ideas throughout the process. I am also grateful to the manuscript's anonymous reviewers. Brian MacDonald edited the final draft for publication. Specific chapters were critiqued at various stages by Tyler Anbinder, Jeff Appelhans, Edward Ayers, Mark Boonshoft, Mary Kupiec Cayton, Carolyn Eastman, Allison Giffen, Mark I. Greenberg, Robert Gross, Daniel Walker Howe, Barbara McClay, Christine Ogren, Gail Radford, Aaron Sheehan-Dean, David Steinberg, J. Mills Thornton III, Kyle Volk, Rachel Wahl, and Jonathan Daniel Wells. Isaac Reed read the entire draft. Jason Opal met with me early on in this project to help me think through my ideas. Lunch conversations with E. D. Hirsch Jr. connected my questions about the past with the challenges of the present. In Charlottesville, I received consistent encouragement and ideas from Christa Dierksheide, Max Edelson, Charles T. Mathewes, Andrew O'Shaughnessy, and Alan Taylor.

The capacity of scholars to complete their research and to learn from colleagues takes time and money. In other words, historians depend on the infrastructure that sustains the American academy—colleges and universities; libraries, museums, and archives; conferences, journals, and academic presses. I want to acknowledge the help that I received from the librarians and staff at the Massachusetts Historical Society, the New-York Historical Society, and the University of Virginia and Western Washington University libraries.

Scholarly societies are vital for incubating new ideas. My intellectual home is the Society for Historians of the Early American Republic (SHEAR). My understanding of the early American republic has been enriched immeasurably through conversations with my SHEAR colleagues. In this book, I aim to bring a broader understanding of the early American republic to the history of education. Simultaneously, I hope that the history of education can further our understanding of the early American republic. That would not have been possible if it were not for another scholarly society, the History of Education Society, which has cultivated important scholarship influencing every chapter of this book.

I received feedback on some of the key ideas in this book during a panel presentation at the Society for U.S. Intellectual History's 2015 annual conference. I thank Rosemarie Zagarri for her queries as commentator, James T. Kloppenberg for serving as chair and offering his own thoughts, and my co-panelists Leslie Butler and Kyle Volk for their ideas. Early iterations of my work were also presented to the Early American Seminar, convened by the University of Virginia History Department and the Robert H. Smith International Center for Jefferson Studies at Monticello; the Dublin Seminar for New England Folklife at Historic Deerfield; and brown bag seminars at the Massachusetts Historical Society and the School of Policy, Government, and International Affairs at George Mason University.

As anyone in this field knows, the prospect of writing a new book on the origins of American public schools is not only a daunting task on its own terms but made more so by the fact that one is standing on the shoulders of giants. The most important predecessor to this book is Carl Kaestle's 1983 *The Pillars of the Republic: Common Schools and American Society, 1780–1860*. I have read and reread Professor Kaestle's book. My copy is underlined and dog-eared and held together by rubber bands. It is well loved. I was almost finished with my book before I had the opportunity to meet Professor Kaestle in Providence for lunch last year. I thank him for his generous encouragement.

In many ways, this book is a return to my roots. I wrote my senior thesis on civic education in a democracy for historian and education professor Ted Sizer and education policy expert Don Ernst. Ted and Don were inspiring mentors for a young person aspiring to be a scholar. Ted is no longer with us, but I thought of him regularly as I wrote. I hope that this book will be a testament to how much I learned from him. I miss him dearly.

I have been supported by my colleagues and friends in the History Department at Western Washington University. I appreciate Western's willingness to allow me two years leave to write this book. My chair Kevin Leonard's support has been indispensable. Conversations with Kevin, Steven Garfinkle, A. Ricardo López, Niall Ó Murchú, Jennifer Seltz, and Mart Stewart remind me how lucky I am to have ended up at such a good institution.

Teachers matter, and I have had the good fortune to have had many wonderful teachers, from preschool through graduate school. My PhD adviser Peter Onuf remains a model for me. As a teacher today, I can only hope that I have some of the impact on my students that my teachers have had on me. I thank all of them.

My partner, Kate Destler, and I met in college. Both of us were interested in education reform. Today, she writes about it as a public policy scholar. In conversation and in her comments on various drafts of this book, Kate consistently encouraged me to clarify my ideas. Our children, Rylan and Avery, are now in the public schools. As a parent, I realize how much trust it takes to send one's children off to school. Parents must have confidence that schools will keep children safe, encourage their intellectual development, foster their character, and nurture their souls. Our children have had teachers and administrators who have earned that trust through their hard work, intelligence, and care.

DEMOCRACY'S SCHOOLS

Introduction

SCHOOLS COMPOSE THAT PART OF EDUCATION not provided by experience, other institutions, or families. They prepare us for the world and acculturate us to the values and norms of our society. They express our values at their best as well as at their worst since they are institutions that are part of our larger history. Because they are devoted to children, they also reveal our dreams, our aspirations, and our anxieties.

At their most basic level, public schools exist because the quality of our democracy depends on the quality of our citizens. Are we intelligent and thoughtful? Do we seek the common good? Yet a democratic education comprises even more than citizenship. It embodies an aspiration. Thomas Jefferson, in the Declaration of Independence, proclaimed that all people have the right to pursue happiness. This meant creating a society in which people could pursue private goods as well as public ones. It also meant endowing each American with the capabilities to engage in these pursuits. A democracy, then, owes something to every young person.

The origins of American public schools lie in the connection between these two democratic imperatives—preparing citizens and enabling each person to pursue her or his happiness. Colonial education had been haphazard and largely took place in churches and families, not schools. By the Civil War, however, most young free Americans attended public elementary schools, and a growing number entered public high schools. By the eve of the Civil War, most northern states had made schools free, paid for by taxes, and many southern states were heading in the same direction. Americans had come to see education as a public good worthy of public investment.

The rise of mass public education was not limited to the United States; state-sponsored education was a transatlantic phenomenon as nation-states turned to schools to foster a common culture. Across Europe, governments began investing more resources in schools. Yet the fact that America was a democracy—and, for white Americans, a particularly egalitarian democracy at that—made a difference.

Our schools were democracy's schools in four important ways. They were local in their origins; they promoted a curriculum designed to prepare people for citizenship and self-culture; disagreements over public schools became part of democratic politics; and citizens struggled to balance the needs of the broader community with the rights of religious and other minorities in a diverse society.

In the decades after the Revolution, American schools were truly local institutions. This mattered. They were organized, run, and built by the labor of ordinary citizens who pooled their time and resources to provide a public good. Localism was, on the one hand, a strategy for building public institutions at a time when state legislatures had few resources of their own and, on the other hand, a democratic principle. Committed to self-rule, American citizens wanted public schools that were funded by local taxes, overseen by locally elected trustees, and closely tied to the communities that they served.

This localism was successful. In the new United States, the greatest growth in school attendance before the Civil War took place before there was significant government oversight and taxes. And even when state governments mandated longer terms, certified teachers, or higher taxes, these mandates were passed by popularly elected legislators and implemented by schools run by locally elected officials.

Ordinary Americans saw the value of education—especially elementary education—and cooperated to provide it for their children. Americans enrolled more students in public schools, as a percent of population, than most European countries (see appendix, tables 1 and 2).[1] According to the 1850 census, about 56 percent of all white children aged five to nineteen were enrolled in schools, but there was significant regional variation.[2] Northern states had among the highest enrollment rates in the world. One study concludes that by 1850, around 80 percent of eleven- to twelve-year-old white children were enrolled in schools in the Northeast, and a little over a half of eleven- to twelve-year-old white children were enrolled in the South.[3]

In 1850 boys and girls up to age fourteen enrolled in school at the same rate.[4] More girls attended high school than did boys (in part perhaps because they did not have the choice of getting a job).[5] African Americans' access to public schooling was much lower than that of white Americans and limited to free states. In New York on the eve of the Civil War, about 28 percent of black children were in school, compared to about 38 percent in Pennsylvania, and about 40 percent in Ohio. In the entire South, on the other hand, only 3 percent of free black children were enrolled. In 1850 only 2 percent of black children aged five to nineteen were enrolled in schools (black and white enrollment did not equalize until around 1970).[6]

It was not just their local quality that made them democracy's schools. Their curriculum was designed to provide a democratic education. Initially, the focus was on citizenship, but by the 1830s reformers had also started to emphasize schools' cultural purposes. Reformers like Massachusetts's Horace Mann argued that public schools must not only bring together a diverse society but also encourage what Mann and other reformers called "self-culture." This was the age of the self-made American. America, it was said, was a land where one could make it if one was independent and worked hard. The new United States would have no aristocracy or nobility. Ordinary people could determine for themselves what they wanted to do with their lives and what kind of people they would become.

Yet self-made men and women, educators argued, did not make themselves out of nothing. They needed help. Public schools were vital to developing each child's potential. Education reformers sought to provide ordinary Americans access to the kind of education that, in much of Europe, would have been considered appropriate only for an elite. Every child, reformers argued, deserved a liberal education, one designed to offer children the riches of knowledge and to enable them to seek higher learning if they were capable of doing so.

To many Americans, reformers' efforts to make an elite education accessible to every child was in itself elitist. To these Americans, the kinds of schools reformers wanted were expensive and unnecessary. They disagreed that every American needed as much education as the educated seemed, condescendingly, to think. To reformers, education was the source of freedom. To other Americans, common sense, life experience, and actions mattered more than formal schooling.

These disagreements entered politics, the third way in which the schools were democracy's schools. Reformers tried to bring America's schools, which were rooted in local communities, under the supervision of public professionals. They believed that professional educators knew better what to teach and how to teach it than did ordinary people. They worried that the quality of American public education would never improve if schools remained local institutions. In short, in order to achieve their vision of democratic education, they challenged the local foundations of education in American democracy. And many Americans resisted, ensuring that the content and form of schools would become a perpetual subject of public deliberation and party politics.

Finally, in an increasingly diverse society, Americans sought to balance the rights of individuals and minorities with the needs of a democratic social order. As the number of immigrants increased during the 1830s, diversity became a political issue. Many of the new immigrants were Catholics in a country that had taken Protestantism for granted. Many came from nondemocratic nations. Some Americans argued that a democracy's respect for minority rights meant allowing parents to choose their children's schools. Others argued that a diverse society depended on common institutions so that citizens could learn to care for each other and to sustain a common world. African American leaders agreed, arguing that common schools were the precondition for equality. These disagreements also found their way into public conversations and democratic politics.

Our public schools have been at the center of our concerns because education is so important to shaping the hearts and minds of young people, and because it is so important to our collective life as well. So let us begin in the days immediately following the Revolution, when Americans could not take the republic for granted. Education was at the center of Americans' concerns then, as it is for so many of us today. Let us think about why so many American reformers wanted to expand access to schooling, and what they hoped public education, in its ideal form, might have looked like (chapters 1–2). And then let us follow the story out as the reformers' vision entered the world of democratic politics (chapter 3), real-life classrooms (chapter 4), and the complicated realities of a diverse society (chapter 5).

1 Citizenship and Self-Culture

A Republic, if You Can Keep It

EDWARD TIFFIN, OHIO'S FIRST GOVERNOR, argued in 1804 that while republican government is "instituted for the benefit of the governed, yet, if they have not the means of acquiring a knowledge of their rights, they will never feel their value, and will, consequently, not be careful to guard against their invasion."[1] America's leaders across the land echoed Tiffin's sentiment. In a society in which the people are sovereign and responsible for choosing—and watching over—their own leaders, every citizen needed an education.

For the Founders, a republic could only be as good as its citizens. The Constitution had been written in secret, but when the authors of the Constitution emerged from their heated debates in humid Philadelphia, Benjamin Franklin, the elder statesman, was asked what kind of government they were proposing. "A republic, if you can keep it," Franklin supposedly replied.

History offered cause for concern. Well read in the classics of ancient Greece and Rome, as well as in the history of seventeenth- and eighteenth-century England, the Founders believed that republics were fragile and hard to maintain over time. The success of the United States was not to be taken for granted. Faced with threats from without—both European and Native American powers—the republic had to be strong from within. Everywhere one turned, the founding generation invoked the need for educated citizens. "The throne of tyranny is founded in ignorance," one observer commented in the 1790s. "Literature and liberty go hand in hand."[2]

If most Americans agreed that an educated citizenry was essential to a free society, a second question proved more difficult to answer. Did a person need an education to be free? In the 1830s, more and more Americans answered yes. Education, they argued, was vital to helping people form an understanding of themselves and their world. Education was thus the precondition for self-making or, in the words of the time, "self-culture." A person was not born free but made free through learning. A good education was like "lighting up a central sun in the imagination where all was darkness before."[3]

Yet this ideal was contested. Many Americans argued that it was not taxpayers' responsibility to do more than the basics. Starting in the 1830s, then, education divided Americans as much as it brought them together.

Citizens

The lessons of history were mixed. The ancient Greek historian Polybius taught American leaders that republics fail when citizens or leaders lose civic virtue, or the desire to put the good of society ahead of their own self-interest. The Roman historian Livy argued that all free societies face constant conflict between elites and the people at large—the plebeians. The Greek philosopher Aristotle argued that any government, whether by the few or the many, had its own virtues and vices. Aristocratic governments had the virtue of being run by wisdom but suffered from the vice of placing the interests of the few over the many. A pure democracy, on the other hand, was in danger of succumbing to popular passion. Americans worried that the people might be swayed by a charismatic demagogue, a Julius Caesar or Oliver Cromwell.

The risks to the republic thus came from both the few and the many, from the elite and the people themselves. Finding a way to prepare both people and their leaders for self-government was a fundamental—perhaps the fundamental—challenge facing Americans after independence. Education was a central component of their efforts to meet this challenge.

Everywhere—in the letters and writings of the Founders, in magazines, and in parlors—Americans discussed education. Many of the new state constitutions asserted the importance of an educated public. Massachusetts's 1780 constitution considered it "the duty of legislatures and magistrates . . . to cherish the interests of literature and the sciences, and all seminaries of them," including "public schools." Georgia's 1777 constitution proclaimed, "Schools shall be erected in each county, and supported at the general expense of the State." Americans thus asserted that it was the responsibility of the public—of legislators—to increase access to schooling for all citizens.

This was a profound and transformative claim. Although we still have much to learn about schooling before the American Revolution, evidence suggests it was limited, informal, and sporadic. This is not to say that children did not receive an education, but that structured schooling in special buildings subsidized by tax dollars and composing a large part of a child's life did not yet exist.

The major exception was New England. In 1642, the Massachusetts Bay Colony required all children be taught to read and to "understand the principles of religion & the capitall lawes of this country." Five years later, the colonial legislature required that towns with more than a hundred families support a public grammar school. Connecticut, too, devoted public funds to schooling so that all children could gain basic literacy and knowledge of religion. In other colonies, education was more haphazard. Most children learned basic literacy—if they learned it at all—at home. Private schoolmasters would keep school in colonial cities or travel the countryside charging parents tuition for lessons. Colonial laws often required master craftsmen to provide their apprentices with religious instruction and teach them how to read. Because education was tied to faith, churches were often the most important educational institutions. Whether lessons were transmitted orally from the pulpit to the entire community or in church schools for younger children of the parish, the goal was to ensure that young people were raised in piety.

Most colonists simply did not expect every child to have a formal education. Basic literacy could be learned in a variety of places, and children picked up the skills that they needed for work or to care for the home by watching their parents or being apprenticed to others. The community's most important concern was faith, not citizenship, which is why churches rather than the government were responsible for education. While religion remained important after the American Revolution, the Revolution added a new urgency to expanding and formalizing the institutions through which Americans were educated. The new republic now depended on it.[4]

The Few and the Many

American leaders approached education from two perspectives. To some, the real risk to the republic lay in the people, who were ignorant, selfish, and easily swayed. Schools were needed to make them fit for a free society. To others, like Thomas Jefferson, the real risk to freedom came from the leaders. Elites, Jefferson believed, tended to corrupt governments by using political power to serve themselves. The people were moral but needed education to be effective guardians of their liberty. Freedom had to be protected not from the people but from their rulers.

Both perspectives guided Americans, and both were equally important to shaping Americans' commitment to education between the Revolution and the Civil War. Given the weakness of human nature—the sinfulness of post-Edenic humanity—it was vital that all Americans be taught the "Love of the Deity" and "Love of their Country," Samuel Adams wrote his cousin John in fall 1790. The "Virtues of the Christian system," Adams hoped, would "subdue the turbulent passions of Men."[5]

To Benjamin Rush, a Philadelphia doctor, signer of the Declaration of Independence, and friend to both John Adams and Jefferson, all American boys and girls must receive an education grounded in Christianity to correct for human weakness. If the people cannot otherwise be trusted, they must be made trustworthy so that the new American republic could avoid the tragic fate of all previous republics, ancient or modern.

In his widely read pamphlet *Of the Mode of Education Proper in a Republic* (1798), Dr. Rush made his case for increasing access to education. In his native Pennsylvania, the Revolution had been particularly divisive. Because long-standing tensions between different political and religious factions came to the fore, reestablishing political stability after independence was challenging. Pennsylvanians had embraced one of the most egalitarian constitutions of any state after independence, but critics, concerned about the lack of checks on popular passion, struggled to develop a more complicated system that balanced popular control with elite influence. In addition, Pennsylvania was among the most religiously diverse of the colonies; at the time of independence, perhaps about a third of the state's population spoke German and attended German Lutheran or Reformed churches.

Rush wondered how to bring together such an ethnically and religiously diverse and politically fragmented state. He believed that Pennsylvania would remain free if and only if its citizens could work together to serve their common good. Unlike in a monarchy in which the common good was the responsibility of a single sovereign, in the new United States every citizen, through voting, influencing public discussions, and running for office, had a role to play.

Education must encourage citizens to serve their community. Left to their own devices, Rush concluded, people were more likely to pursue their immediate self-interest than to think about their neighbors. A devout Christian, Dr. Rush believed deeply that citizens must learn to care about their neighbors. He thus urged schools to encourage patriotism among young people. He also believed that patriotism—the love of Pennsylvania and the United States—would overcome some of the state's divisions, rendering a pluralistic society "more homogeneous." Every young person must "be taught to love his fellow creatures in every part of the world, but he must cherish with a more intense and peculiar affection, the citizens of Pennsylvania and the United States." In fact, Rush famously wrote, a good education would "convert men into republican machines," who would put the common good ahead of their own economic, ethnic, or religious interests.[6]

To others, history taught a different lesson. American poet Joel Barlow, writing in 1801 from France, reminded his fellow Americans that "ignorance is everywhere such an infallible instrument of despotism." The only way to sustain free societies was by "diffusing universally among the people that portion of instruction which is sufficient to teach them their duties and their rights."[7] South Carolina's governor Henry Middleton noted in 1811 that "a system of general instruction is essential to the preservation of our political institutions."[8]

This was Thomas Jefferson's perspective. The author of the Declaration of Independence believed that history proved that the people were more often the wronged than the wrongdoers. To Jefferson, political elites and church leaders had conspired to maintain their power at the expense of ordinary people. A good education would give all young people the skills and knowledge that they would need to understand and to protect their liberties. For too long the knowledge necessary to undertake a meaningful life and to secure liberty had been kept locked up by the few. Jefferson hoped to "diffuse" it to the many—he anticipated a fundamental redistribution of knowledge so that every American, no matter how poor, would have access to it. To educate the few and leave the rest in ignorance, Jefferson thought, not only violated God's creation of us as equal but also threatened liberty by denying each of us the ability to police our leaders.

Like Rush, Jefferson hoped that the American Revolution would lead to an education revolution. He wanted his home state of Virginia to offer free schools to every Virginian or, to be more accurate, every white Virginian. Jefferson was a slave owner, and while he believed that enslaved African Americans were also entitled to life, liberty, and the pursuit of happiness, his racism prevented him from embracing a multiracial republic. On the other hand, Jefferson wanted every white Virginian (including immigrants) to be able to go to school. He proposed a pyramid structure in which elementary schools would teach every boy and girl in Virginia the basic skills (such as reading, writing, and arithmetic) and knowledge (such as history, science, and ethics) necessary both for their own private pursuits and for effective citizenship. Elementary education would endow every Virginian with the ability "to judge for himself what will secure or endanger his freedom."[9]

Jefferson did not assume that all students were equally gifted. He anticipated that the better students would become the state's leaders and would need more education. Students continuing into higher education—beyond the elementary level—needed access to cultural literacy, or the knowledge offered by the liberal arts, if they were to have the capacity to make smart decisions about the public welfare. He proposed teaching advanced students not just critical thinking and ethics but also ancient and modern history, mathematics, physics, chemistry, anatomy, medical theory, zoology, botany, mineralogy, philosophy, legal ethics, the law of nature and of nations, and the principles of government and political economy.

Jefferson worried that only the rich would have access to the liberal arts, so he proposed that local officials choose each year one poor but promising boy to attend grammar school (where he would learn Greek and Latin) at taxpayer expense. The best among them would attend Virginia's then only college, the College of William and Mary, at public expense. Jefferson hoped that making higher education free for those students who displayed academic talent and good morals would encourage the next generation of leaders to come not just from rich families but from families of all incomes from all regions of the state.[10]

Whether they saw the people as corrupt or noble, American leaders agreed that a republic would fail without education. Civic motives dominated the founding generation's commitment to public education. The goal was to prepare citizens to govern themselves and to watch over their leaders. The people were not naturally able to govern, but instead had to be made capable of carrying out their civic duties. For Americans, this tension would never go away: education in a democracy simultaneously would seek to make the people safe for free government and to make the people capable of participating in free government.

Equally notable, the founding generation was committed to educating both boys and girls, and for civic reasons. Jefferson's proposals for public elementary schools explicitly included girls. Noah Webster, who is famous for his effort to simplify the English language for Americans, wrote in 1790 that women, responsible for educating "their own children," must be educated so that America's youngest were brought up with "such sentiments of virtue, propriety, and dignity as are suited to the freedom of our governments." Women needed an education not just to teach their own children but because women shaped "the manners of a nation."[11]

Dr. Rush agreed. Because women were partners on the farm and responsible for rearing children, girls should be introduced to all the important subjects—language, grammar, writing, numeracy, bookkeeping, geography, history, morality. Rush still wanted these educated American women to be pleasant company, so he also urged them to study music and dancing.[12]

The Idea of Equality

"We hold these truths to be self-evident, that all men are created equal." Americans took Jefferson's words from the Declaration of Independence seriously. They meant more than having rights. By the 1830s, ordinary Americans thought of themselves as equal to elite Americans. Such a thing had never been seen in the history of the world, and it took foreign observers by surprise. Europeans were amazed that ordinary Americans did not defer to their social betters. Alexis de Tocqueville, a French aristocrat whose family had suffered during the French Revolution, came to the United States in the 1830s because he believed that democracy was the future. He then returned to France to compose his two-volume classic *Democracy in America* (1835, 1840). Tocqueville considered "the equality of conditions as the original fact" of American society. Not only were Americans more equal to each other than the rich and poor of Europe, but they also actually thought that they were equal to each other.

Equality had a more limited meaning than it does today. It obviously did not apply to enslaved people. Moreover, free African Americans continued to face racism in law and culture. With the exception of New Jersey, where women could vote until 1807, women in post-Revolutionary United States lacked formal political power. Despite its limitations, this idea of equality was still profound. It transformed social relations by abolishing centuries-old presumptions that the better sort were in fact better than others. It meant that in growing cities and in the

West, social order was hard to read since it was unclear where people belonged. And who was to say where someone belonged? And who had the right to?

Moreover, the world around Americans was changing quickly. By the 1830s, American society looked very different from the world in which the Revolutionary generation had grown up. Industries developed, particularly along New England's rivers, where there was fast-running water to turn factories' mill wheels. More Americans moved west. International trade increased, and, as foreign demand for cotton skyrocketed, Americans increasingly invested in slavery. In such a mobile world, individuals were cast adrift from the agrarian structures that had once defined life. People had not only the opportunity but, in a market economy, the obligation to figure out how to make it on their own. Thus, equality brought new responsibilities. Self-making was an awesome opportunity, but failure was as much a possibility.[13]

But what did it mean to make a self? This was the question that educators sought to answer. Education is always about forming people, but by the 1830s, new ideas, many shaped by European intellectual currents, had provided new answers. Would Americans be able to shake off what one historian has called the psychology of dependence and become true individuals? Or would democracy lead to a world in which an individual's potential was left fallow and undeveloped? Tocqueville worried that it would be the latter. "I see two very clear tendencies in equality," he commented. "One impels each individual toward new ways of thinking, while the other would induce him to give up thinking voluntarily." In short, would equality enable and inspire "the human spirit" or would it instead lead to a mass society in which each person became subject to "the sway of public opinion"?[14]

American education reformers wagered that they could achieve the former, a society in which, through schools and other cultural institutions, from museums and historical societies to local libraries, Americans would take the opportunity of self-making seriously. They would lead lives that mattered. But this challenging task would require support from the community. Ultimately, it required broad access to education.

Self-Culture

Educators came to see young people as lamps, not mirrors—as subjects who must shed their own light upon the world rather than reflect what they observed. Each person, in short, must be a work of art. Developing her or his inner potential required a new kind of education.[15] In a world in which the old hierarchies had been rent asunder, Americans now had the opportunity to use their newfound freedom and rights to make themselves. People would have to pull themselves up by their own bootstraps, but self-making for Americans meant more than economic success. It meant that people had the opportunity to develop their innate capabilities, revealing souls of amazing potential.

The most influential advocate of self-culture was Rev. William Ellery Channing, a founder of American Unitarianism, who was born in the seaport town of Newport, Rhode Island, in April 1780. His father, a lawyer, died when Channing was thirteen. When he was just under fifteen, Channing entered Harvard College. After graduation, he worked as a tutor in Virginia. In 1802, he received his MA in theology, and in February 1803 he was called to Boston's Federal Street Church, where his ministry commenced.

In the 1820s Channing challenged New England ministers by arguing that ideas dating back to Calvin about original sin and depravity denied each individual's power to shape her or his own character. Called Unitarians because they claimed that God was singular (thus denying the trinity), the movement Channing came to represent divided churches up and down New England. Channing was at the center of the storm. His claims about the innate goodness of the human soul were controversial. While he shaped the ideas of many of the leading educators of his day, he was also a source of division, and thus many Americans would challenge his—and his followers'—efforts to reform education.

As a young person in the 1790s Channing found himself deeply moved while reading the Scottish moral philosopher Francis Hutcheson's work on what, in the eighteenth century, was known as the "moral sense" or "conscience." That each of us has a conscience within us was an inspiring thought to Channing. Who put it there? What is it for? How does it develop? What does it mean if it is not developed? Ultimately, Channing went beyond the limits of the moral sense to the soul itself. He was influenced by discussions among New England ministers about the relationship between free will and God's absolute power, by ideas that crossed the Atlantic from Scotland, and, increasingly, by new European ideas that emphasized the importance of people's inner experiences.[16]

To Channing and his followers, education had an even nobler purpose than preparing people to be citizens. Education must also enable each person to engage in self-making. Self-making was not about getting ahead or making money but about developing oneself in the image of God. Born equal before God, endowed with a shared nature, each person was entitled to an opportunity to develop her

Figure 1.1. William Ellery Channing (ca. 1842). Collection of the
Massachusetts Historical Society

or his inner potential. A democratic society—a Christian society—would therefore offer more than civic education; it would help human beings develop themselves.

Channing's most important lecture, which was excerpted and reprinted in
education journals, was "Self-Culture," given in 1838. It was intended as part of
a series of lectures for the working people of Boston.[17] Channing believed that
everyone was inherently equal. He told his audience of working men that he was
not interested in them for their "usefulness to the community" but rather for
"what they are in themselves." Ordinary people could not stand out "from the
multitude," but this did not matter since "every man, in every condition, is great."
Each person was endowed with "powers of intellect, of conscience, of love, of
knowing God, of perceiving the beautiful, of acting on his own mind, on outward
nature, and on his fellow-creatures." The elements shared by all human beings are
most worth celebrating: "The common is the most precious."

Because each person was "the image of God, the image even of his infinity,
for no limits can be set to its unfolding," within each person were "germs and

promises of a growth to which no bounds can be set." To make good on this potential, we were endowed with "a still nobler power, that of acting on, determining and forming ourselves." To form a self, however, was no easy feat. The capacity to engage in self-culture was, Channing admitted, "a fearful as well as glorious endowment." All our potentialities could be guided and managed by our efforts, in order to take what is native to us and "cultivate" it. "Growth, expansion is the end." Every person can and must do all he can "to unfold all his powers and capacities, especially his nobler ones."

Every person deserved an education, Channing concluded, "because he is a man, not because he is to make shoes, nails, or pins." To educate some for work and others to appreciate beauty was to commit a crime against human nature. "A rational, moral being cannot, without infinite wrong, be converted into a mere instrument of others' gratification." That meant that every human being was entitled to a "liberal education."

Some say, Channing added, that "a liberal education is needed for men who are to fill high stations, but not for such as are doomed to vulgar labor." But, Channing responded, no person was just a worker; every person was a human being. Every person thus "has close, tender, responsible connections with God and his fellow creatures." Each of us is "a son, husband, father, friend, and Christian." Each person "belongs to a home, a country, a church, a race." Americans therefore should not tolerate a "social order" in which a few were entitled to develop themselves to the fullest, and the rest were left to toil. No society was just when it "can only be upheld by crippling and blinding the Minds of the people," not simply because free societies required educated citizens but because the very dignity of human beings required that they be allowed to cultivate their powers.

Channing considered self-culture the essence of being American—it was the ability to develop one's capacities to their fullest to gain the most of one's experience. A democratic education would open the riches of the natural and human worlds to all people—to allow each young person to gain insight into the nature of things. To offer some such a rich experience of the world and to leave others without it was an abrogation of the idea that all people in a democracy are equal.

Channing's presumption that every person was equal was radical. While the ideal of self-culture circulated among thinkers on both sides of the Atlantic, Americans went beyond their European counterparts to argue that self-culture was the right and duty of every child.[18]

Intellectual and Moral Formation

Not all American reformers were as romantic as Channing, but they shared with him a belief that democratic education must encourage self-culture. Thus, Dartmouth professor C. B. Haddock argued that, while educating citizens is essential in a democracy—"no community," he wrote, "has long existed, or can long exist, without intelligence and virtue"—we come together in society to ensure "intellectual and moral progress." In other words, "we seek not to live for the sake of living, but for what there is to live for." We cannot do that alone. Thus, the real goal of living together in society is "the development of the faculties and the perfection of the character of man as man,—as an intellectual, a moral, and religious being, capable of indefinite progress, of boundless attainment, of an intense personal and spiritual life." Because we were not intended to be mere "hewers of wood and drawers of water," Haddock believed, "the education of the many, is, next to the spiritual salvation of the race, ultimately, even as a means of this salvation itself."[19]

Nobody made the case for self-culture more strongly than Horace Mann. Born in 1796 in Franklin, Massachusetts, the fourth of five children, Horace received his early education at home and in a local district school. His father, Thomas, died of consumption when Mann was only thirteen. When Mann was nineteen, he started taking lessons to prepare for college. In 1819 he graduated from Brown University and entered the world ambitious but uncertain. After studying law, Mann embarked on a legal career in Dedham, which prepared him to enter politics. He served on the town school committee and, in 1827, was elected as the town's junior representative to the state legislature. He supported John Quincy Adams and later joined the Whig Party. In contrast to Democrats like Andrew Jackson, Whigs like Mann believed that the state had an obligation to improve individuals and society by developing their moral, intellectual, and economic potential.[20]

After the death of his beloved wife Charlotte in 1832, just two years after their marriage, Mann felt lost and alone. Realizing the depth of Mann's depression, his good friend Elizabeth Peabody, herself an important intellectual and teacher in Massachusetts, introduced him to the Rev. Channing, who was to have a profound influence on Mann's understanding of education. When Massachusetts established a board of education in 1837, Mann became its first secretary. During his first year, he not only read widely about education and pedagogy but also trav-

Figure 1.2. Horace Mann. Library of Congress, LC-USZ62-109928

eled more than five hundred miles on horseback to learn about conditions in the state's schools and to build support for their improvement.

Mann, like others, believed that a democracy depended fundamentally on educated citizens. But schools also had to promote self-culture, which Mann, like Channing, believed was a democratic right. Access to science and literature must be *"spread amongst the people,"* he argued: "Let not the quest for new discoveries cease; let philosopher after philosopher reveal more and more of the wonderful works of nature, and thus present to all men new reasons for adoration of the Creator."[21]

Mann saw in every human being a plant worthy of cultivation—of internal development. All the faculties of the mind must be developed in the proper order to ensure "natural order and progression," just as plants grow from seeds in natural progression. People were not empty vessels to be filled but rather untapped potential who must be fertilized to grow. Because reading can open up new worlds for students when they analyze the texts themselves, Mann condemned those who taught reading by focusing solely on "pronunciation, emphasis, and cadence"—an emphasis that too often robbed students of their love of writing. Writing is a form of creation, Mann believed, and "young students desire to be composers." Thus, reading and writing—all learning—must foster insight, to help people see the world with fresh eyes.[22]

The Imagination

Because self-making was creative, it was ultimately imaginative, and thus one of the goals of public education was nothing less than democratizing access to imagination. Education reformers hoped that by giving Americans access to the richness of the liberal arts, they could help students to imagine new worlds—to truly create their lives. Self-making could not be done without knowledge—it required it. Imagination would be enriched by studying subjects like history, which revealed the ideas and experiences of others, and science, which provided knowledge of God's creative force in nature. The arts and sciences would offer students perspectives not available elsewhere, providing knowledge students could draw on as they sought to make worlds of their own. The liberal arts were thus necessary to enable people to be effective citizens and to foster self-culture.

American educators were influenced by the ideas of Scottish philosophers like Dugald Stewart, who concluded his exhaustive volume on *Elements of the Philosophy of Mind* (1792) with an examination of how imagination enabled the mind to move beyond what we perceived with our senses "to form a new creation of its own." "All the objects of human knowledge" inspired imagination, Stewart believed. Milton and Shakespeare took all that they had learned and then used their imagination to produce beautiful works of art. This poetic ability belonged by nature to every child, but education was required to cultivate it.[23]

In the eighteenth century, people also believed that imagination was vital to morality. According to Adam Smith, imagination allowed us to put ourselves in others' situations and to feel their joy or pain, which, in turn, enabled us to regulate our own actions according to how others might perceive them, something that neither the senses nor reason alone could do.[24]

Some Americans worried that formal education risked "impairing the imagination" because schools offered dry material that did not inspire young people to learn. But, one observer responded, it took knowledge to foster imagination.

Why would one want a young person to imagine "nothing but fogs and false-hood"? It was a "strange notion" that "the imagination, in order to act well, must act blindly." The works of Homer and Shakespeare were "built of the solid materials of human knowledge," the writer asserted. "The only way to enrich the imagination, and enlarge the pleasures derived therefrom, is to store the mind with well ordered and distinctively comprehended truth."[25] Ohio lawyer and public speaker Samuel Eels agreed. A good teacher revealed to young people "not the visible world only, but the empire of thought and imagination."[26]

In fact, if disconnected from truth and morality, imagination could be a dangerous faculty. There was a real battle over the imagination in the decades before the Civil War. Some even worried that fairy tales would corrupt the imagination with false images.[27] Americans believed in "the direct influence of the imagination on the moral feelings" and thus urged teachers to ensure that children filled their imaginations with "stories exemplifying correct moral principles, and benevolent sentiments."[28] Horace Mann worried that imagination, if divorced from good morals and knowledge, would lead to "impure images."[29] If imagination was not tied to knowledge and morality, students would not be able "to determine the fitness and relevancy" of an argument.[30] In fact, Mann called the proliferation of novels an "epidemic" because, he believed, most novels appealed to people's passions without engaging their minds. "The intellect" sets the boundaries, "shows what things can be and what things cannot be, and thus arrests the imagination when it would otherwise soar or plunge into the impossible and the preternatural." Otherwise, imagination would be liberated "from all responsibility of consequences."[31]

Thus, one teacher urged her peers to foster an "educated imagination," by which she meant "one whose conceptions are conformed to the standard of nature and which does not indulge in wild extravagances and fancies wholly unlike in kind to known realities."[32] Scientist Louis Agassiz urged teachers to remember that imagination must be informed by "what exists in nature."[33] Chemist John Griscom argued that a "judicious teacher" would avoid "the two extremes" of, on the one hand, "dull and rigid formality" and, on the other, "merely superficial attention to those things which cultivate the imagination at the expense of the reasoning powers."[34]

Imagination was perhaps the most highly valued outcome of education because, some Americans argued, it distinguished people from animals. "Our age gets very little credit for poetry or music or indeed for art in any of its branches," former slave Frederick Douglass told an audience in the closing days of the Civil

War. But, he continued, "man is the only picture-making animal in the world." Although "reason is exalted," other animals can reason. "Imagination"—that "sublime, prophetic, and all-creative power of the human soul"—was the "glory of man" alone. With imagination "a new life springs up in the soul." Thus, imagination is "the divinest of human faculties." Douglass, who had been denied an education as an enslaved child, knew what it meant to be dehumanized and took seriously the importance of education for human dignity.[35]

That was certainly what an anonymous writer in the *US Democratic Review* thought. To this writer, imagination distinguished humanity "from the lower creation." Imagination ultimately made up "*soul*" since it could not be understood by measurement alone. Reason was concerned with "analysis," whereas imagination engaged in "synthesis"—in putting back together what reason had torn apart, but putting it together in a new way that allowed each person to experience the "beautiful." Thus, this writer concluded, "if science discovers, it is art that invents."[36]

Speaking before an Indiana audience, author J. Willis Westlake defined imagination as that "spiritual and mysterious power of the human mind which defies the limits of time and space . . . [and] . . . gives us glimpses of those great truths which lie beyond the regions of science and of sense."[37] A southern writer called imagination the "power by which he combines into a thousand varying creatures the separate impressions he has received from the world."[38] Imagination was truly "the Creative Power."[39]

Imagination served society by fostering creativity. People could use math, science, literature, and history to come up with new ideas. Those whose insight earned them the title "genius" were true heroes since they offered something new to all people, a new way of seeing the world. And this was how progress took place—acts of creation by imagination. Thus, Joseph K. Edgerton, a Vermont-born lawyer and railroad advocate, who went on to serve in the U.S. House of Representatives, urged those whom God had endowed with particularly strong creative powers to serve humanity by developing new knowledge.[40]

Yet creativity would never happen without society. Thus, Orange County's Charles Borland Jr., a Union College graduate who would serve in the New York State Assembly and in the U.S. Congress, argued that although "the great advances . . . made in the arts and sciences, as well as the more practical operations of the day . . . have been the suggestions of single noble minds," a person could have great ideas because "society in its associated capacity, have come forth with its treasures and encouragements." Genius was nurtured, was brought into being, through public schools.[41]

Because it was understood as the telos of human beings to develop their capacity to gain insight into the world, magazines devoted to teachers consistently urged teachers to encourage students' imaginations. The *Connecticut Common School Journal*, edited by Henry Barnard, stated in 1840 that all Americans had the right to have their imagination "sedulously cultivated" since imagination was "a constituent part of the universal mind" from God. "We have no sympathy," the *Journal* made clear, "with those who would exclude the bulk of society from communion with the greatest and best of our race through their written thoughts, or from the enjoyment of the glorious sights and sounds of which nature is so full, and which no extent of participation can diminish."[42]

Education and the Economy

Many scholars have accused Horace Mann and his generation of school reformers as being motivated primarily by economic concerns. During an era when New England, in particular, was becoming more urban and industrial, historians once assumed that the development of public education must have been connected to the economic interests of New England's factory owners. Factories required disciplined workers capable of spending hours working the factory floor. Scholars thus concluded that education was oriented toward social control rather than human freedom.[43] Yet Mann did not seek to create docile workers for American factories. Instead, he hoped that education could counteract the degrading tendencies of modern work.

Mann echoed Scottish economist Adam Smith, who had argued that the division of labor made possible huge gains in productivity. In the past, manufacturers had been artisans who undertook every step of the production process. A shoemaker, for example, made an entire shoe from cutting the leather forward. In modern factories, tasks were divided up. Managers took control of production, and workers did the same repetitive tasks. While this made factory owners wealthy and shoes cheaper, it also meant that a factory worker had "no occasion to exert his understanding."[44]

If Smith was right, then high profits came at a high cost. That was certainly Mann's conclusion. While he had argued in 1841 that educated workers were more productive, he made clear that he did so reluctantly. After seeking feedback from various factory owners around Massachusetts, he wrote that "I have novel and striking evidence that education is convertible into houses and lands, as well as into power and virtue." Mann hoped to convince the rich that it was in their interest to pay taxes for public education, and the poor that it was in their interest to send their children to school. But Mann never allowed economic purposes to substitute for the civic and cultural goals of education. He closed his report by reminding readers that economic reasons are the *least* significant ones justifying public schools, and in fact, a good education would help Americans resist the "more dangerous seducements of prosperity."[45]

Mann condemned factory owners and managers, most of whom were in his own Whig Party, for putting their wallets ahead of their democratic, Christian duties. Rather than promote the moral, spiritual, and intellectual development of human beings, he argued, employers "pursue a course of action by which the god-like powers and capacities of the human soul are wrought into thorough-made products of ignorance and misery and vice." Mann was equally frustrated with the state's working citizens who sent their children to toil in factories. What kind of parent, Mann wondered, would "sell his child into ransomless bondage for the pittance of money he can earn." Of course, in many families, children went to work because families needed the money, but, to Mann, owners and parents alike were to blame for depriving young people of "all the means of intellectual and moral growth."[46]

After a decade serving as the secretary to the state board of education, and traveling around Massachusetts extolling public schools, urging local communities to support taxation, and struggling to convince rich and poor alike that schools were worth it, Mann was exasperated. He had made much progress, but he was uncertain whether the people got it. Did they realize that public education was a fundamental democratic and Christian principle? Did they know that to educate a human being was an obligation because every child was created in God's image? In his tenth report to the state board of education, the usually stolid Mann let the board, the state's political leaders, the factory owners, and the broader public have it.

Mann was frustrated that so many Americans, especially well-off Americans, did not wish to pay taxes to support universal free public education. He argued that their refusal stemmed from their "false notions" concerning "their right to property." Too often people thought that they had earned their property on their own. But this was simply not true, Mann pointed out. No man is an island. He condemned the "arrogant doctrine of absolute ownership or sovereignty."

Instead, every one benefited from what they inherited from others. God had created nature, which was the basis for all wealth and knowledge. Second, prior generations had cleared the land, built the structures, developed the knowledge, and thus had made it possible for people to do what they do today. Third, Americans were members of a community. The only person who might claim an absolute right to his property was one who was born and lived his entire life on a desert island "having no relations to a community around him, having no ancestors to whom he had been indebted for ninety-nine parts in every hundred of all he possesses, and expecting to leave no posterity after him." Of course, such an "isolated, solitary being" never did and never could exist. We are not "hermits," Mann wrote. Finally, since all wealth stemmed from God's bounty, no person had the right to claim more property than he or she could use; to do so was "embezzlement."

Because success was made possible by God, the gifts of our ancestors, and the health of one's community, all property was social, and members of the community had a legitimate claim to it. The only question was when that claim could be made. For Mann, a child's claim to public support "begins with the first breath he draws." It was not enough for a child to be given food and shelter. Since God designed people with innate capacities, including the capacity to appreciate the beauty of His creation, "to preserve the animal life of the child only" would be a "fearful curse."

Mann's frustration led him to state his case as clearly as possible. It would be better, he said, that we deny a child food and shelter and let her or him die than ignore "the higher interests of the character." The rich, by denying young people access to public education, the generally mild-mannered Mann wrote, "are guilty of infanticide." Society exists not just "to protect the natural life of children" but to nurture their moral and spiritual lives as well. "The natural life of an infant should be extinguished as soon as it is born" if the community would not ensure a young person access to the education necessary to develop her or his capacities.[47]

Would Americans embrace the ideals of citizenship and self-culture, educators wondered. They worried that their efforts would be challenged by what North Carolinian Lee M. McAfee called Americans' "utilitarian spirit." McAfee worried that Americans cared only about "the dry details of profit and loss." "The cold and calculating spirit of business" pretends that "poetry is only a mere toy—an embellishment," rather than—as many educators saw it—"the true excellence of humankind." Educators like McAfee believed that in a democracy children must have access to the poetic spirit, to their innate "creative power." Especially in a world that seemed to value getting ahead at all costs, education must endow citizens with "public spirit." In short, schools must help Americans become effective citizens and engage in self-making.[48]

Popular Roots of Self-Culture

The ideal of self-culture was not just expressed by elite reformers but was embraced by the thousands of Americans who, after the Revolution, formed voluntary associations committed to "self-improvement." People signed up for classes in academies and formed and joined "literary associations" where they shared ideas with each other. Throughout America, ordinary people engaged in the effort to become more informed about public affairs, with or without schools. Newspapers proliferated as more and more people identified with political parties and voted.[49]

What had once been the preserve of the urban elite worked its way down to more modest middle-class families around the country in what has been termed the post-Revolutionary "Village Enlightenment." Artisans formed mechanics' institutes that combined practical knowledge with cultural knowledge or, better, argued that cultural knowledge was practical. The hunger for knowledge was widespread—Americans subscribed to magazines to bring culture into their homes, and they flocked to lyceums, library societies, and young men's societies to hear lectures by community members and by famous figures such as essayist Ralph Waldo Emerson, abolitionist Frederick Douglass, or scientist Louis Agassiz. There was a widespread desire to make sense of the world—to become literate and worldly. Lectures were so popular that one commentator noted that, although lectures had once been "*luxuries*, they are now the *necessaries* of life."[50]

Americans wanted access to knowledge, and they wanted their children to have access, too. Behind this all was the premise that who we are is not fixed, that education could change us. For children, this meant that schools were not just useful but necessary. Over the course of the eighteenth century, more and more people came to believe that children were born neither good nor bad but were malleable. Developing adults therefore required proper socialization and education. Creating the right kinds of schools took on a heightened importance because external influences shaped inner character.

And that external world was changing—becoming, or at least experienced as, more unstable, unpredictable, precarious, and thus frightening. The early American republic was a time of social, economic, and demographic change. In shaping their destinies, people were expected to pull themselves up by their own bootstraps in a market that was, supposedly, governed by natural economic laws. In practice, however, the market was capricious, and people in the antebellum decades could go from rags to riches, but often enough they found themselves subject to the "freaks of fortune." Society was bustling—immigrants arrived and native-born youth moved from their small hometowns to the nation's growing cities or out to the West. Everything seemed to move, and all that was solid felt like it was melting into air.[51]

As adults confronted the dislocations and instability of the world, they sought shelters for their children. Middle-class parents sought to turn their homes and schools into safe zones where children could be socialized free from the dangers of a world for which they were ill prepared. As parents struggled to make sense of a changing world, they idealized childhood as a time of safety and security, a place free of the economic anxieties and pressures of the real world. In the past, childhood had not been seen as a place of innocence and ease. By the 1830s, however, childhood was considered "as a distinct stage of growth and development in which a young person was prepared for emergence into adulthood," and parents were convinced that "early departure from the homestead is a moral crisis that many of our youth do not show themselves able to meet."[52] Thus, one author in the *Southern Teacher* reminded readers of "the days of sunny childhood" when "care was unknown, nor sorrow felt," and everything was "perfect bliss."[53]

Schools served as shelters wherein the human spirit could be nourished without the overwhelming pressures of the adult world. Yet mixed in with this aspiration were also more mundane concerns. At a time of economic uncertainty, parents were reasonably concerned about their children's financial security. While scholars continue to debate whether more education paid off before the twentieth century, parents and many young people certainly believed that better literacy and numeracy skills would offer access to the increasing number of white-collar jobs available in America's expanding commercial institutions— stores, banks, factories, and corporate offices.[54]

Most young men did not require much schooling to get a job, and as a result boys tended to leave school earlier than girls to seek employment.[55] Yet, increasingly, schools served as a credentialing system for families who could afford to keep their children out of the workforce or did not need their help on the farm. As a result, just as education reformers pushed to increase the time children spent in schools at taxpayer expense, many Americans started to wonder who benefited.

High Schools and Liberal Education

William Ellery Channing had urged his audience of mechanics to use their spare time to engage in self-culture—to read books and to talk about them, to observe nature, and to make the best use of the time before them. Many working Americans agreed with this ideal, but they questioned whether it was applicable in a world in which, as one writer in Philadelphia's *Mechanics' Free Press* put it in 1830, "we are fast approaching those extremes of wealth" and "ignorance, poverty, and wretchedness" that would re-create the "unnatural and oppressive distinctions which exist in the corrupt governments of the old world." When factory owners had more power than workers, advocates of working people argued, inequality had to be addressed first. Unless, for example, legislators limited the workday to ten hours, few Americans would have time for cultural pursuits.

Working people demanded greater tax support for public education, but their emphasis was on increasing access to the lower common schools, not high schools, academies, or colleges. Education should not, as a workers' committee in Philadelphia noted, foster "an aristocracy of talent." Public schools must promote equality. Despite reformers' rhetoric, many working Americans wondered whether the schools were serving democratic purposes.[56] Were calls to expand access to education, especially at the higher levels, masking new ways to justify elite privilege?

Nowhere were these tensions exposed as clearly as in debates over public high schools. For many Americans, the civic and cultural goals of public education, which required students to study the liberal arts—subjects such as ancient and modern languages, literature, history, and natural science—seemed disconnected from what people needed in the real world. Elementary education was widely supported because most parents agreed that students needed basic skills—reading, writing, arithmetic—and good moral character. But as more and more students completed the common school sequence—akin to up to middle school or so for us today—education reformers sought to provide public access to higher learning. The debate over public high schools pitted those who sought to democratize access to culture against those who believed liberal education was a luxury for the few that did little to help working people's more pressing needs.

The first public high schools were established in cities where the population was large enough for there to be sufficient demand. High schools were often established as upper "departments" of the regular common schools before moving to buildings of their own. Boston led the way in 1821. By 1839, Massachusetts had twenty-six public high schools, and Philadelphia, Baltimore, and Charleston followed suit. In 1851, at least eighty cities had established public high schools. From the very beginning, public high schools had an unclear mission. Should they serve as college preparatory schools—as grammar schools had—by focusing on ancient languages and literature? Or should they be more practical, preparing young Americans for their adult lives? The classical track had prestige on its side, but the practical track, which emphasized English language and literature and science, seemed more in tune with the world in which people actually lived. Since few Americans would in fact attend college, many high school advocates envisioned high school as "democracy's college," where graduates would be prepared to enter the adult world.[57]

To their advocates, high schools would expose the most talented children to the kind of education before available only to rich children. Access to the liberal arts, whether classical or modern, would allow young people from all walks of life to develop the knowledge they would need to become civic leaders, to develop more fully their own moral and intellectual potential, and to succeed in the workplace. The Boston committee that recommended the nation's first public high school noted that the lower common schools did not fully "bring the powers of the mind into operation" or effectively prepare promising young people for "those stations, both public and private, in which they may be placed."[58]

Middle-class young women were in a good position to take advantage of these new opportunities, whether in public high schools or in private academies. Because they did not need to be, nor were expected to be, breadwinners, they could more easily embrace the civic and cultural goals of liberal education, and many did.[59] But other Americans were skeptical. Everyone recognizes the value of elementary schools, noted one observer in 1848. It was harder for ordinary Americans to see the value of "liberal education" in "our high schools and colleges." Certainly, the personal benefits to individuals of a higher education in the liberal arts were significant. Through higher studies, "the mind is liberalized," but the benefits extended beyond the individual. The "general interests of society" were served by "cultivation of the liberal arts." Graduates would go on to become leaders, professionals, and scholars. All of society was "ennobled by the possession, or by the influence of enlightened minds."[60]

Public high schools would replace an aristocracy of wealth with a meritocracy. In a democracy, many argued, merit ought to determine one's social position rather than one's parents' background. As the Lowell, Massachusetts, school committee put it in 1840, public high schools would "place within reach of the poorest citizen such means of preparing his children for college, or for giving instruction, or for any branch of active business, as the richest shall be glad to avail themselves of for their own children."[61] Advocates of public high schools in Illinois argued in 1844 that "the child of the cottage and of the palace shall meet on terms of perfect equality, except as one excels the other in scholarship."[62]

But why, many Americans wondered, should taxpayers foot the bill? First off, education in the liberal arts—in history, literature, moral philosophy, math, biology, and chemistry—did not have any clear practical purpose.[63] Other critics reminded Americans that inequality could not be solved by more education but by a fairer economy. For this reason, many Democrats opposed free public high schools. Charles Smart, Ohio's state superintendent in the 1870s, called the high school a "palace of extravagance" and pointed out that working people faced other challenges—long hours, low pay—and "the offer of a liberal education to the poor, as well as to the rich, sounds well, but of what worth is a thing offered to those who can not accept it, though they have aid in paying for it?"[64] To such critics, high schools increased rather than diminished inequality.

High schools thus remained on the margins of American public education, unlike the lower common schools; by 1890, only 6.7 percent of fourteen- to seventeen-year-olds were enrolled.[65] A legislative committee in Connecticut in 1842 questioned whether higher learning ought to have public support when compared to subjects "which may the most readily be brought into action and enter into our business concerns."[66] An 1856 Norwich, Connecticut, observer worried that the people would not long support taxing themselves for high schools. Americans loved their "lower schools," "but the studies of the high school, Algebra, Geometry, Chemistry, Natural Philosophy, Ancient History, Latin, Greek, French and German were a perfect 'terra incognita' to the great mass of the people."[67]

Illinois citizens in the 1870s questioned the constitutionality of using public funds to pay for higher learning. Michigan citizens argued that their state constitution did not authorize funding high schools. "Instruction in the classics and in living modern languages," such critics argued, was "in the nature not of practical and therefore necessary instruction for the benefit of the people at large." While the state circuit court disagreed in 1873, and the state supreme court concurred the following year, clearing the way for school districts to use public funds for high schools, the jury was still out in the court of public opinion.[68]

Americans pushed back against high schools. In March 1860, voters in Beverly, Massachusetts, chose to abolish their two-year old public high school and return the money to the lower common schools. For Beverly's working-class citizens, the new high school was a gift to the wealthy; the high school's supporters tended to be wealthier and better educated than those who opposed it. Statistics bear out that the children of middle-class and wealthy parents were more likely to attend high school than were working-class children. Working-class families may have lacked the money to keep their children out of the labor market, or perhaps they did not see the high school curriculum as practical. Whatever the reason, Massachusetts's new public high schools tended to serve the children of the privileged, reinforcing rather than overcoming inequality.[69]

Yet access to high schools may have been more widespread in other communities. In Lynn, Massachusetts, a city undergoing the dramatic changes associated with industrialization, the *Awl*, a working-class newspaper, supported establishing a public high school and argued that it was "the rich and influential" who opposed it.[70] And in Newburyport, almost one-third of children from eleven to sixteen years old attended high school between 1857 and 1863, a number much higher than one might imagine, although only about a third of these ultimately graduated. Of these students, nearly a sixth were children of unskilled fathers, suggesting that access was not entirely dependent on family wealth or educational background. Newburyport was in Essex County, and the numbers there too are higher than one might expect—around 15 percent of children went, for at least some time, to a high school. Most small towns did not have high schools, but in those that did, small-town children were much more likely to enroll.[71]

One of the ironies of the expansion of American democracy, with its idea that all human beings are created equal and equally endowed by the Creator with the rights of life, liberty, and the pursuit of happiness, is that Americans quickly looked for ways to stand out from the crowd. In a society in which the old forms of distinction—inherited positions and titles—were no longer permitted, money and access to culture became the way the few sought to rise above the many.[72]

High schools dangled the promise of all these things. To have your teenaged son or daughter in high school meant that you were wealthy enough not to need their labor. In high schools, children gained access to the liberal arts, those subjects that historically have been associated with elite status. Most public high schools had entrance exams to ensure that students had the academic skills necessary for success. High schools were not intended to be universally accessible. As a result, high school functioned as a sign of merit, even if, in practice, a student's success was in large part a function of their family's economic standing.[73]

Thus, the civic and cultural functions of schooling were at risk of being overwhelmed by credentialing.[74] At a time when things were insecure and unstable, parents looked for ways to make their children stand out from others. Whether they cared about the civic and cultural purposes of education or not, having their children excel in school sent a signal that their children were both bright and capable of working hard. In other words, perhaps the subjects studied mattered less than the credentials. In turn, working-class and rural parents argued that the civic and cultural ambitions of education reformers were impractical and that the benefits accrued to the well-off anyway.

An Overlapping Consensus

Since its inception, American public education has served many masters. It sought to educate citizens, to promote self-culture, and simultaneously to prepare people for success in the workplace. The public schools reflected the complicated aspirations of policy makers, education reformers, citizens, parents, teachers, and students. In America, schools benefited from an overlapping consensus in which the various stakeholders did not always agree on why schools existed but agreed that they ought to exist. This overlapping consensus fueled the dramatic growth in public school enrollment between the Revolution and the Civil War.

But since Americans did not always agree on the purposes of education, public schools also generated intense political conflicts. Perhaps for most Americans, schools were practical institutions. They gave young children basic skills, reinforced the community's morals, and prepared them to be citizens and productive members of society. But to reformers, public schools would also elevate the human spirit. To do that, the following chapters argue, reformers sought to transform the content of the curriculum and how teachers taught and, ultimately, to make public schools free and universal.

2 Democratic Education

The Poets of Humanity

REFORMERS OFFERED AMERICANS AN IDEAL—and idealized—curriculum for a democratic education, one that went beyond the basics in order to develop the potential of each human being. Like all ideals, theirs was a vision, reflected in speeches, pamphlets, and books. They believed that public schools would help each young person come to see herself or himself as a subject worth taking seriously and would orient young people to higher purposes. They believed that in a democracy liberal education could not be just for elites but must be made available to every American.[1]

Reformers defined liberal education in two ways: education in those subjects which provided the skills and knowledge necessary for effective citizenship, and an education for self-culture. From this perspective, individual freedom depended on democratizing access to the liberal arts. Reformers aspired for young people to develop the skills and knowledge necessary to live meaningful and worthy lives.

Education thus developed "the human faculties" and offered the "necessary knowledge" for an American to "discharge his duties as an individual, as a member of society, and as a citizen of a free State," proclaimed James Henry Jr., the superintendent of schools in Herkimer County, New York.[2] Members of the Illinois Ladies' Association for the Education of Female Teachers believed that women,

no less than men, needed an education that "enlarges, strengthens, and invigorates the mental powers" by teaching them to "reason, reflect and act."[3]

Schools would be the "grand machinery" through which the "'raw material' of
human nature can be worked up into inventors and discoverers, into skilled artisans and scientific farmers, into scholars and jurists, into the founders of benevolent institutions, and the great expounders of ethical and theological science,"
proclaimed Horace Mann. With access to public schools, "embryos of talent may
be quickened" not only to "solve the difficult problems of political and economical law" but also to kindle "the genius . . . which will blaze forth in the poets of
humanity."[4]

Reformers sought to orient public schools around preparing young people
for citizenship and self-culture. This meant that teachers should pay more attention to what happened inside students' hearts and minds and less on their
external performances. Character education, for example, should encourage self-
discipline, not obedience, so that young people could make good choices about
the kinds of lives that they would lead. Reading, writing, and arithmetic must
be treated not just as useful skills but as the building blocks for self-formation.
A liberal education in academic subjects ought to provide students insight into
themselves and the world around them.

The Year 1828

The reformers' vision was contested by other Americans, who questioned
whether educated elites knew better how to raise children than they did themselves. These Americans believed that the people's common sense should govern
in a democracy. When Tennessee's Andrew Jackson gave voice to their vision in
1828, it marked the beginning of a new era for American democracy. Four years
earlier, Jackson, despite winning the popular vote, claimed to have been denied
the White House by a "corrupt bargain" between newly elected president John
Quincy Adams and Kentucky senator Henry Clay. Jackson subsequently joined
forces with Adams's opponents around the country to form what would become
the Democratic Party. Jackson's supporters challenged the elitist assumptions of
Adams, Clay, and their National Republican Party. They proclaimed that elites
served their own interests, that elites could not be trusted to act for the people.
Americans wanted a leader who seemed to be one of them. While, in reality,
Jackson was anything but ordinary—he was one of the largest slaveholders in
Tennessee—he came to represent the common person.[5]

The new order symbolically began with President Jackson's inauguration. "Throngs of people" came to see Jackson become their president, although, some skeptical observers noted, many of these well-wishers were office seekers "soliciting rewards."[6] Margaret Bayard Smith, a DC scion, in a letter to one of her friends described the "majestic spectacle" of "thousands and thousands of people, without distinction of rank, collected in an immense mass round the Capitol, silent, orderly and tranquil," as they awaited Jackson's arrival.

Things fell apart once the party began. "The Majesty of the People" gave way to "a rabble, a mob, of boys, negros, women, children, scrambling[,] fighting, romping." The president was "*literally* nearly pressed to death and almost suffocated and torn to pieces" by his admirers. "Cut glass and china" lay shattered on the floor, "ladies fainted, men were seen with bloody noses." What would this mean for the future of American democracy, Smith wondered. "It was the People's day, and the People's President and the People would rule," but "God grant that one day or other, the People do not put down all rule and rulers." The scene, Smith told her friend, reminded her of "the mobs in the Tuileries and at Versailles" during the French Revolution.[7]

This new era posed a challenge for educators. Jackson's Democratic Party was suspicious of elites, yet the very premise of education is that the educated have something to teach others. Jackson and his followers, however, trusted the common sense of ordinary people more than the refined ideas of the educated.[8] What role was there for uncommon sense in an era of the common man? To observers like University of North Carolina's president Joseph Caldwell, it seemed that just because many Americans had managed to raise their families without formal education did not mean that Americans should "become avowed partizans of mental darkness against light" and celebrate "glorying in ignorance."[9] But education did in fact come under attack. Critics called it old fashioned and elitist. Did every American need a liberal education in a society in which the needs of the common person should trump those of the educated?

Nowhere was this attack felt more than in the classics. In its ideal form, classical education prepared students to interpret texts thoughtfully through close study of grammar, logic, and rhetoric, while also introducing them to conversations about the meaning of liberty and the good life. Some students entered a world where the ancients lived, where their debates about citizenship and freedom were thrilling, and where those debates could inform America's experiment in republican government. For most students, however, the classical curriculum was a boring slog through Latin and Greek grammar without any clear payoff.

Moreover, many wondered whether a curriculum designed for intellectuals was appropriate for the broader public.[10]

Yale's professors were forced to answer this question in 1828. Recently established Amherst College had criticized older colleges for being "stationary," or refusing to change with the times. Amherst offered students college degrees without requiring Greek and Latin, allowing students to take chemistry, anatomy, and civil engineering instead.[11]

When the Yale Corporation met in September 1827, Noyes Darling, who came to be known for research about insects and corn, supposedly proposed a motion "to leave out of said course the study of the *dead languages*." Darling was a state senator, and perhaps he thought making college more practical would appeal to voters. Nonetheless, Yale responded by forming a committee composed of members of the corporation (the college's governing board) and faculty members.

The committee presented its *Reports on the Course of Instruction in Yale College* to Yale's governors in September 1828 and then published it in order to defend not just classical education but liberal education. Yale's faculty felt besieged by the democratic advocates of common sense. They needed to explain—and, to be honest, to justify—what education was for.

First, they argued, it was simply wrong to suggest that Yale had not changed in the past century. The faculty had introduced not only new "modes of instruction" but also new subjects: "chemistry, mineralogy, geology, political economy, &c." Faculty members did not oppose change but believed that any change must be true to the higher purposes of education. A college education, according to Yale's professors, had two equally important goals: "the *discipline* and the *furniture* of the mind," a distinction akin to today's distinction between skills (critical thinking, creativity, etc.) and knowledge of subjects (history, literature, physics, etc.). One needed to be able to think, and one needed things to think about.

In making their case, the authors relied on what was called faculty psychology. The word *faculty* refers to a human "ability or aptitude" or a "capacity."[12] Americans at the time believed that the human psyche was composed of multiple faculties, each of which had a different function. A proper understanding of human faculties, and how they related to each other, provided the foundation for what it meant to be a free person. Faculty psychology, in other words, provided a general framework for the development of free individuals.

Philosophers were confident that psychology could be a guide to understanding God's vision of human freedom. Scottish philosopher and University of Edinburgh professor Francis Hutcheson wrote in his influential *System of Morals*

(1755) that understanding how to conduct our lives requires "knowledge of the constitution of this species, and all of its perceptive and active powers [or faculties], and their natural objects."[13] His fellow philosopher Henry Home, Lord Kames, agreed that "acting according to our nature, is acting so, as to answer the end of our creation."[14] Dugald Stewart echoed this point: understanding human faculties "enables us to form any reasonable conclusions concerning the ends and destination of our being, and the purposes for which we were sent into the world."[15]

While human beings had multiple faculties, not all faculties were equal. Humans shared appetites and instincts with animals. Other faculties, like passions and emotions, spurred people to act for good or for ill. At the top of the hierarchy stood humanity's capacity to engage in critical and ethical judgment, which was linked to the faculties of reason, imagination, and morality. A free human being was one who had developed fully these higher faculties.[16]

A good curriculum, Yale's professors argued, would therefore rely on "those branches of study . . . which are best calculated to teach the art of fixing the attention, directing the train of thought, analyzing a subject proposed for investigation; following with accurate discrimination, the course of an argument; balancing nicely the evidence presented to the judgment; awakening, elevating, and controlling the imagination; arranging, with skill, the treasures which memory gathers; rousing and guiding the powers of genius."[17]

A good education would develop all "mental faculties," but Yale's professors made a special plea for humanity's creative potential. "However abundant may be the acquisitions of the student, if he has no talent at forming new combinations of thought, he will be dull and inefficient." The real signs of education "consist in the creations of the imagination, the discoveries of the intellect, the conquests by which the sciences are extended."

Developing the faculties was hard work, and Yale professors knew that most of their students preferred "escaping the demands of mental exertion." Good teachers must force lazy students to use their minds whether they wanted to or not. Lectures thus were less important than recitations and disputations in which students used their own minds to have their own thoughts, develop their own ideas, and reach their own conclusions.

But critical thinking was not enough. On its own, in fact, it was meaningless. In addition to developing the higher faculties, education must also provide the "furniture" of the mind—knowledge that fuels insight. Yale's faculty was adamant that education "in the arts and sciences" was necessary "both to strengthen and enlarge the faculties of the mind, and to familiarize it with the leading principles of the great objects of human investigation and knowledge." No good college ought to offer undergraduates "a professional education."

Yale's professors admitted that most Americans did not see the value of students studying higher mathematics, the sciences, history, or modern and ancient languages. Nonetheless, they proclaimed, knowledge "enlarges the circle" of thought. People who study science and literature can see the world more clearly and deeply and ask better questions of it. Whether in their working or personal lives or as citizens, the "mind is thus far liberalized by liberal knowledge."[18]

Whether in the classics or more modern subjects like the sciences or history, Yale's faculty argued that liberal education was vital not just to the republic but to individuals as well. Public school reformers agreed. They hoped to introduce all Americans in public schools to subjects that would discipline and furnish the mind. But they would have to make the case to a sometimes skeptical public that a broad education in the arts and sciences was valuable not just for some but for everyone.

Education for Autonomy

Just as Andrew Jackson became the people's president, and as the Yale faculty defended liberal education from its populist critics, Rev. William Ellery Channing was asked to give an address in Providence, Rhode Island, on the occasion of Rev. F. A. Farley's ordination. Channing chose for his text a passage from Ephesians: "Be ye therefore followers of God, as dear children."[19]

Channing took this moment to describe his idea of human nature, which would shape his understanding of self-culture a decade later. Channing believed that each of us was made in "likeness to God." To Channing, God was not some being out there whom people must adore but "a being whom we know through our own souls, who has made man in his own image, who is the perfection of our spiritual nature." To make one's self therefore was "the perpetual unfolding and enlargement of those powers and virtues by which it is constituted in his glorious image." True religion "is to feel the quickening and transforming energy of his perfections" and to "thirst for the growth and invigoration of the divine principle within us."[20]

What this meant was that people needed to align what was inside of them with a vision of perfection. The highest development of a person's faculties would enable her or him to gain insight on God's universe. Educators thus linked the cultivation of the faculties of morality, reason, and imagination with Channing's telos: the purpose of education was to develop human beings in God's image, which meant to bring out and nurture what was best within them. It was to see each person as a project—and to endow each person with the discipline or autonomy to make herself or himself in relation to a higher ideal. "Education, in the broadest sense," stated Rev. Samuel May in 1826, "may be understood as the complete and harmonious development of all the intellectual and moral powers of our nature—the subjection of ourselves to the supreme control of right principles, and the acquisition of all knowledge that may be necessary, in order to our filling well the sphere of duty, in which God has placed us."[21]

The purpose of education is "no less than to develop all the faculties of the human soul to the utmost extent of which they are susceptible in this temporal life and condition," proclaimed Edward Mansfield, author of *American Education: Its Principles and Elements*. This was the "ultimate" purpose, but schools had to confront the "practical" fact of educating students. Here too the same principles applied. First, education should teach young people about the nature of "republican government" and offer the knowledge and skills necessary for effective citizenship. But, then, education must move beyond the citizen to perfect the human being through the "physical and spiritual development of all the faculties in each individual."[22]

But to what end? Here, Mansfield confronted a serious problem in a diverse society. To educate human beings requires some understanding of what it means to be a human being. In a society as religiously plural as the nineteenth-century United States, this was no easy task. Mansfield did not shy away from the issue. He recognized that "it is impossible for an individual or society ever to improve, without placing before it the ideal beauty of something better than exists, or has existed, in our experience."[23] To Mansfield, the ideal of perfect goodness came from "scripture," which "places before us, for imitation, the character of God, the beauty of excellence, and the loveliness of holy society."[24]

Horace Mann, who as secretary of the board of education in Massachusetts was a bit more careful about how he invoked religion, nevertheless echoed Channing's and Mansfield's conclusions. Since "the mind of every man is instinct with capacities above the demands of the workshop or the field," a democracy must develop each person's inner potential. Each person must have access to "the language of poetry and art." A society educated to work but to nothing more "will be disrobed of many of its choicest beauties."[25]

Alonzo Potter's 1842 *The School and the Schoolmaster*, a book sponsored by

New York State's superintendent of schools and distributed widely, considered the primary purpose of education nothing less than "the drawing out or development of the human faculties." A child was born "a stranger alike to himself, to the world, and to God." Education must slowly develop each child's appreciation and understanding of the world around her or him. A good school would develop intellect, morality, and what Potter called "taste."[26] North Carolina superintendent of schools Calvin Henderson Wiley argued that those who believed "that the chief end of man is to make money and acquire power, and to use them for the indulgence of his passions, will in the end first become slaves to their appetites and then to a more self-denying race." Teachers must help young people "improve the heart and subdue its passions, as the mind is enlightened." To Wiley, a good education granted each young person the discipline to become "a responsible free agent, each individual accountable for his own life and opinions, to the One Divine Master of all."[27]

Ultimately, even Horace Mann did not beat around the bush. "Perhaps it is in the order of nature that a people, like an individual, shall first provide for its lower animal wants,—its food, its raiment, its shelter,—but the demands of this part of our nature should be watchfully guarded, lest in the acquisition of sensual and material gratifications we lose sight of the line which separates competence and comfort from superfluity and extravagance, and thus forget and forfeit our nobler capacities for more rational enjoyments."[28] We must "cultivate the higher faculties" and resist "the lower instincts and selfish tendencies" of the human race. We must celebrate humanity's "conscience, its benevolence, a reverence for what is true and sacred," not "wealth, luxury, preferment."[29]

Mann's friend, British author George Combe, taught Mann about the science of phrenology, which claimed to assess intellectual capacity and moral character from the structure of a person's brain and skull. Phrenology sanctioned Mann's confidence in the brain's plasticity and his belief that social influences fundamentally shaped human beings. While phrenology had a dark side—suggesting that negative traits were housed in physiology and might be inherited—it also reinforced Mann's egalitarianism: if brains were malleable, then education mattered even more, both for individuals and for society.[30] Many African Americans reached the same conclusion, including famed antislavery activist Frederick Douglass.[31]

Ohio's superintendent of common schools, in defending coeducational buildings, argued that boys and girls were both endowed with the faculties "of memory, of reason, of conscience, of imagination, and of will" and that schools must ensure that "all these powers are to be developed."[32] Calvin Henderson Wiley called a person who could not resist immediate desires a "slave"; Mann referred to such a person as an "animal." Education must cultivate the best within us. Otherwise, people would not be free, or self-made, but remain an unformed bundle of impulses with no ability to resist immediate temptation.

Francis Wayland, Brown University's president and author of the best-selling textbook *Elements of Moral Science* (1835), wrote that a moral act is the "voluntary action of an intelligent agent, who is capable of distinguishing between right and wrong, or of distinguishing what he ought, from what he ought not to do."[33] Discipline was considered the precondition to individual freedom.

William Holmes McGuffey and His Readers

It was not easy to become a citizen and to engage in self-culture. The world was full of temptations that would distract or disrupt the road to autonomy. People's passions and emotions could lead them to seek immediate pleasures rather than the long-term pleasure that comes from developing themselves in relation to higher goods. Young people had to learn to control themselves and to resist immediate impulses in order to nurture and develop their potential. They needed good character.[34]

The core of character education in America's common schools was the lessons embodied in *McGuffey's Readers*, written by Rev. William Holmes McGuffey. McGuffey was born in Washington County, Pennsylvania, in 1800, into a family with Scotch-Irish roots. In 1802 his family moved to the Western Reserve in the now state of Ohio. McGuffey's early education came from his mother and from scattered sources until he was noticed by a minister who saw his promise and prepared him for college. While attending Washington College in Pennsylvania, he taught school and earned a reputation for being not only an innovative teacher but also a hard disciplinarian. He impressed Miami University's president Robert Hamilton Bishop, who urged him to move to Ohio to join his faculty. Thus, young McGuffey became a professor of ancient languages in 1826.

McGuffey's relationship with Bishop deteriorated over the next decade. The president was liberal on religious issues, whereas McGuffey was conservative. Moreover, McGuffey was stern. He expected good behavior and tolerated nothing less, both as a schoolteacher and later as a college professor. He believed in character and was troubled by the amount college students—especially the southern ones—drank.

In the late 1820s, McGuffey undertook a study of the spellers used to educate young children and began to develop his own ideas on elementary education. Unhappy with the quality of existing school readers, he recognized the growing demand for something better for the nation's expanding common schools. Publishers too recognized the potential to make real money in this growing market. Cincinnati publishers Truman & Smith approached educator Catharine Beecher to make a reader for western schools, but she instead directed them to Professor McGuffey.

Although McGuffey made little money—his contract entitled him to a 10 percent royalty on up to ten thousand copies—his publishers had a hit on their hands.[35] *McGuffey's Readers* became the best-selling schoolbooks of the nineteenth century. Across the nation, school districts adopted *McGuffey's Readers*, offering American students a common set of experiences. As many as 122 million copies of *McGuffey's Readers* may have been printed between 1836 and 1920, when revised versions were widely used.[36] These numbers downplay their influence. Since siblings would share copies, and neighbors would hand them to neighbors, it is likely that even more people had access to them. One scholar has gone so far to conclude that McGuffey was responsible for "making the American mind," while another writes that "outside of the King James Bible, *McGuffey's Readers* were the most widely read books in 19th-century America."[37]

McGuffey himself went on to become president of Cincinnati College and then of Ohio College. His stint at Ohio College (now Ohio University) was unsuccessful, in part because of his strict discipline. He instituted a daily schedule that began with a faculty meeting at five o'clock each morning and then student recitation at six. McGuffey expelled students if they swore or violated the rules. After expelling sixteen students between June 15 and July 14, 1841, only one out of fifteen seniors remained to graduate. Professors complained, and some resigned. But other students recalled McGuffey as a demanding but caring teacher who took a real interest in his students.

McGuffey resigned his position after Ohio's legislature responded to farmers' protests about paying taxes to support the university. He returned to teaching in 1843, serving as a professor at Woodward College and then as chair of the Department of Moral Philosophy at the University of Virginia, a position he held until his death in 1873.[38]

McGuffey's Readers sought to encourage those dispositions of character that McGuffey considered vital for a free society and for free people. Without these personal and public virtues, individual and public freedom would be at risk. The

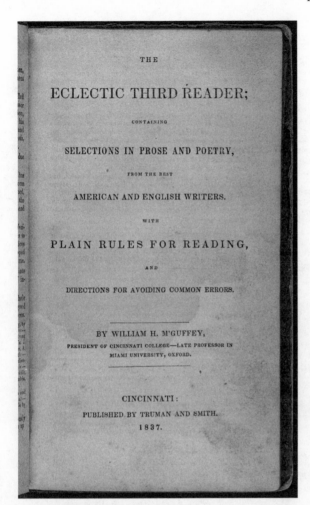

Figure 2.1. William Holmes McGuffey, *The eclectic third reader; containing selections in prose and poetry, from the best American and English writers. With plain rules for reading, and directions for avoiding common errors* (Cincinnati, 1837), title page. Courtesy of Albert and Shirley Small Special Collections Library, University of Virginia

readers, composed of selected essays and excerpts from larger works, were designed to develop students' faculties, dispositions, and skills year by year. The fourth volume thus included a "wider range" of selections than earlier ones to encourage "a more vigorous exercise of thought."[39] The readers made two essential points: people must learn to resist immediate impulse to have the discipline to pursue higher things, and they must care about those around them. *McGuffey's Readers* sought to implant in children an internal gyroscope that allowed them to orient their interior lives to principles and aspirations outside their own experiences.[40] They sought to cultivate the character necessary for public duties and private pursuits of happiness. Thus, one passage taught young people that they,

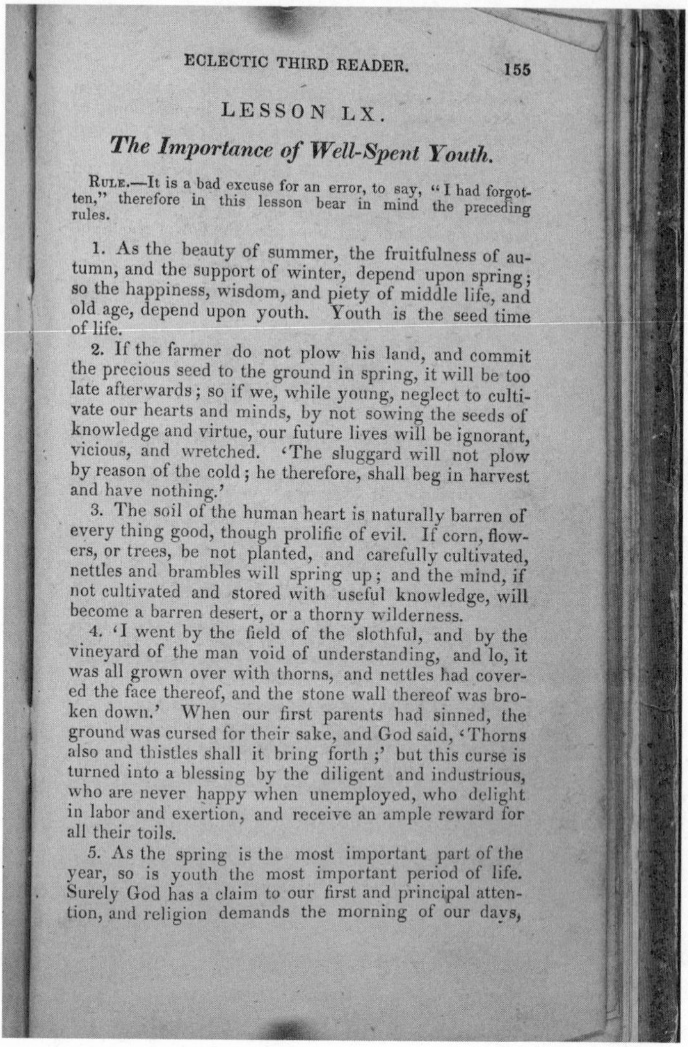

LESSON LX.

The Importance of Well-Spent Youth.

RULE.—It is a bad excuse for an error, to say, "I had forgotten," therefore in this lesson bear in mind the preceding rules.

1. As the beauty of summer, the fruitfulness of autumn, and the support of winter, depend upon spring; so the happiness, wisdom, and piety of middle life, and old age, depend upon youth. Youth is the seed time of life.

2. If the farmer do not plow his land, and commit the precious seed to the ground in spring, it will be too late afterwards; so if we, while young, neglect to cultivate our hearts and minds, by not sowing the seeds of knowledge and virtue, our future lives will be ignorant, vicious, and wretched. 'The sluggard will not plow by reason of the cold; he therefore, shall beg in harvest and have nothing.'

3. The soil of the human heart is naturally barren of every thing good, though prolific of evil. If corn, flowers, or trees, be not planted, and carefully cultivated, nettles and brambles will spring up; and the mind, if not cultivated and stored with useful knowledge, will become a barren desert, or a thorny wilderness.

4. 'I went by the field of the slothful, and by the vineyard of the man void of understanding, and lo, it was all grown over with thorns, and nettles had covered the face thereof, and the stone wall thereof was broken down.' When our first parents had sinned, the ground was cursed for their sake, and God said, 'Thorns also and thistles shall it bring forth;' but this curse is turned into a blessing by the diligent and industrious, who are never happy when unemployed, who delight in labor and exertion, and receive an ample reward for all their toils.

5. As the spring is the most important part of the year, so is youth the most important period of life. Surely God has a claim to our first and principal attention, and religion demands the morning of our days,

Figure 2.2. William Holmes McGuffey, *The eclectic third reader; containing selections in prose and poetry, from the best American and English writers. With plain rules for reading, and directions for avoiding common errors* (Cincinnati, 1837), page 155. Courtesy of Albert and Shirley Small Special Collections Library, University of Virginia

and the first season, the spring of our lives: before you are encumbered by cares, distressed by afflictions, or engaged in business, it becomes you to resign your soul to God.

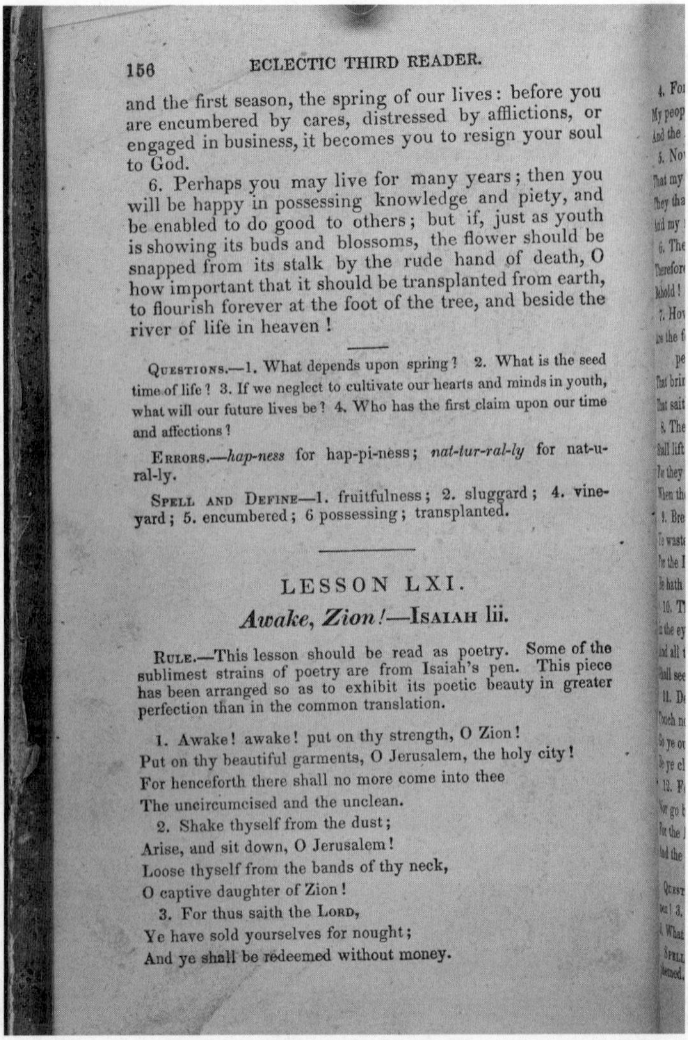

6. Perhaps you may live for many years; then you will be happy in possessing knowledge and piety, and be enabled to do good to others; but if, just as youth is showing its buds and blossoms, the flower should be snapped from its stalk by the rude hand of death, O how important that it should be transplanted from earth, to flourish forever at the foot of the tree, and beside the river of life in heaven!

QUESTIONS.—1. What depends upon spring? 2. What is the seed time of life? 3. If we neglect to cultivate our hearts and minds in youth, what will our future lives be? 4. Who has the first claim upon our time and affections?

ERRORS.—*hap-ness* for hap-pi-ness; *nat-tur-ral-ly* for nat-u-ral-ly.

SPELL AND DEFINE—1. fruitfulness; 2. sluggard; 4. vineyard; 5. encumbered; 6 possessing; transplanted.

LESSON LXI.

Awake, Zion!—ISAIAH lii.

RULE.—This lesson should be read as poetry. Some of the sublimest strains of poetry are from Isaiah's pen. This piece has been arranged so as to exhibit its poetic beauty in greater perfection than in the common translation.

1. Awake! awake! put on thy strength, O Zion!
Put on thy beautiful garments, O Jerusalem, the holy city!
For henceforth there shall no more come into thee
The uncircumcised and the unclean.

2. Shake thyself from the dust;
Arise, and sit down, O Jerusalem!
Loose thyself from the bands of thy neck,
O captive daughter of Zion!

3. For thus saith the LORD,
Ye have sold yourselves for nought;
And ye shall be redeemed without money.

Figure 2.3. William Holmes McGuffey, *The eclectic third reader; containing selections in prose and poetry, from the best American and English writers. With plain rules for reading, and directions for avoiding common errors* (Cincinnati, 1837), page 156. Courtesy of Albert and Shirley Small Special Collections Library, University of Virginia

like New England's rocky soil, needed to be "carefully cultivated" if they were to produce beautiful and worthy things.[41]

Because McGuffey wanted to develop students' faculties, the readers encouraged conversation and deliberation. McGuffey hoped that the lessons would not be accepted passively; they were to be internalized only once students really understood them. The readings should open up "questions" to "lead the mind of the pupil, as often as practicable, beyond the pages of the book." While they should inspire students "to make discoveries," McGuffey hoped the lessons in the readings would also be "interrogated."[42]

We must be capable of good works, not just passionate outbursts, McGuffey believed. Thus, he included a reading by "Miss Beecher" contrasting the lives of Anglican missionary Henry Martyn and the English poet Lord Byron. Like others of her era, Beecher believed that "by reasoning from the known laws of the mind, we gain the position that obedience to the Divine law is the surest mode of securing every species of happiness." If we were to be happy, we must forge our lives in ways that were true to human nature, which was divine nature.

Henry Martyn did just that. He left England to preach the Gospel in India and Persia, even though he was "the object of many affections" and "won the highest honors" at university, and before him lay "the road to fame and honor." He chose not to pursue these lower worldly goods but to live a life truly worth living. He devoted himself to others, and suffered for his religious convictions. "He died *alone*—a stranger in a strange land," but because he chose to live a good life, he died in "*true happiness.*"

The poet Byron, on the other hand, was "one of the most mournful exhibitions of a noble mind in all the wide chaos of ruin and disorder." Byron did not allow the higher faculties to reign over his lower ones. His imagination was not tempered by reason and morality. Instead, he "passed through existence amid the wildest disorder of a ruined spirit." Byron's mind was "utterly unbalanced, teeming with rich thoughts and overbearing impulses, the port of the strongest fancies, and the strongest passions." He was "bound down by no habit, restrained by no principle." Unable to distinguish between the base and the noble, Byron's personal life was a combination of "manly dignity and childish folly." While he had moments of true genius, he was a "wounded spirit" who lamented on the eve of his thirty-third birthday, in his own words, "I go to bed with a heaviness of heart at having lived so long and to so little purpose."[43]

McGuffey's selections also reminded young people that they had duties to others. They reinforced the Golden Rule: "Therefore all things whatsoever ye would that men should do to you, do ye even so to them; for this is the law and the prophets" (Matthew 7:12). The Golden Rule relied more on the moral sense than reason. One must learn early to empathize with the suffering of others. In one selection, a boy turned over a turtle, and his friend asked, "What if you were a turtle, and somebody should put you on your back?" We must respect others' feelings, even a turtle's, for "a turtle can feel."[44] Another selection featured a boy stealing a robin's nest. His sisters asked him to think about the poor mother robin's feelings: "Who can describe her distress when she returns to feed her helpless little ones." The boy's "heart was touched," and he quickly returned the nest. To cause others to suffer for our own happiness was wrong.[45] Real happiness came not from seeking superficial "beauty" or "wealth" but offering "kindness."[46]

To educate was to produce a human being, and this meant offering young people the tools to determine what was right and wrong, and ultimately to distinguish between worthy and unworthy ways of living, McGuffey believed. To some extent, concerns about new immigrants and poor people animated reformers' emphasis on character.[47] But reformers did not target the poor alone. Horace Mann, as we saw in the previous chapter, saved his harshest, angriest, and most colorful language for the selfish rich who were not good stewards of society. One southerner, writing to Mann in 1846, complained that opposition to public schools came "principally from property-holders who have educated their children or have none to send to school."[48]

McGuffey's Readers too aimed at the moral sentiments of the rich. Gluttony, in particular, was condemned. Some scholars have argued that McGuffey did little more than reinforce middle-class values of hard work.[49] There is some truth to this. The *Readers* celebrated those who worked hard and earned what they had and condemned both the rich and the poor alike who did not. Students were told that they were responsible for their own success and failure, that they must be self-made. In one selection, former U.S. attorney general William Wirt advised that "the education, moral and intellectual, of every individual must be, chiefly, his own work." Those who took advantage of their opportunities would make it; others would not. That's why "young men who have had precisely the same opportunities" ended up in different places.[50]

Yet at the heart of *McGuffey's Readers* was a reminder that individual success was linked to the health and well-being of one's community. Various selections invoked the beauty of America's landscape and its ideals of liberty to foster in students a love of their country.[51] But McGuffey never equated patriotism with blind devotion, as some of his critics have concluded.[52] As with everything else,

McGuffey wanted his students to use their minds and hearts to reach the right conclusions. Thus, in the *Fourth Reader*, students were warned about "political corruption" and the "irresistible power of temptation." Far from deferring blindly to leaders, citizens were encouraged to watch over their leaders to ensure their honesty.[53] A few lessons later, students would have learned that what made George Washington great was not his accomplishments but his virtue, his willingness to put the public good ahead of his own.[54]

Character is about not what you know but who you are. The *Readers* sought to form young people into adults capable of living worthy lives. They sought to foster virtues or dispositions. The virtues they emphasized were autonomy (one's capacity to resist temptation in order to pursue higher goods), empathy, and the Golden Rule (living up to one's duties to self, community, and God). To orient one's life around something worthwhile—to be good citizens and to lead a good life—one needed to be able to say no to temptation. Discipline was, McGuffey argued, the basis for self-culture.[55]

McGuffey offered young people a charmed world—one with chirping birds, happy turtles, and good children. It was a utopia where the Golden Rule ruled, where the better angels of human nature helped create a perfect society in which individuals cared for each other, and in which, through their caring, the world was made more beautiful for all its inhabitants. McGuffey's *Readers* taught that each human being had the capacity to reason, imagine, and love. The purpose of education was to develop this innate potential.

The Bible and Public Schools

For readers today, the presence of biblical references—and even biblical passages—in the nation's most popular public school readers may be surprising. Even during McGuffey's era, the role of the Bible in the public schools was a controversial issue. Catholics worried not just about the use of a Protestant translation —the King James Bible—but also an implicit pro-Protestant perspective (see chapter 5).

Trained as a minister, McGuffey shared with many of his Presbyterian fellows a firm belief in the Bible's centrality to American life. At the same time, by including biblical selections alongside secular readings, McGuffey made it possible for the Bible to be read as a shared cultural text for teaching moral principles rather than as a sacred text that required religious instruction. McGuffey was also purposefully ecumenical. American diversity required a text that was premised on

Christian principles but was not so narrow that it could not be used by families from different denominations.

McGuffey himself made "no apology" for using scriptural passages "in a christian country." The Bible should be taught as part of "general education" and not used to preach a particular religious viewpoint. To McGuffey—Catholics would have disagreed—"the Bible is the only book . . . which is not sectarian," since any other text would reflect the theological assumptions of particular denominations.[56] As he revised new editions, he cut or edited selections deemed offensive to Catholics or Jews, seeking to uphold the very Golden Rule that his *Readers* conveyed to young Americans.[57]

That McGuffey felt the need to make "no apology" suggests that there was a need to apologize. Still, one can exaggerate how often the Bible was read, not for moral purposes as in *McGuffey's Readers*, but as a devotional. While some schools opened their days with readings from Scripture, many did not, causing concerned observers to worry about the absence of the Bible and religion from public schools.

St. Louis citizens rejected schoolroom Bible reading in 1840, and the school board in Watertown, Wisconsin, decided to eliminate Bible readings in 1858. In Allegany County, New York, in 1844, only 27 schools out of 105 opened with a passage from the Scriptures. In 1850 Bible reading was much more common in the Northeast than in the West, Midwest, or South.[58] In 1842 Detroit's new school board decided to prohibit Bible reading, but the negative response spurred the board to reverse itself three years later. Given the growing number of Catholic immigrants, the board determined that teachers could read from the Bible of their choice if they wished. Of course, almost all the city's teachers were Protestants.[59]

Horace Mann struggled to find the right balance. An 1827 Massachusetts law prohibited using public funds for sectarian texts, but most agreed that there was a difference between religious and sectarian content. Mann insisted, as did McGuffey, that public schools only purchase and use books that offered the general principles of Christianity—but what did this mean? At a time when Massachusetts was deeply divided between liberal Unitarian and conservative Congregationalist factions, and when new migrants were starting to come from predominantly Catholic Ireland, it was unclear whether citizens could agree even on Christianity's general principles. Some of Mann's opponents suspected that a general Christianity was really nothing more than code for Mann's own Unitarian interpretation, which, of course, was, to its detractors, sectarian.[60]

Mann's efforts were similar to those made around the nation. Most Americans took for granted that America was a Protestant nation, and American national identity was premised on this shared religious heritage.[61] Yet they also faced several issues surrounding religion. The first was the growing number of Catholics and the small but influential number of "free thinkers" who challenged Americans' Protestant assumptions.[62] The second was how to reconcile Americans' deep commitment to the separation of church and state with their equally deeply held belief that public schools must teach character, and that character had its basis in religion. The third was the simple fact that, even as most Americans took Protestantism for granted, they disagreed on the specific tenets that mattered.[63] While American culture might be broadly Protestant, what to do or say about the Bible in schools was less easy to figure out.

Reading, Writing, Arithmetic

In addition to character, the elementary curriculum emphasized reading and writing (literacy) and arithmetic (numeracy), but to what end? The ultimate goal was to form a good person, one capable of putting knowledge and virtue into action. This goal required rethinking both the purposes of reading, writing, and arithmetic and how they should be taught. In the era immediately following the Revolution, the purpose of literacy was to form citizens who combined wisdom and virtue with rhetoric, or public speaking. In the Roman Republic, rhetoric was the highest art because citizens would have to engage each other on the Senate floor. Some Greek and Roman rhetoric teachers had considered rhetoric independent of knowledge, but Roman statesman Cicero believed that good citizens not only needed to know how to convince other citizens but also had to do so on the basis of what was correct (knowledge) and what was right (virtue).[64]

After the American Revolution almost all reading textbooks—called spellers —emphasized oratory. Their goal was to create citizens who could participate in public life. Thus, they focused on teaching students to speak clearly, with proper emotion, intonation, and body language. The spellers celebrated Greek orator Demosthenes, who was seen as a role model for young Americans because of his selfless commitment to using speech to serve the common good.[65]

The best-selling textbook in post-Revolutionary America was Lindley Murray's 1799 *The English Reader*. Reading might be "productive of improvement both to the understanding [wisdom] and the heart [virtue]" but, ultimately, learning to read well must be connected to learning to speak well. Citizens must offer each other "clear communication of ideas and feelings." In other words, the purpose of reading well was connected with speaking with others in the public places of a democracy; it was oriented outward toward other citizens.[66]

Reading and writing were linked to oratory. Students would engage in public speaking to demonstrate their mastery, which would also prepare them to be effective citizens capable of influencing their fellow citizens in a society in which public opinion determined who got elected and which laws were passed.[67] Most instruction in reading and writing itself was mechanical—the emphasis was on correct grammar and intonation.[68]

That was how Elizabeth Buffum Chace, who was born in 1806 in Rhode Island, remembered it. Chace was an opponent of slavery and allowed her house to be used as a stop on the Underground Railroad, the secret network of homes that enslaved people relied on as they made their way from bondage in the South to freedom in the North or in Canada. She was also an advocate of women's right to vote. She was not fond, however, of how reading and writing were taught. "In grammar we were obliged to recite every word of Murray's large volume over and over, for a long time, before we were set to make practical application of it in the analysis or parsing of a sentence."[69]

An Ohio critic remembered that the "reading lesson accomplishes little for the pupils beyond an indifferent drill in vocal culture. It is not generally regarded as a means of cultivating expression and stimulating thought."[70] Author William Russell, who migrated to the United States from Scotland in 1819, argued that schools "invert the order" by teaching writing and speaking before students learned to think.[71]

By the time *McGuffey's Readers* entered the market, the ways Americans read had been transformed. Reading—like everything—has a history. Why we read, what we read, and how we learn to read are not constant over time, but change with new social contexts.[72] Immediately after the Revolution, reading, and the places where reading took place—such as libraries, lectures, and even social clubs—were sites in which citizens engaged in public exchange. Literacy was directed outward, to others, rather than inward, to the experience one personally had of reading.[73]

Not just in schools, but everywhere one turned, Americans in the nineteenth century started to focus equally on what was happening inside them. People now read in domestic settings, symbolizing the private rather than the public importance of reading. More Americans were reading novels, many of which—like Jane Austen's—emphasized what people felt and thought, rather than actions.[74]

In turn, many American men and women learned to have similar conversations within their own minds as they sought to develop their own identities and enrich their experience of their interior lives.

Reading other people's autobiographies and diaries helped Americans understand how other people made sense of their lives; writing their own helped them do the same.[75] Life, it seemed, had become not a series of roles to perform—as elocutionary textbooks had emphasized—but something to experience, and the more literate one was, and the more knowledge one had, the deeper and more profound that experience could be. Moreover, lives were seen as continuous—where earlier experiences shaped later ones and people developed a discrete identity. To create a life then meant to be able to interpret and make sense of one's own inner world—for which reading and writing were fundamental.[76]

Students should read and write not just to gain basic skills but, reformers argued, to make themselves. Reading and writing well improved students' ability to make meaning out of the world—in fact, to impose meaning upon the world.[77] The better one could read and write, the more fuel there was inside to light one's internal fire, and the brighter that fire, the more illuminated would be the outside world. Democratizing access to self-making required giving all children the skills and knowledge that would then transform the external world—they would make not just themselves but the world they inhabited, both for themselves and, through their creative energies, for others too.

Self-culture cannot be achieved unless every person is taught "the power of Utterance," Channing believed, in order to help her give her mind "voice and to exchange it for other minds." Through mastery of language, "we understand ourselves better, our conceptions grow clearer, by the very effort to make them clear to another."[78] Words "should be looked at as a medium, not as an end," Horace Mann proclaimed.[79] An author in the *North American Review* argued that "the first thing" schools should do is enable "children and youth to understand what they learn." To understand meant to engage the mind, to process material, and to make meaning out of it. Too often, students were expected to rely on "memory" in order to "recite," which made it look like they knew something when they "know nothing."[80]

McGuffey condemned the old ways of teaching literacy, as if reading was nothing but "an exercise of memory" that need not engage the faculties of reason and imagination. Good teachers needed to "awaken the attention" of students, not have students passively repeat what the teacher or the books said. In fact, the whole point of reading was to develop the child from the inside. "Let the child be encouraged to tell over the story, which he has just read, in language of his own," making the knowledge his and coming to his own conclusions.[81] According to an advertisement for *McGuffey's Readers* in a Berkshire, Massachusetts, newspaper, "The leading principle of this system is, that the child should be regarded not as a mere recipient of the ideas of others, but as an agent capable of collecting and originating and producing most of the ideas which are necessary for its education, when presented with the objects or the facts from which they may be derived."[82]

This was a democratic understanding of what it meant to read. In the past, the words in a book were to be accepted without too many questions. Students memorized them and recited them. Now reformers like Mann and McGuffey wanted students to "understand the meaning of the words they read."[83] Teachers should ask young people not to repeat but to interpret what they read. This reflected in part a new recognition of citizens as active participants in public life, but the importance of reading for understanding and meaning went beyond citizenship to cultivating the intellectual and creative capacities of human beings. Language was considered vital to help people express themselves not just to each other but to themselves. We formed ourselves—we engaged in self-culture—through language, educators argued. We must learn from reading ways to imagine life, but we must also reflect on our own lives through language.

The ability to use language well was therefore "an indispensable condition of our existence as rational beings." Self-culture could not happen without a real understanding of language. Each person was considered a unique individual who must learn to make sense of and refine her or his internal life. If self-making required "a creative mind, revolving, searching, reforming, perfecting within its own silent recesses," how could a student really search within herself or himself without a language that "can bring into life whatever was prepared in darkness?" Horace Mann wondered. True individual freedom came when each student made knowledge her or his own, understood it with reason, and transformed it with imagination. "Knowledge is not annexed to the mind like a foreign substance" but must be made knowledge by the mind's "own vital powers." Thus, every American "must think with his own mind, as every singer, in a choir, must sing with his own voice."[84]

In short, to engage in citizenship and self-culture required going beyond recitation of what others thought to thinking on one's own. Public schools should seek to graduate not just critical but creative thinkers. Reading and writing were not simply mechanical exercises, but rather spiritual ones, by which the mind was cultured, and people, by taking what they learned, processing it, and articulating it to themselves and to others, transformed what they read from mere words to something meaningful. Someone who could read but not understand was "a mere grinder of words."[85]

The same kinds of changes can be seen in how educators understood arithmetic. For most of the colonial era, very little arithmetic was taught; it was seen as unnecessary except as a practical skill for merchants. Farmers needed only basic counting skills, and elites associated math with the low work of making money, not the high work of politics and culture. Most colonial schools focused on reading and writing. Basic arithmetic would be introduced to students, usually boys, who went on to academies.

Boston's schools first required arithmetic in 1789.[86] As the century progressed, arithmetic came to be seen as more important since more Americans were engaged in commerce. Everyone now needed basic numeracy. But, like reading, math had long been taught through recitations, where external performance mattered more than internal experience. Caleb Bingham, author of one of the era's best-selling textbooks, accused one respected New England academy teacher of not even understanding the math himself but hiding his ignorance by asking students to copy problems from a book: "Any boy could copy the work from the manuscript of any other further advanced than himself, and the writer [Bingham] never heard any explanation of any principle while he was at school."[87] This was also how a North Carolina author remembered math instruction. Teachers would provide rules, and students would do math by "memory." Students had to perform, but they never had to understand "why."[88]

Like reading and writing, the goals of math also changed in order to encourage self-culture. Warren Colburn, born on a Massachusetts farm in 1793, worked in factories in Pawtucket, Rhode Island, before enrolling in Harvard College in 1816. After Harvard, Colburn taught school, like many recent college graduates did. He then went on to work in manufacturing, but he had a deep interest in science. Influenced by new ideas about how children learn, in 1821 Colburn published a new textbook, *First Lessons in Arithmetic on the Plan of Pestalozzi, with some Impressions*.[89]

The title of Colburn's book invoked Johann Pestalozzi, a Swiss educator who influenced the shape of American education. To Pestalozzi, young children should not be treated as sinful, passionate beasts to be tamed but rather as tender plants to be carefully cultivated in loving nurseries. Rather than fostering obedience, education must develop students' moral and intellectual potential. Children needed to think for themselves and feel for themselves before they could understand for themselves; good teachers tapped into students' natural curiosity and slowly and methodically developed their minds and character.[90]

Colburn's new book was "a sign of life from the dead."[91] Colburn, following Pestalozzi, argued that we must follow children's natural inclinations and foster their innate curiosity. "As soon as a child begins to use his senses, nature continually presents to his eyes a variety of objects; and one of the first properties which he discovers, is the relation of number." Children in fact often learn to count well before they can use letters. Math would develop students' reasoning powers. "Few exercises strengthen and mature the mind so much as arithmetical calculations." If math was taught "to be understood," then students increased their power of "reasoning."[92]

Speaking to Boston's American Institute of Instruction in 1830, Colburn argued that math is eminently practical; everyone had to use arithmetic "in the ordinary routine of business." If taught properly, arithmetic also encouraged "discipline of the mind" and thus strengthened reason. Students needed to do more than simply calculate, however; they must be able to understand math's insights. Math was not about applying "a rule" but about understanding how numbers work, and how nature works. By "exerting his own powers," a student would internalize mathematical reasoning and knowledge, would make "his own rules," which were a "generalization of his own reasoning, and in a way agreeable to his own associations." In short, education's impact on what happened inside a person mattered as much as her or his external performance.[93]

Charles Davies, who taught math at West Point, reinforced this point in his book *The Logic and Utility of Mathematics* (1850). Math was one of the first ways in which students engaged with nature. Children early started to count, and over time children developed "notions of number." As students learned to think about the world through math, they would start to see the world with more insight. They would move beyond simple observations to "a system of symbols," which, like language, "not only enables us to express our known thoughts . . . but is a potent means of pushing our inquiries into unexplored regions." Finally, drawing on the ideas of Locke, Davies argued that math would help students develop their reasoning skills by developing exact ideas.[94]

Thus, reading, writing, and arithmetic became more than skills necessary to getting ahead in life. They were the building blocks on which all other learning would take place. Words and numbers formed the language through which students deepened their appreciation of Creation, enriched their experience of the world and their own inner lives, and developed the higher faculties of their minds.

Academic Subjects

Reading, writing, and arithmetic provided the tools necessary to make sense of the world, but it was through engaging with academic subjects that abstract skills could be turned into insight. Educators believed that true insight required a curriculum rich in content. Thus, as students progressed into upper grades, schools would introduce the arts and sciences.

By 1860, there was broad consensus on what subjects constituted a high school education.[95] Eighty-five percent of high schools offered arithmetic, and more than 90 percent offered algebra and geometry. Over half offered grammar, analysis, and composition. After having long been relegated to the margins, science became part of the core, with 70 percent of high schools teaching botany, astronomy, and geology, 85 percent teaching chemistry and physiology, 90 percent teaching physical geography, and 100 percent teaching natural philosophy.

Classical languages still reigned, with 80 percent of high schools offering at least one year of Latin, and 30 percent offering three years. Greek was taught in 35 percent. Modern languages, however, were on the rise. German was taught in 35 percent of schools, and French in 20 percent. Other subjects included bookkeeping (40 percent), necessary for success in business, mental philosophy (60 percent), and moral philosophy (55 percent).[96]

History lagged behind other academic subjects. Only 40 percent of schools offered ancient history, 30 percent modern history, and 15 percent U.S. history and English history. In 1840 about half of Massachusetts's primary schools taught history, but it became required in 1857. Only a third of New York State's academies taught history in 1825, but 92 percent did by 1860. That year, most high school students in America would have about three years of history.[97]

To Edward Mansfield, the purpose of studying academic subjects—the arts and sciences—was threefold: it "is the best exercise to improve the reason to the highest point"; studying academic subjects "gives the most complete idea we can have of form, order, beauty, and harmony"; and, "as the works of creation are exhaustless, and the spirit of man immortal, science affords an exhaustless field for the investigations, the improvement, the strengthening, and enlargement of the human mind."[98] In other words, academic subjects improved critical thinking skills; gave students insight into themselves, their society, and nature; and provided the raw materials for them to imitate Creation through self-culture—through the "exhaustless" world before them, which they analyzed with reason and then imagined anew.

Every subject was designed to further these three goals. To understand "the world of matter and the world of mind," students must study the "various departments of knowledge," believed A. S. Welch, principal of Michigan's normal school, or teacher's college, in Ypsilanti.[99] No one subject alone could offer insight into the world. For Mansfield, "The illumination of the mind . . . is made up of *many* lights, each shining in its own sphere."[100] Students must therefore see the world from different perspectives, from the perspective of mathematics, or history, or literature.

A student should study higher mathematics not because of "any practical use" but because it would "develop the faculties of abstraction, reason, and imagination."[101] A student with knowledge of mathematics could see deeper into the structure of the world, understand better the causes for actions, and thus experience the world more profoundly than one who relied on experience without knowledge.[102]

Critical thinking, imagination, morality, and insight: this was why the arts and sciences mattered. By reading "history, poetry, criticism, essays, novels, stories, biographies, travels," students gain, through the "*written expression* of thought," access to perspectives before unavailable. Each work of literature was "a small, broken, vista-like picture" of the internal life of the "soul." More than anything, literature was "the guide of the imagination," the "originating faculty of the human mind."[103]

History was a "fertilizing stream" for "the poet" and the novelist. It connected the imagination not with fantasy but "the right, the beautiful, and the glorious." History also provided insight into "human nature" in action. Finally, by studying the history of nations past and present, citizens were prepared to understand where liberty thrived, and where it did not.[104]

Like other subjects, the focus in history shifted from memorization to understanding and imagining, in order to ensure its impact on each student's internal development. Early history textbooks, like one in 1807, had urged students "*to commit all the historical facts to memory*," and an 1840 book echoed by asking students to recite the material "exactly in the language of the textbook."[105] In contrast, Emma Willard, in her widely assigned *History of the United States*, believed that history should engage all the "faculties" by offering a "frame-work" to connect facts to something larger. Students should start with their own nation's history because, as Pestalozzi had taught her, "the natural order of the thoughts must be regarded," and children start local and move outward.[106]

Like mathematics and the natural sciences, history would both improve general thinking skills and provide insight. History had the added burden of fostering the patriotism necessary for good citizenship. Students must be placed not just in time but in American time. Like McGuffey, North Carolina's Calvin Henderson Wiley believed true patriotism was not "an arrogant and self-sufficient egotism" but instead "a proper self-respect and love of home."[107]

Cultivating a sense of American patriotism—what Willard called "national virtue"[108]—was particularly important at a time when white Americans were divided not just by religion and class but between the slaveholding South and the free North. History textbooks affirmed that America's future depended on the vigilant protection of liberty and the union of the states. From the seventeenth century forward, American settlers had struggled to protect their liberty and achieve unity, textbook writers claimed, somewhat erroneously. Studying American history would help Americans come to see themselves as "one people" united "by the identity of their language, laws, and customs, and the ties of a common kindred," as well as by their commitment to "republican" principles. American history's lesson was clear: would you, American citizens, carry the legacy forward?[109]

The natural sciences were a new addition to the basic curriculum. Well after the Civil War, Harvard's president Charles Eliot still complained that the sciences lacked the prestige and respect given to the humanities.[110] Most observers believed that by studying nature, students gained access to God's Creation. Science was also seen as modern and useful. Reformers like Thomas Jefferson had hoped that science—because it was the progressive uncovering of truth—would serve the larger cause of liberty by replacing myth with knowledge. It was seen as useful—an industrializing society needed technical innovation. Thus, science worked its way into the curriculum for multiple reasons. Educators might have appreciated science's ability to provide insight and to develop the faculties, but many appreciated its practicality.[111]

Studying the natural world encouraged students' "powers of observation" and improved the "faculty of discrimination," proclaimed Harvard scientist Asa Gray, who would go on to introduce and popularize Charles Darwin's ideas in America.[112] To learn science did not mean to memorize facts, any more than it did in math, history, or literature. It meant, instead, to engage in the scientific method, to learn to observe facts in the world, and to draw conclusions from them. Educators urged schools to equip themselves with microscopes and other scientific apparatus to help students do science themselves.[113]

In sum, academic subjects would not just develop the faculties of reason, morality, and imagination; they also would provide knowledge, what Yale's professors in 1828 had called the "furniture" of the mind. Together, these two outcomes would cultivate young Americans' capabilities for citizenship and self-making.[114] The "first duty" of all Americans remained citizenship, proclaimed Massachusetts governor Edward Everett. Public schools thus must ensure all Americans "the capacity of deriving knowledge, with readiness and accuracy, from books and documents." But education aimed beyond citizens to human beings, enabling people "to rise above the dust beneath their feet, to the consideration of the great spiritual concerns of immortal natures."[115]

The Ambiguities of Economics

During the decades that witnessed the expansion of the ideal of self-culture and the self-made man, economic inequality was on the rise. Industrialization brought great wealth to investors but also relied on a poorly paid and an increasingly immigrant workforce. The number of Americans employed in manufacturing grew from 3.2 percent in 1810 to 14.5 percent by 1850. The wealth held by the top 1 percent of Americans grew from 12.6 percent in 1774 to 29 percent by 1860.[116] Americans, in other words, were becoming less equal. People were confused. They were told they could pull themselves up by their own bootstraps but discovered that even if they worked hard, the laws of the market could bring them down.[117]

You would not learn this from *McGuffey's Readers*. Their purpose was to develop individual character, and they did not address questions of structural inequality. In his *Readers*, McGuffey condemned any person who did not empathize with the sufferings of others or who sought to gain at the expense of another. Being a good person required each American to do her or his duties regardless of wealth.[118] In a revised edition of the *Second Reader*, two selections sit side by side, "the rich boy" and "the poor boy." The rich boy, to the manor born, is aware of his luck and responsibility. He and his parents help the less fortunate, and the boy thinks to himself that no person ought to be poor and that, if he could, he would buy for the poor "cottages" and "clothes" and ensure that "they should all learn to read and write, and be very good." For his part, the poor boy works hard, helps his parents, and does not engage in idleness. He is thankful for what he has, and "when he sees little boys and girls riding on pretty horses, or in coaches," he does not "envy" them, recognizing that they too are people with problems and duties.[119] While the poor should work hard without envy, the rich must make a better society for everyone, not just for themselves. Thus, McGuffey, focusing on individuals, condemned both greed and envy.

The kind of discipline McGuffey taught was considered vital to making it in a market economy. Success required hard work and the ability to save and to plan ahead. This kind of discipline was, paradoxically, quite difficult to achieve because the market constantly threatened to undermine the very character traits on which economic success depended. Everywhere one turned, sellers sought to separate people from their money. Temptation for immediate pleasures was ever present. Markets encouraged impulsive behavior. *McGuffey's Readers* hoped to teach people how and why to resist sellers' appeals to our basest desires.[120]

The focus on individuals was built into the assumptions of economics. Thus, in high school one might read in the popular textbook *Elements of Political Economy*, by Brown University president Francis Wayland, similar ideas to McGuffey's. Success depended on self-discipline and hard work; if you did not make it, you had no one to blame but yourself.[121] Wayland proclaimed the principles of economics to be "analogous" to those of morality. Like human psychology, the economy had "determinate laws," the most important being that "no man can grow rich, without industry and frugality." These laws derived from God, who had "excited us to labor by sufficient rewards, and deterred us from indolence by sufficient penalties." Thus, all that was needed in economics was "to give to these rewards and penalties their free and their intended operation."[122] Or, according to Rev. Henry Ward Beecher: "I never knew an early-rising, hard-working prudent man, careful of his earnings, and strictly honest, who complained of bad luck. A good character, good habits and honest industry, are impregnable to the assaults of all the ill luck that ever fools dreamed of."[123]

This commitment to a connection between external rewards and internal ordering had to do with economics textbook authors' presumption that the world was divinely created and that a well-ordered soul would thrive in a well-ordered universe.[124] In reality, it took a lot more than hard work to make it in the nineteenth century. Government investment was vital for prosperity, and public policies and court decisions determined many aspects of economic life.[125] American law, for example, allowed investors to pool their resources in a corporation but did not permit laborers to do so by forming a union.[126] Who you were mattered too. Opportunities were very different if one was poor, Catholic, black, or a woman.[127] Certainly, many hard-working Americans could save enough to achieve what Abraham Lincoln aspired for them—land and independence in the West.[128] But even then, whether on farm or in city, the vagaries of the economy could bankrupt people who made all the right decisions and embodied all the right virtues. Fortune, not hard work, had a lot to do with success; the laws of the market were rarely rational.[129]

Wayland did not address these questions any more than did McGuffey. To be sure, Wayland was no libertarian. He, like Adam Smith and McGuffey, was a moral philosopher. He would no doubt condemn greed. His textbook argued that the rich ought to pay proportionally more than the poor since they have more property and wealth to protect. And Wayland argued that every American had to fulfill her or his civic obligations by paying taxes for public goods: "the support of civil government, education, national improvements [roads, canals, railroads, &c.], the support of the institutions of religion, war, and pauperism [the sick, the destitute, and the helpless]."[130]

Authors of economics textbooks furthered the ideal of self-culture by teaching people to think of themselves as responsible for their own destinies. Life was not handed down or inherited; it was something achieved. Success required the discipline to resist immediate desires in order to achieve long-term goals. Young people had to become responsible adults capable of making it in a market economy. None of the textbooks celebrated greed or self-interest; they promoted the kinds of virtues—thrift, honesty, hard work—that were good in any person at any level of society. They never proclaimed that wealth was the end of a good life. They aspired to endow young people with the capability to thrive in a market economy so that they could engage in meaningful pursuits of happiness. Yet there was always the risk, because textbook authors linked wealth to moral worth, that the former would come to stand in for the latter, or even become more attractive.[131]

Self-Made Men and Women

Mobile, Alabama, superintendent of schools W. T. Walthall condemned Americans' "Vandal spirit." Americans "would tear down the fairest fabric of art," he believed, "if it stood in the way of a railroad" or "cotton factory." The result was a society robbed "of all its amenities, science of all its beauties, and life of all its poetry."[132] Walthall worried that many Americans did not support the kind of liberal education that reformers promoted. Indeed, it seemed to reformers, many Americans questioned the necessity of it.

But everyone needed a liberal education, reformers believed. That was hard for many Americans to get. "Give us *self-made* men," Americans proclaimed. We need more men like Washington and Franklin, who "never studied Greek or Latin." Why, they wondered, does anyone need more than an elementary education? In response, one exasperated observer countered, nobody can make himself through "efforts purely and personally his own." How could Americans really think that by choosing to "not study what Washington and Franklin do not study" they will somehow "become Washingtons and Franklins"?[133]

Free individuals are made, not found, proclaimed a professor before a teachers' convention in Ohio. That's why "*schools are necessary.*" Yes, "there are men who have educated themselves, but they are exceptions."[134] Indeed, wrote one Alabama educator, public schools "would not weaken the self-reliance of the citizen" nor "destroy his individuality," but "teach him to feel it."[135] To the antebellum advocates of democratic education, the self-made person was not a rugged individualist who went out to conquer the wilderness using nothing but brute strength and common sense. Far from it. Self-making—self-culture—required schools to nurture young people, to develop both their character and their minds. Self-making was not something one did alone; it required the community.[136]

3 Politics of Education

The Social Principle

WHEN HORACE MANN ACCEPTED THE POSITION of secretary of the Massachusetts Board of Education, mounted his horse, and rode around the state, he was appalled. In his *First Annual Report*, Mann painted a sorry picture of the state's schools. Most teachers did not meet basic quality standards, despite an 1826 law requiring local school committees to be vigilant. No efforts were being made to ensure children had access to the best textbooks; instead, children continued to come to school with whatever was at hand. In any case, students did not attend regularly, and those who did received too little instruction—an average school year was six months and twenty-five days.

This proved, Secretary Mann concluded, the "apathy of the people." Rich parents "turn away from the Common Schools" to send their children to a "private school or academy" and ignored their obligations to public schools. Out of forty-three towns (not including Boston) that made up two-fifths of the state's population, only fourteen maintained all the schools required by law—elementary, secondary, and grammar.

"The maintenance of free schools rests wholly upon the social principle," Mann scolded his readers.[1] Mann and his allies aspired for schools that were truly public—overseen by public officials and funded by public dollars. He worried that too many Americans were unwilling to devote the time and resources necessary to educate every child in every community. To make it happen would require the state to get more involved.

But what Mann saw as a failure of the social principle was in fact proof of a different social principle at work, what we today call social capital. Social capital is a measure of citizens' capacity to work together. It is generated by "social networks and the norms of reciprocity and trustworthiness that arise from them." In other words, communities with high levels of social capital are places where citizens trust each other and are in the habit of working together. This makes it easier for them to cooperate to promote public goods like education. In towns around the nation, citizens tapped into their local reservoirs of social capital to organize schools for their children.[2]

And it worked. By the 1830s, more children were going to more schools than ever before, because ordinary Americans had come together to do it, without much aid from the state or from the likes of Horace Mann. The origins of public education in America, despite what Mann may have thought, lay with ordinary citizens who pooled their labor, time, and resources to organize schools well before Mann arrived on the scene.

Americans organized two kinds of schools, academies and common public schools. To organize, oversee, and fund these schools, Americans gave time and money. In short, citizens worked together. Modest-sized communities boasted high levels of social capital. In fact, it was in America's small towns—in 1830, 91 percent of Americans lived in towns of less than twenty-five hundred people —where public education really took off.[3] By 1826, it was estimated that more than 70 percent of Massachusetts children up to age nineteen were enrolled in common schools in towns of less than twenty-five hundred residents, and more than 50 percent in towns with fewer than five thousand residents. Larger towns lagged. In towns between five thousand and ten thousand residents, only about 38 percent of children enrolled, while the cities of Salem and Boston had enrollment rates of 20.9 and 30 percent, respectively. New York State had a similar negative correlation between town size and percentage enrolled.[4]

The social principle in action was marvelous, or so it appeared to French visitor Alexis de Tocqueville as he traveled across America in the 1830s. "Americans of all ages, all conditions, and all minds are constantly joining together in groups," he wrote in awe. In Europe, a lord or noble would do the work, but in America people banded together in associations. "This is how they create hospitals, prisons, and schools."[5] Thus, a paradox. To Mann, the schools were in crisis. To other

Americans, the schools were a triumph, proof that ordinary citizens, working together, could do great things.

Age of the Academies

After the Revolution, American leaders everywhere had extolled an educated citizenry, but it was far from clear how to achieve one. State governments lacked the capacity to do it themselves. There was no state or local bureaucracy to carry out public education, and there were few public common schools. One approach was to work with private corporations. For example, if the state wanted to build a bridge, it offered a group of investors corporate privileges and the right to profit from tolls. In return, investors risked their own money and mobilized resources to build the bridge and to run it.[6] State governments' approach to education was similar. States wanted colleges, but they could not establish and run them. Instead, colleges received corporate charters authorizing them to hold property, charge tuition, and grant degrees. States subsidized colleges with land and other endowments but did not directly control them. Even as policy leaders sought to build public schools, they simultaneously encouraged citizens to organize themselves into chartered schools called academies. Indeed, the era between the Revolution and the Civil War has been called the "age of the academies."[7]

Academies sought to serve communities' diverse educational needs. Many offered elementary education to young children. For older children, academies provided both a classical curriculum in Greek and Latin and an "English track" with such subjects as rhetoric, history, math, modern languages, moral philosophy, various sciences like chemistry, botany, and geology, and often vocational subjects like bookkeeping and surveying. Academies were both academic and practical—since few of their students would go on to college, academies prepared them for various stations in life.[8]

Academies proliferated in the decades before the Civil War. According to one account, 6,100 academies were operating in 1855 (compared to 239 colleges and 80,978 common schools), but there were probably more.[9] Ohio chartered 100 academies between 1803 and 1840. Between 1818 and 1848, Illinois incorporated at least 125 academies. Historians have found 24 academies in Alabama and 55 in Virginia in 1830. By 1860, the number of Virginian academies increased seven times, as demand for schooling increased and Virginia, unlike other states, failed to establish a common school system. Georgia may have chartered more than 580 academies between the Revolution and Civil War.[10] The South by 1850 boasted more academies than did the North or Midwest.[11]

Between 1780 and 1800, Massachusetts incorporated at least 17 academies.[12] To subsidize academies, the legislature offered citizens a charter, authorized fund-raising lotteries and, in 1797, provided academies with vacant lands in Maine (then part of Massachusetts) to sell for the proceeds.[13] New England had at least 168 chartered academies by 1830.[14]

Most academies were coeducational, but new academies focused on girls also opened. At the time of the Revolution, few girls had received a formal education, but Americans after the American Revolution believed that women also needed to be educated. As a result, the number of schools serving girls increased dramatically, transforming women's lives by providing access to knowledge and skills that had long been reserved to men: history, languages, civics, math, and science. Between 1790 and the 1830s, at least 182 female academies and 14 other female seminaries opened. Many female graduates would become teachers and leading citizens at the local level and beyond, promoting such causes as temperance and antislavery.[15]

Academies were not-for-profit, open access, and supported by local and state funds. They were funded by a combination of private and public money. Private donations helped academies meet their capital needs—land, buildings, start-up costs. Their operating expenses depended on tuition and state support. State subsidies included one-time grants, lotteries, and the interest from permanent school funds derived from state and federal land sales and corporate stock.[16]

States sought to make sure that poorer students could attend. Indiana's constitution required that all academies be free for poor students and incorporated at least seventy-five academies between 1830 and 1850.[17] Ohio's 1803 constitution committed the state to increase access to education by promoting academies. Academies were "entitled to receive letters of incorporation," and in return must ensure that poor students could attend.[18] Some recent studies have suggested that academies were run in a "free-market context," but such a claim is inaccurate.[19] True, they had to bring in enough money to pay their bills, but they were also philanthropic enterprises, and their expenses were paid in large part by private donations and public subsidies. Moreover, they did not seek profit. Instead, they provided a public service for tuition fees.[20] States intended academies to use their resources to serve students. Thus, Massachusetts, New Hampshire, and Connecticut all limited the amount of revenue an academy could generate from land to ensure that academies did not become shells for profit making rather than for serving the public good.[21]

Academies were civic institutions, the product of local voluntarism and philanthropy. Raleigh Academy in North Carolina, founded in 1801, received the patronage of local elites and the broader community, which held fund-raisers to raise money for a new building.[22] In New York, almost all academies originated when town elites sought pledges from various citizens for land, labor, building materials, and cash.[23] In Deerfield, Massachusetts, around forty donors contributed in the 1790s to the establishment of its new academy.[24] Citizens took pride in academies, and their patrons intended to serve the public good. The founders of New Hampshire's Haverhill Academy promised, in return for a state charter in 1793, to be of "great Utility to the Publick."[25] Academies not only served communities by providing education but could improve local land values and encourage people to settle in western areas.[26]

Academies reflected the aspirations of upwardly mobile families. This also created tensions as academy teachers sought to inculcate young people with values and aspirations for life "beyond the farm."[27] They offered a higher education in the arts and sciences and encouraged students to think of themselves as part of the nation, not just of their communities, challenging the locally rooted ethic of the farming families from which many students originated. And until the Civil War, they were the primary institutions through which both boys and girls gained access to higher learning at a time when few attended colleges and public high schools were just being established.[28]

Because few states devoted as much effort to its academy system as did New York, it remains a good case study for today. Like other states, New York encouraged academies by offering citizens charters in return for raising donations. The legislature also provided relief for struggling academies, including grants, loans, and land. In 1784 and 1786 the legislature set aside land in each town for primary and secondary schooling. In 1792 it authorized the Regents of the University of the State of New York, which oversaw education for the state, to distribute £1,500 for five years to aid the state's academies, subject to state visitation. In 1801 a state lottery provided $12,500 for academies. In addition, many towns offered local tax support to academies in return for their public services.

In 1817 the Regents passed an ordinance allowing academies to receive income from the state's literature fund (a state fund to subsidize education) in proportion to the number of students enrolled in the classics and preparing for college; it extended its support to advanced English education in 1827, responding to public demand.[29] That year the legislature also increased the revenue available from the state literature fund from $4,000 to $12,000. Between 1820 and 1839, the legislature incorporated ninety-six academies, and the Regents chartered an additional fourteen. An 1838 law directed a large portion of federal dollars to New York's fund to support common schools, academies, and colleges. State subsidies increased substantially and, after 1838, a new law required all academies to meet the Regents' requirements—to have built a suitable building and sufficient apparatus and funds—before receiving public funds.

The legislature also targeted land or money to specific academies. Between 1820 and 1850, 231 new academies were chartered, thanks to state support and growing public support for education, and because the growing numbers of public elementary schools ultimately increased the number of students seeking higher education. By 1850, 161 academies received state aid.[30]

Although New York's academies received public support they still relied on tuition. Between 1825 and 1853, approximately three-fourths of an academy's operating expenses were paid for by student fees; the state contributed about 14 percent.[31] After 1836, even as New York's public schools expanded, the state increased its support of academies for higher (high school) learning. At its highest point, the median share of public support for academy teachers' salaries in 1840 was about 22 percent.[32]

Other states made similar efforts. In 1806, for example, the young state of Tennessee received a large amount of land from the federal government on the condition that one hundred thousand acres be set aside to support an academy in every county. Land sales endowed a college fund, an academy fund, and a common school fund. Thirty-eight academies were quickly established under 1806 legislation, largely for boys. In 1838 Tennessee required the newly incorporated Bank of Tennessee to pay eighteen thousand dollars per year to support academies, and in 1840 certain academies were declared "county academies" eligible to receive support from the bank. In short, Tennessee subsidized a robust charter school system.[33]

Although academies charged tuition, they sought to maximize access while remaining solvent. Students tended to be middle or upper class, in part because their families could afford higher learning and to keep their children out of the workforce. In the 1840s, academies charged an average of three to four dollars per term for common subjects, four to six dollars per term for advanced education, and five to seven dollars per term for classical education. Moreover, academies were flexible, allowing students to come and go as their lives and their funds allowed.[34]

Academies provided many Americans, especially in rural areas, with their first opportunity to gain an advanced education. They thus helped popularize the ideal of liberal education and fostered a generation of students who had experienced it. But American leaders ultimately concluded that academies were unable to meet the nation's need for an educated public and, worse, that they exacerbated the division between the haves and the have-nots.[35] In the post-Revolutionary era, Massachusetts governor Samuel Adams asserted that academies increased inequality because well-off families who sent their children to academies would be less willing to pay taxes for the state's common schools. Citizens, Adams argued, "will never willingly and cheerfully support two systems of schools." Given that academies could not serve all students, Adams wondered whether they would "grind the public school to the wall."[36] To education advocate Noah Webster, "in several states we find laws passed establishing provision for colleges and academies where people of property may educate their sons, but no provision made for instructing the poorer rank of people even in reading and writing."[37]

In the 1830s, Massachusetts legislator James G. Carter argued that free public education in common schools was vital at a time when the rich were segregating their children in private academies.[38] New York governor George Clinton suggested in 1795 that, while academies served "the opulent," all children deserved access to "common schools throughout the state."[39] New Yorker James Henry agreed with Clinton's assessment, concluding in 1843 that academies served those who think themselves "of nobler origin and of higher race than the common masses of humanity" while "equally deserving children of honest manual labor" attended common schools.[40] North Carolina state senator Archibald Murphey, in an 1816 report, reminded legislators that "a republic is bottomed upon the virtue of her citizens." To make education universal "requires a system of public education" since "private effort has not been entirely successful."[41] Connecticut governor Oliver Wolcott argued that public support was necessary to ensure access to quality schools for every citizen, not just "the opulent." "The poor and improvident," he worried, "are in greatest danger of being neglected."[42]

Grassroots Public Education

If academies provide evidence of social capital in action, the true roots of America's public schools lie in local district common schools, to which policymakers turned to equalize educational access.[43] Nineteenth-century districts were small: large enough to encompass several families and small enough for children to walk to school.[44] One-room schoolhouses, often unpainted clapboard buildings, were located at the edge of someone's property or on a vacant town lot.[45] Yet these schoolhouses were local products and, as such, reflected the best of their communities. Some started as "subscription schools" where parents agreed to share the cost of a teacher. James Herring, who had recently migrated from the United Kingdom, told of how he found himself in 1810, when he was about sixteen, in the small village of Wantage, New Jersey. Having spent the night at the home of one his traveling companions, he was asked the next morning to cut wood. The family quickly "discovered that I was better qualified to teach than to cut wood." He was hired to instruct the family's children. He was then urged to "prepare an agreement to be offered to all the residents in & around the village of Wantage." Herring asked for "a quarter for each scholar, and my board in each family for a proportionate time." After visiting the neighborhood's families, he "took possession of the School-House and started on my new track."[46]

Timothy Flint, a Harvard graduate doing missionary work in the West, was amazed at how quickly parents in 1820s frontier Indiana set up schools: "Among the first works of an incipient village, is a school house, and among the first associations, that for establishing a school."[47] The same was true of the settlers of Kenosha, Wisconsin, who in 1835 constructed a building to serve as a school and church, even as families continued to live in log shanties. Two years later, they pooled resources to build an academy building.[48] Similarly, in frontier Alabama, Clarke County, early settlers pooled resources to run a school out of a neighbor's home; a few years after, they built a schoolhouse.[49]

Over time, subscription schools gave way to district schools, organized by law, and funded through tuition and taxes. Yet the schools remained decidedly local institutions, and most school officers remained closely tied to their communities in ways that blurred the line between government and civil society. But because district schools were public institutions, they had the coercive authority to collect taxes. Since school districts were experienced simultaneously as community institutions and tax authorities, the annual school meeting became a major event. Citizens came together to discuss whether to have a school, what it would cost, and how to pay for it. They would reflect on the past year and plan for the coming one.[50] Darwin Atwater, a school trustee in Mantua Village, Ohio, commented in 1841 on "what has been done during the year that has past and what can be done during the year to come in the school in our neighborhood to forward the great enterprise of educating the human race."[51] At an 1849 annual meeting of School District No. 8 in North East, Dutchess County, New York, the "freeholders and legal voters" chose school officers and circulated a subscription list "for the purpose of raising the necessary funds to build an out-house." The following year they approved a thirteen-dollar tax "to repair the School House and defray incidental expenses."[52]

Tough decisions awaited citizens. After all, schools cost money, the district had to agree to foot the bill, and citizens often disagreed among themselves. Some farmers, especially the better-off ones, wanted the same kind of education provided in towns and cities. Others, perhaps poorer, or less committed to liberal education, wanted just the basics and thought parents should pay for anything more than that.[53] Throughout America, citizens divided between those who supported the reformers' program of liberal education and those who did not.

Controversial decisions had political ramifications. The school committee in District No. 4, Lima, New York, voted to allocate half its public money to summer-term teachers. This broke from a precedent that reserved most money for the winter term, when more students attended. Summer school served daughters, younger kids, and boys whose labor was not needed. The committee's decision upset the community, and two weeks later the decision was revoked at a special meeting.[54]

In Boylston, Massachusetts, in 1829, the town school committee decided to allocate public school money according to student enrollment, rather than by each district's tax contribution. Many citizens were upset, and over the next decades, competing proposals emerged. Wealthier districts sought to spend more than outlying districts, suggesting that not all agreed on what kind of education to provide.[55]

Districts did not always act quickly, often because voters did not want to pay taxes and because they did not see the need for them. In Boxford, Massachusetts, for example, the town school committee consistently urged better buildings, schoolbooks, and teachers, and even better attendance, but their appeals were ignored at the local level.[56] Rock County, Wisconsin, took years to fund and build a schoolhouse in the 1840s.[57] But whatever its drawbacks, relying on social capital had benefits. People showed commitment to the schools that they had organized themselves and funded out of their own pockets. Yes, voters could be parsimonious, but the spread of schools also suggested generosity. By 1839, just as Horace Mann was entering the picture, 38 percent of all Massachusetts children up to age nineteen were enrolled during the summer term and almost 46 percent in the winter term. In the state of New York, already more than 60 percent of children were enrolled in public schools by the 1820s.[58] As early as 1800, in fact, 37 percent of New York's children younger than age nineteen were enrolled in school. If we assume that schoolchildren range from four to thirteen years old, it rises to 75 percent.[59] In the Midwest, it reached about 55 percent in 1850, much of the growth taking place before schools received major tax support.[60]

Small towns and rural communities led the way. More than 70 percent of America's schools and 70 percent of teachers in 1850 were in rural areas. Cities spent more per student, but it was outside the city, in places where social capital was highest, that the greatest proportion of children attended schools.[61]

Nudge, Push from Government

Local control reflected the scale and tempo of small town and rural American life. It allowed schooling to be cheap and offered the curriculum most Americans wanted—reading, writing, and arithmetic, with some civics and character education. The proliferation of common schools depended on citizens' capacity to cooperate. Yet increasing access to common schools was not spontaneous. It relied on nudges and ultimately mandates from state legislatures. Moreover, only the legislature could endow districts with the legal authority to tax and to hold elections. Even if many of the earliest schools were organized locally, as Rev. Flint observed during his Indiana travels, they ultimately required the state.

Indeed, localism was a tactic for state building. From one perspective, legislators relied on citizens to act locally to form academies and district schools. But, from another perspective, by providing charters and grants to academies, and by mandating the formation of school districts and taxes, legislators also encouraged Americans to work together, replenishing, and perhaps even increasing, localities' stock of social capital. Even the federal government played a role, beginning with the passage of the Northwest Ordinance, which required land in new territories to be set aside to raise funds for public schools.

In the era between the American Revolution and the Civil War, legislators knew that state governments had significant formal authority to serve the public welfare—known as the "police power"—but they had to rely on citizens and local governments to carry out government's dictates. Colonial governments had required people to devote time to the militia and road maintenance. Then, like today, people were expected to serve on juries. And when it came to schools, successful states tapped into local social capital, treating citizens' ability to work together as a resource for state building. Localism was not just a principle but a strategy for legislators to build public institutions when state governments lacked the capacity to do so.[62]

For example, Massachusetts had a long tradition of local schooling, since the Puritans had required that each person read the Bible, but the schools needed a jump-start after the Revolution. The new state constitution mandated Massachusetts to "cherish the interests of literature and the sciences."[63] The legislature responded in 1789 by requiring all towns to hire schoolmasters. It empowered larger towns to raise taxes for schoolhouses in 1800. By the 1820s, towns had broken up into districts, elected school officials, and ran schools for at least part of the year.

In 1795 New York authorized twenty thousand pounds in education subsidies, but required localities to raise half the amount through local taxes. Citizens responded, and demand for state funds outran supply, obliging the state to pass an unpopular statewide tax in 1799.[64] Although money came from the state, the actual work was done by ordinary New Yorkers at the local level. Towns elected between three and seven commissioners, but the schools themselves were run by neighbors who, according to the law, should "associate together" to hire teachers and maintain schoolhouses.

New York's leaders remained dissatisfied. They wanted to enroll more children in better schools. Lacking the cash to do it, they, like other states, relied on the major resource that they had—land. They established a school fund from public land sale revenue and, in 1812, used the money as matching grants to nudge more communities into acting by requiring districts to raise in taxes an amount equal to the state subsidy.[65] The law was made mandatory in 1814; by 1816 New York had about 5,000 districts with tax-aided common schools, not including New York City and Albany. By 1849, the number may have reached 11,400.[66] The success, in fact the existence, of each school in each district was evidence of social capital working.

Ohio's governor Ethan Brown, who had studied law under Alexander Hamilton, was impressed by the eastern states' accomplishments and hoped to have the same success. However, land sale revenue was insufficient for quality schools. In 1821 Ohio passed a law to nudge citizens into action by allowing townships to divide into smaller districts where citizens could elect school committees and tax themselves. Sweetening the deal in 1825, legislators required counties to collect a twentieth of a percent of their overall taxes for education and distribute those funds to townships. To ensure that citizens acted, legislators required townships to form districts, and required districts to form schools. Another act created a school treasurer and authorized committees to levy up to three hundred dollars to build schoolhouses, if three-fifths of householders agreed.[67] In 1829 the legislature mandated a minimum school term of three months.[68]

Samuel Lewis, Ohio's first state superintendent, counted 7,748 school districts in 1837, approximately 7 per township.[69] As many as 150,000 students might have been enrolled by then.[70] Another source lists 4,336 schools enrolling 146,400 children in 1837, or about 31 percent of the school-aged population. Following a dramatic decline in the years following the financial Panic of 1837, in 1850 the number reached 52 percent, or 421,733 students.[71]

In Pennsylvania, an 1824 law permitting the creation of districts and taxes faced strong opposition and was overturned two years later. A decade later, in 1834, a new law required Philadelphia and every county to create school divisions. Within each division, every ward, township, or borough would form school districts overseen by elected officers. To receive state funds, counties had to vote to collect in taxes a sum double the state subsidy. If the vote failed, they got nothing.[72]

State governments thus were not idle. They encouraged and then mandated localities to act. But the action itself took place locally, community by community.

Social Capital in the South

Middle-class white southerners were frustrated by their political system's failure to respond to their aspirations. They blamed rich elites and ignorant farmers. They rightly felt that many did not want to pay for schools. But the slow development of southern public education also reflected the political system's initial inability to tap into what southern communities could do.

For a long time scholars have assumed that most southerners did not want schools. Rich planters did not want to pay to school the poor, and the poor did not really want an education. Because of the South's agrarian geography and social structure, it was argued, public education struggled to gain traction.[73] A new picture is now emerging. Southern towns, like their northern counterparts, had high levels of social capital. Southerners voted in similar rates as voters in the North.[74] Southern communities mandated that citizens give time to slave patrols, militias, and road upkeep. They formed thousands of churches.[75]

In other words, white southerners participated in public life and were able to work together. And middle-class white southerners joined together in everything from literary and historical societies to social reform, especially in commercial towns and cities. The South had more local chapters of the American Bible Society per white person than the North.[76] Most of these joiners were middle-class people—commercial farmers, shopkeepers, professionals, and government workers. They sought the same economic and cultural opportunities for their children as did parents in the North and actively worked together to achieve them.[77]

If the South did not lack social capital, why did it lack common schools? It may be because the southern political system initially failed to tap into local communities' reservoirs of social capital. One challenge was that southern society was governed at the county level instead of at the town level, and many local offices were appointed rather than elected.[78] Political power at the state and county levels thus tended to flow from the top down rather than from the bottom up.[79] Citizens were less involved in daily governance.

This started to change in the 1830s, as part of a broader democratization of local politics. Not only did suffrage expand, but more state and local offices became elected.[80] Southern states also authorized citizens to form school districts and elect their own trustees. And, as in the North, once southern states tapped into local social capital, public schools took off. And where legislators did not rely on local action, enrollment lagged.

Take South Carolina as an example. Many South Carolinians wanted free schools; Governor Henry Middleton reminded the state legislature in 1811 about the importance of "free schools" for all citizens. Petitions from various communities pressured the legislature to act, and that year a free-school act was passed, well before northern states established free schools. Rather than relying on citizens acting locally, however, the law authorized the state legislature to appoint a board of school commissioners in every election district, which in turn was responsible for establishing schools. Each school would be administered by three trustees. Unlike in the north, authority flowed from the top down, as did money. Each district would receive three hundred dollars from the legislature, but there was no provision for local taxation, and citizens were not asked to do much. The effort soon faltered. Many citizens saw the schools as charity for the poor rather than, as in the North, common institutions for the good of the entire community.[81]

Tennessee offers a similar lesson. In the early 1820s, legislators passed a law to use state funds to support "poor schools" or to pay "the tuition of poor children." This linked common school support to charity. In 1830, however, Tennessee shifted gears and tapped into local social capital. The county court would now appoint a commissioner for each "captain's company," but the commissioners would divide each company into smaller school districts in which voters would elect their own board of trustees. The trustees would be responsible for providing a schoolhouse and other duties in return for state money. While Tennessee allowed for local governance, it did not authorize local taxation, which limited the law's potential. But in 1854 the state authorized more funding and also permitted counties to tax themselves. The result was "a popular wave in favor of schools."[82]

Arkansans in 1843 devoted funds from land sales and private contributions to education, and, unlike in South Carolina, voters elected their own trustees; however, the law made no provision for local taxation, limiting its effectiveness. Nonetheless, by 1860 around 652 common schools may have been organized.[83] Alabama, on the other hand, tapped into local social capital early on. In 1823 a new law divided townships into school districts; voters elected their own school overseers. This approach unleashed, in the words of one historian, "an army of public support for public education." The state would offer funding in 1839 in return for local action.[84] By the 1850 census, about a third of Alabama's white children were enrolled. At this point, Alabama did what other states did and sought to balance local autonomy with state oversight, creating in the mid-1850s a state superintendent and county superintendents. The combination was successful, and the number of public schools tripled. By 1860, nineteen hundred of the state's twenty-one hundred schools were public, and expenditures had increased by about one-third, much of which came from local sources.[85]

Mississippi too relied on both bottom-up and top-down efforts. In 1824 control of schools and school land funds was given to an elected board of trustees in every township. In 1846, frustrated by lack of progress, legislators turned to a top-down process by authorizing county boards of police to appoint school commissioners and levy school taxes, assuming the consent of the majority of household heads in each township. The secretary of state was charged with oversight, but the act was voluntary and achieved little.

The real decade of growth was the 1850s. School expansion followed the same process as in the North—governance was returned to townships, starting in 1848; the state provided a nudge by offering in 1850 one dollar in state funds for every twenty-five cents raised by local taxes; and by now teachers, parents, and policymakers had become boosters. By 1860, public funding—from taxes as well as from fees and interest—still made up less than half of school income, but the number of schools increased by about a third. The state had started down a path toward greater enrollment and public support.[86]

As southern states tapped into local social capital, enrollments and tax revenue increased. On the eve of the Civil War, the South had made huge gains. One study suggests that attendance in southern common schools increased 43.2 percent between 1850 and 1860, and the number of schools by 50 percent, even if the South still trailed the North.[87] Yet a few southern states failed to establish common school systems. Virginia, for example, educated only about 13 percent of its students in publicly supported common schools;[88] according to the 1840 census, Kentucky was at 1.4 percent.[89] Georgia, despite a promising effort in the early 1830s, did little until 1858, when the legislature authorized counties to tax themselves a percent of the state tax, but only a bit over half took advantage of the opportunity.[90]

North Carolina, on the other hand, made real strides. Education reformers spent decades trying to convince legislators to establish common schools. Their opportunity came in 1836 when the Whigs were swept into office with support from the western part of the state, thanks to recent constitutional reform. Whigs devoted federal surplus money to education; Democrats would have preferred to use it to pay down debt. An 1838 report recommended emulating Massachusetts, noting that the Tar Heel State was rich in natural resources but "in the relative dissemination of intelligence it must be admitted that superiority is not with us."[91]

An 1839 school law provided a nudge by authorizing state subsidies to localities that voted to raise one dollar in local taxes for every two state dollars. Districts raising twenty dollars and erecting a schoolhouse would get forty dollars. The Courts of Pleas and Quarter Sessions would appoint five to ten county superintendents, who would in turn appoint between three and six school committee members. Failure to comply was fined. In 1841 the law was revised to allow school district committees to be elected by free white voters.[92] In other words, North Carolina, like Massachusetts, built the public education system from the local level. And, again, it worked. All but seven counties chose to tax themselves, and enrollment increased from 19,483 in 1840 to 130,000 in 1856.[93] By 1860, two-thirds of North Carolina's young white people were being educated in common schools, a number not that different from Massachusetts.[94] Clearly demand for public schools in the South was comparable to demand in the North.

Professional Government

Nonetheless, Horace Mann was unconvinced of the advantages of localism. He had a grander vision for public schools. He wanted to offer all children a democratic education, one that enabled them to be effective citizens and to engage in self-culture. He wanted better teachers, better buildings, better supplies, and longer terms—tuition free—for every American.

Mann's dream would cost money. It was hard enough to get citizens to pay for a basic elementary education with bad buildings, poorly prepared teachers, short school terms, spotty equipment, and almost no high schools. Moreover, Mann and other reformers did not acknowledge that the success of American schools reflected their status as local institutions. Reformers paid even less heed to the fact that parents might not have wanted to have distant elites tell them how to educate their children. In their rush, ambition, and idealism to offer every child a democratic education, they did not always respect what it meant to educate in a democracy.

In Massachusetts, Mann blamed his state's 1789 law, which delegated responsibility to localities. "The most unfortunate law," he called it.[95] He overlooked the fact that, absent local action, there would have been no schools in the 1830s. Yet, he had a point. As long as education was in the hands of amateurs, so long as few Americans saw the need for what he was proposing, there was little he could do. If the grassroots did not want what Mann aspired for them, how could he make it happen?

Mann found himself facing one of the fundamental challenges of democratic government. It is based on the premise that the people are sovereign but also requires faith that the people's decisions will serve the common good. But what if they do not? What then?[96]

Mann sought to balance popular control with wisdom, a goal shared by others in the 1830s, especially in the Whig Party. Whigs believed that effective government depended on educated public servants authorized to do their jobs well, without the intense pressures of partisan politics and public opinion. This belief reflected broader trends toward professionalization in the nineteenth century. Professionals are communities of experts whose decision-making authority stems from their knowledge and an obligation to serve the public welfare.[97] Medicine was professionalized in the nineteenth century, as was law. Doctors and lawyers set entry standards for their profession, devised codes of ethics, and pursued their public good—medicine or law—with relative autonomy.

Mann wished that teaching would also become a profession, as detailed in the next chapter. He, like other Whigs, also believed that professionalism should animate government more broadly. Whigs created agencies to regulate banks and railroads, to provide public health, and, with the board of education, made up of appointed members, to improve schools.[98]

The process of professionalizing government began in cities undergoing a "municipal revolution." Cities replaced volunteer boards with salaried staff overseen by independent agencies, first in public health, but then in fire and police protection.[99] This approach acknowledged the scale and complexity of many city tasks but also insulated experts from popular control. In New York City, where Democrats relied on city offices for patronage, reformers sought to make school offices appointed rather than elected.[100] In Boston, which had recently replaced its open town meeting with a new government composed of elected ward representatives, city leaders aspired to professionalize city services. The all-volunteer school board, feeling overwhelmed, asked for a full-time salaried superintendent "with permanence, personal responsibility, continued and systematic labor." The city council agreed in 1851.[101] Other cities followed this trend. Louisville appointed a salaried superintendent in 1837; Cincinnati in 1851; Chicago in 1854.[102]

Mann hoped that state boards of education with secretaries like him or with salaried superintendents would similarly make education responsive to knowledgeable officials rather than amateur volunteers. At one level, his hopes were realized. By 1861, of the thirty-four states, nineteen had state superintendents, and nine had designated a state officer to serve *ex officio*. In 1870, twenty-seven cities in thirteen states had their own superintendents. But the backlash had begun.[103]

Education in a Democracy

Leading the charge against the reformers was New Englander Orestes Brownson. Brownson was born in 1803 into a farming family in Stockbridge, Vermont. He received very little formal schooling, other than a brief stint in a New York academy. When he was thirty, he became a Unitarian pastor and publisher of the *Boston Quarterly Review*, through which he hoped to publicize the writings of Bronson Alcott, Ralph Waldo Emerson, Margaret Fuller, George Ripley, and other New England Transcendentalists.

Brownson believed that education could never avoid dealing with the ultimate question of what life is for. For this reason, he worried that Horace Mann's approach would allow the state, rather than the people, to determine the meaning of life. In an 1839 *Boston Quarterly Review* essay, Brownson reviewed Mann's *Second Annual Report* as secretary of the board of education. He agreed with Mann that every child "whether male or female, black or white, rich or poor, bond or free," deserved a public education. But he disagreed about how to provide it.

Education is "more than the mere ability to read, write, and cypher" and even more than "moral and intellectual culture," Brownson wrote. It was ultimately "the fitting of the individual man for fulfilling his destiny, of attaining to the end, of accomplishing the purposes, for which God hath made him." This meant that "an education which is not religious is a solemn mockery." But if all good education was ultimately religious—concerned with the purposes of life itself—then the state could not take control over it without threatening religious freedom.

Mann argued that the state could provide a democratic education for all people. But, Brownson countered, almost everyone on the board of education was a Whig and a Unitarian. Would a parent who was a Democrat or a Baptist "entrust my children to the care of those who are to me virtually Atheists?" Brownson's answer was no. By allowing a central board of education to determine curriculum or how teachers were trained, Whigs and Unitarians had given themselves a "self-perpetuating power" that was better suited to "despotic Prussia" than democratic America. Instead of schools being placed "in the hands of the government," Brownson argued for local popular control. Authority must rest in "our present school districts," which are under "the control of the families" whose children will be taught.[104]

Brownson's concerns were shared by Thomas Jefferson. After the American Revolution, Thomas Jefferson wanted nothing more than public education for all Virginia white boys and girls. Most Virginians balked at the idea. By 1809, Governor John Tyler, frustrated by Virginia's unwillingness to pay for schools, commented that "a stranger might think we had declared war against the arts and sciences."[105] But the 1810s brought hope. Virginia was looking for ways to improve its economy, and many leading Virginians felt that their state, once the pride of the original thirteen colonies, was in decline. It might be time to invest in public schools.[106]

That was what Charles Fenton Mercer, a young politician from Loudon County, thought. The only problem was that Mercer was a Federalist, and Jefferson had been elected president as leader of the opposing Republican Party. Mercer and Jefferson might have cooperated in 1814, when Jefferson's nephew Peter Carr published in the *Richmond Enquirer* a letter from his uncle calling for public schools. Jefferson's letter reiterated his commitment to public schools and his belief in a tiered system, in which everyone received a basic education, and the most promising poor students would be offered public support to continue their education.

By that time Jefferson was retired at his mountaintop home, Monticello, and sought to start a public university, the University of Virginia. Mercer supported Jefferson's idea. But when Joseph Cabell, who worked with Jefferson, introduced a bill in 1816, he prioritized the university over the common schools. Mercer disagreed and, as chair of the House Finance Committee, rewrote Cabell's bill to ensure that public money from Virginia's Literary Fund be applied first to elementary schools and only later to higher education.

Jefferson and Cabell turned against Mercer's bill. Why? One reason was partisanship. In his bill, Mercer located a university in central Virginia, rather than in Charlottesville, as Jefferson wanted. But there was something more important at stake. Jefferson believed firmly in local control of elementary schools. Mercer, like other Federalists, worried with Benjamin Rush about the dangers of uneducated people, and he was more willing to use state power. Mercer, like Jefferson, promoted free public schools, but, unlike Jefferson, he also wanted them supervised by a state board of education.

Jefferson, like Brownson, would have none of it. While he hated most things that came from New England, Jefferson loved New Englanders' reliance on local government. In his 1778 proposal for free schools, Jefferson had recommended that every county elect three aldermen, who would divide counties into "hundreds," or districts small enough for children to attend school easily. Voters would govern local schools as they did in the North.[107]

Parents, Jefferson wrote Cabell, are best suited to oversee their children's education. If the state were to take control of education, what's next, "the management of all our farms, our mills, and merchants' stores?"[108] Jefferson's decision to oppose Mercer, then, was not just because Jefferson prioritized higher education over common schools. While he really wanted his university, also at stake was local democracy.[109]

Whereas Brownson worried most about religious diversity, Jefferson was concerned about citizens' power. By creating districts and encouraging citizens to work together, Jefferson hoped to foster social capital and civic virtue in Virginia. Coming together to organize schools, citizens would become more effective. "When every man is a sharer in the direction of his ward-republic, or of some of the higher ones, and feels that he is a participator in the government of affairs, not merely at an election day in the year, but every day," then he becomes invested in his community and its welfare. He will do anything to protect its liberty. He would "let the heart be torn out of his body sooner than his power be wrested from him by a Caesar or a Bonaparte," or a Federalist.[110]

Horace Mann Almost Loses His Job

Americans shared Brownson's and Jefferson's concerns, and Horace Mann almost lost his job as a result.

Slowly, Massachusetts began to centralize authority. Overturning the tradition in which school decisions took place in open town meetings, legislators, in 1826, created a buffer between popular control and expertise. They ordered towns to appoint a five-person committee to inspect schools, certify teachers, choose schoolbooks, and report to the state. (Hiring remained in local hands.) The law was unpopular, at least in the town of Norton, where citizens initially declined to choose a school committee. Other citizens demanded a meeting to comply with the law, which was soon held. After that, angry citizens petitioned unsuccessfully to dismiss the committee.[111]

The following year, state legislators required every local school district to elect a "prudential committee" to oversee district affairs and support the town-level school committee. In 1834 Massachusetts established a new school fund, but to get any of the money, localities had to raise at least one dollar per school-aged resident (those between four and sixteen) and comply with state reporting requirements. In 1837 legislators established the state board of education and, in 1844, authorized school committees to dismiss teachers, thus weakening the autonomy of local districts. As one chronicler observed, "step by step the control of schools had passed from the direct control of the town meeting to the indirect control of the town through some delegated authority."[112]

Marcus Morton, the newly elected Democratic governor, was none too happy with this trend. Morton had graduated from Brown in 1804 and then studied law. He had practiced law in Taunton and then, like Mann, entered politics. Lieutenant governor in 1825 when Governor William Eustis passed away, Morton found himself governor. He ran consistently thereafter, and finally was reelected on his thirteenth try, in November 1839. In the interim, he had served on the state supreme court and as chairman of the state Democrats.[113]

Governor Morton preferred voluntary action to state action. On the state supreme court, he promoted free-market competition over state monopolies.[114] He advocated temperance, but opposed laws prohibiting alcohol sale and consumption. His election, in fact, resulted in large part from Whigs' passage of a law limiting liquor sales. Whigs promoted professionalization by limiting who could practice medicine or law. Now, Democrats argued, Whigs wanted to hand public education over to elites and stop people from drinking.

Governor Morton and his Democratic allies set their sights on the board of education. Morton promoted smaller government (what he called "retrenchment"), and Democrats in the legislature argued that the board was expensive and unnecessary. Others believed it was, as Brownson noted, dangerous. Democrats brought to the floor a bill abolishing the board, and Mann's job with it, but it failed largely along partisan lines, allowing Mann to live to fight another day.[115]

Henry Barnard Loses His Job

Henry Barnard was born in 1811 in Hartford, Connecticut. His father was a prosperous farmer; his mother died when Henry was only four. Barnard attended a "dame school" (a small school run by a female teacher) and then the South District School, which he later referred to as "a miserable district school." At twelve, he planned to run away to sea with a friend, but his father instead sent him to the Monson Academy in Massachusetts, where he studied Greek under a tutor, learned to love reading, and went on to graduate from Yale in 1830.

Barnard began to study law but, on the advice of Yale's president Jeremiah Day, decided to become a teacher at Wellsboro Academy in Pennsylvania. He returned to law, spent some time at Yale Law School, and was admitted to the bar in 1835. Elected to the general assembly, Representative Barnard began a career as a Whig reformer, focusing on issues involving the blind and deaf, poor, and insane, as well as promoting schools, libraries, and other civic institutions. When Connecticut established a board of education in 1838, Barnard agreed to be secretary. He had already condemned the "deplorable state" of Connecticut schools, and now it was his responsibility to improve them.[116]

Connecticut's school system had evolved slowly since the Revolution. A 1794 law authorized school districts subsidiary to existing ecclesiastical societies (church parishes—Connecticut had a public religious system until 1818), and with a two-thirds vote citizens could tax themselves for schoolhouses. In 1795 Connecticut gained the ability to sell its western lands in what is now Ohio and used the revenue for a state school fund. In 1798 school societies were authorized to appoint visitors to hire teachers and, in 1799, to collect a mandatory property tax of two dollars per two thousand. But by the 1820s, the schools seemed to falter. Governor Oliver Wolcott urged more attention, as did an 1826 House of Representatives report urging greater state oversight.[117]

Like Mann, Barnard used his first annual report as secretary to paint a sorry portrait. Formal responsibility for schools had resided in "religious societies," but in practice districts directly ran schools themselves. Because districts lacked clear taxing authority, citizens paid very little attention. Apathy reigned.

Unlike Mann, Barnard sought to counter popular apathy by encouraging local activism. He recommended allowing districts to raise their own taxes, which he hoped would lead to "a new zeal animating her school officers." Yet local action, Barnard agreed with Mann, had to be directed to the right ends. Central officers—like Barnard—needed to offer professional oversight. "There is too much division and subdivision of authority, without any necessary connection or accountability," lamented Barnard. It took six thousand to eight thousand people to run the schools. Such a decentralized approach might work in the countryside but not in cities, where volunteers should be replaced by salaried officials, he believed.

Barnard convinced the legislature to act. In 1841 Connecticut repealed almost all prior legislation and authorized school societies to create districts with taxing authority. It now required school societies to appoint a body of visitors to hire teachers and inspect each district school four times a year.[118]

But then Barnard's fortune changed. A new governor, Democrat Chauncey F. Cleveland, labeled the 1841 laws a failure and the board of education a "useless expense." To Governor Cleveland and his followers, the idea of state officials mediating the will of the people violated the very spirit of democracy. The Connecticut legislature agreed, repealing the 1841 law and abolishing the state board, leaving Barnard unemployed.[119]

"Our worst apprehensions are realized," Barnard wrote Horace Mann. Far from deferring to experts, the legislature was composed of people "unfit to have anything to do with education." He had never witnessed "a more ignorant, rabid set" of partisans.[120] Mann agreed. The purpose of politics was not to do whatever the people wanted but to serve the common good. Mann had urged Barnard to save the "Ark of God from the hands of the Philistines," but, for now, the Philistines had won.[121]

Centralization in Ohio and New York

In Ohio and New York, reformers' efforts to centralize control met the same kind of resistance as in Massachusetts and Connecticut. When Ohio Whigs established a state board of education in 1838, they appointed Massachusetts native Samuel Lewis as superintendent. Like Horace Mann, Lewis rode around the state—traveling twelve hundred miles to Mann's five hundred. Like Mann and Barnard, he too painted a sorry picture of miserable, underfunded schools, horrific schoolhouses, low and spotty attendance, and unqualified teachers.

Whigs responded with ambitious reforms, perhaps too ambitious. They extended Lewis's term to five years, empowered him to collect statistics on enrollments and school terms (to embarrass districts), and required better reporting from the school to the township to the county to the state. Lewis, who had wanted even more accountability, hoped that, as state superintendent, at the top of the chain, he could improve schools' quality. Instead, as in Connecticut, his actions created a backlash. When he retired the following year, Democrats abolished his office.[122]

New York initially led in efforts to centralize supervision at the state level when Gideon Hawley, a Union College graduate practicing law in Albany, became the nation's first salaried state superintendent of common schools in January 1813. Responsible for reporting to the legislature, he urged legislators to require localities to organize schools, which they did in 1814. Hawley consistently advocated more and better schools, as well as the Lancasterian model of pedagogy, in which advanced students taught junior ones. His judgment was respected by legislators.

Until 1821. New Yorkers distrusted executive power; as a result, many state offices were appointed by a council of appointment. That year, enemies of Governor DeWitt Clinton—one of Hawley's allies—dominated the council. The new Bucktails from upstate, led by Martin Van Buren, promoted constitutional reforms and extended the vote to all white men. For partisan reasons, Hawley found himself out of a job. The following year, Hawley's position was abolished, and his duties assigned to the secretary of state.[123]

Hawley's removal showed, for New Yorkers with long memories, that partisanship could undermine educational reform. As the Bucktails morphed into the Democratic Party, the entire state became open for party patronage. Democrats handed out offices to loyal party men, not to the best qualified. In response, reform-minded Democrats joined with their Whig rivals to try to limit the influence of the state's two most powerful officials—the secretary of state and the comptroller. To break the state from party control, reformers established independent offices and agencies—an auditor for canals in 1838, a banking commission in 1851, a board of railroad commissioners in 1855, and an insurance department in 1859.

With the same goal of insulating government from parties, New Yorkers in 1854 reestablished the office of state superintendent for public instruction. The superintendent would be appointed by joint ballot of the legislature rather than voters, in hopes that the office would therefore be less likely to get caught up in popular politics. The new superintendent ideally would be a professional civil servant, acting "independently of all political bias" and uninfluenced by "the polls."[124]

Localism Challenged and Defended

Efforts to impose state oversight were designed to ensure that local control was balanced with the guidance of professional civil servants who understood education. Reformers worried that citizens simply did not have the knowledge to run schools. Vermont's state superintendent in 1846 called small school districts the "paradise of ignorant teachers." He urged the formation of "union" or consolidated districts where more students and taxpayers, as well as better regulation, would allow for better schools.[125] Pennsylvania's secretary Townsend Haines believed it "worse than folly to leave to illiterate men, altogether unacquainted with the progress of knowledge, a power, on the proper exercise of which, depends the vitality of our public schools."[126]

Similar attitudes took hold in the South. North Carolina superintendent Calvin Henderson Wiley believed that only state oversight would ensure "efficiency and uniformity."[127] Alabama's first state superintendent, William Perry, agreed. Without state guidance, Alabama schoolhouses were "destitute alike of every attractive feature," teachers were ignorant, and local communities complacent.[128]

Reformers believed districts should be accountable to county and state leaders, ideally to appointed civil servants. But centralization did not come easy. It remained imperfect, with the bulk of authority still situated at the local level.

In 1853 Massachusetts authorized its town school committees to abolish local school districts unless voters explicitly decided every three years to keep them. Angry citizens secured the repeal of this law in 1857. The state legislature then abolished districts in 1859, leading to a special session of the legislature to reestablish them in time for the next fall. A decade later the legislature abolished districts again, only to decide, the following year, that towns could keep them with a two-thirds affirmative vote. Not until 1882 did reformers in Massachusetts—Horace Mann's home state—succeed in eliminating local districts and securing town- and state-level oversight.[129]

New York's secretary of state convinced legislators in 1839 to authorize him to appoint school inspectors. Legislators also established deputy superintendents appointed by county commissioners (1841) and replaced town commissioners and inspectors with a single town superintendent (1843). Many voters balked, however. The deputy superintendents were abolished several years later, and in 1850 the secretary of state complained that "an efficient administration . . . cannot be secured without this class of officers."[130]

Pennsylvanians in 1834 required the courts of quarter sessions to appoint two independent local inspectors to visit schools and to certify teachers, and added oversight responsibility to the secretary of the commonwealth.[131] The next year, after a senate bill repealing the entire law failed, legislators eliminated the inspectors and authorized districts to decide whether to have schools and school directors certify teachers.[132] Then in 1854 the legislature created county-level superintendents to visit schools and certify teachers. School board directors would recommend a candidate for three-year terms. The county superintendents reported to the secretary, who was allowed to hire a deputy. Neighborhood subdistricts were abolished, making the township the locus of authority.

Pennsylvanians didn't like it. District officials and voters resisted, and several counties convinced legislators to pass a bill allowing them to eliminate county superintendents, but the governor vetoed it. A proposal eliminating all superintendents narrowly failed.[133] In the long term, centralizers achieved their goal; by 1857, education had its own state agency.[134]

Other states had similar histories. Maryland established a state superintendent in 1826, eliminated it in 1828, and reestablished the office in 1864.[135] Tennessee established the office in 1838, but abolished it in 1844.[136] North Carolina created a superintendent in 1852 and, despite fears that Democrats would eliminate it, reappointed Calvin Henderson Wiley two years later.[137] Reformers believed that authority over schools should be balanced between professionals and local citizens, but many citizens were unwilling to allow their schools to be governed by government officials.

The people organized the schools, built the schoolhouses, and paid for them. And many of them did not want the reforms men like Mann offered. They also did not appreciate being told that educated officials knew better how to educate their children. They valued the close ties between teachers and local parents that reinforced rather than undermined familial authority.[138]

Thus, while northern rural and small-town communities had led their states in enrollment into the 1830s, many citizens turned against education reform. They did not simply oppose greater taxes, though that was part of it. For example, a small district in upstate New York resolved "not to raise no money for teacher's wages." Residents of Onondaga County argued that legal requirements to raise taxes for schools enabled people "to put their hands into their neighbors' pockets."[139]

Americans were committed to local control. The schools were public institutions directly accountable to citizens and run by citizens. They did not appreciate having the schools, products of their own labor, alienated from them and handed over to Mann.[140] But behind questions of governance were also ones of culture. Critics also rejected Mann's vision of education's purposes. When he lost his job in Connecticut, Barnard called the state's Democratic legislators "radical and ignorant demagogues . . . utterly unfit to legislate" on schools.[141] But many Americans did not think that citizens needed to defer to educated leaders. Schools should teach the basics and localities were qualified to decide upon a teacher to do it.

Moreover, many Americans did not agree with Mann and his supporters that schools were the most important places to learn how to be a responsible and successful member of the community. Instead, they believed that the most important lessons were learned from life—common sense and experience were the crucibles that turned a child into an adult.[142] Tax-supported schools, according to an editorial in a rural Pennsylvania newspaper, took money from "the honest, hard-working farmer or mechanic" to pay for the education of "idle drones too lazy for honest labor" and their "pauper, idle, and lazy schoolmasters."[143] Another Pennsylvanian wrote that farmers and mechanics had better uses for their children "during the busy season of the year," and thus schooling must be limited to "the winter months." This system of "economy and education" was good enough even if it was "sneered at by those enthusiasts who have dreamed of a community of learned men."[144] A North Carolinian wondered, "Would it not redound as much to the advantage of young persons, and to the honour of the State, if they should pass their days in the cotton patch, or at the plow, or in the cornfield, instead of being mewed up in a school house, where they are earning nothing?

Such an ado as is made in these times about education, surely was never heard of before."[145]

Communities across America divided because other small-town and rural citizens shared the same ideas about childhood and culture as Mann and other reformers. They were the local boosters and constituents for education reform. They became activists and served on school committees. They were often from families that had a bit more resources and thus different aspirations. They were men like Genesee County, New York's Delos Hackley, a commercial farmer who, after learning that the local schoolhouse had burned down in 1862, worked tirelessly to rebuild it. He became a regular at school district meetings and, when his eldest son was seven in 1868, he was elected a school trustee. He took his duties seriously, urging neighbors to pay their school taxes, interviewing a potential teacher, and overseeing school expenses. Men like Hackley sought, in district after district, to convince their neighbors to support better schools.[146]

From Tuition to Taxation

If the reformers' program was not always embraced, nonetheless, momentum for free common schools continued to build. Traditionally, common schools had been funded by a combination of local taxes, state subsidies, and tuition paid by parents, along with in-kind donations such as room and board for itinerant teachers and wood for schoolhouse stoves. By the Civil War, however, taxation replaced tuition fees (called rates) in northern states (see appendix, table 3). Moreover, between the 1830s and the Civil War, spending per student increased dramatically, even as the population was growing.[147]

Most taxes came from local sources, reflecting legislators' reliance on localities to organize schools. Although local taxes can increase inequality between districts (one reason why Democrats often tied expanding public schools to statewide taxes), they were also more popular since citizens controlled how the money was used, saw where it went, and had a direct a stake in their schools.[148]

School spending was correlated with the proportion of people who could vote, making clear that school taxes were popular with voters. People wanted schools. But why? First, schooling had become an expectation, so parents had an incentive to shift the cost burden to the community at large, from parents to property.[149] Second, citizens were more likely to support public spending when they were the beneficiaries. Local schools and local taxes led to local results; the investments were clear, the beneficiaries often known to the taxpayers. Finally, local taxes for schools improved property values and the cultural and civic life of a community, so all voters had an incentive to support them.[150]

Cities led in the move for free schools. New York's major cities started offering free schools well before the rest of the state, as did Providence, Baltimore, Charleston, Chicago, Cincinnati, Detroit, Mobile, and New Orleans.[151] While rural areas had led in enrollment, they were slower to embrace free schools. Lower property values and a dispersed population made it more difficult for rural and small-town residents to afford free schools.[152] In Lima, New York, for example, only a fifth to a third of school costs between 1825 and 1845 was covered by public funds; the rest was tuition.[153] To the east in Glenville, tuition brought in one to three times what public funds offered.[154] Even in Massachusetts, in-kind payments made up 7.3 percent of school income in 1841, declining to 2 percent in 1850, and disappearing in 1880.[155]

Local school board members trying to implement state laws often met resistance. They complained, as did the board members of a joint district in Iowa and Dane counties, Wisconsin, that voters were hopelessly divided over taxes. Indiana's state superintendent Caleb Mills lamented in 1855 that districts used public funds for schoolhouses but relied on tuition to cover ongoing school expenses.[156] But, as communities organized schools, built schoolhouses, hired teachers, bought supplies, and learned how to run the schools, their investments of time and money made further investments seem necessary and appropriate. In other words, the development of schools themselves helped foster a commitment to greater spending. It made little sense to turn back the clock. Instead, as more and more children went to school, and as more and more Americans were involved in overseeing them and funding them, access to public education became a widely shared expectation.[157]

We must remember that the local nature of schooling demanded the building of thousands of buildings, and thousands of people had to get involved. Barnard estimated that it took six thousand to eight thousand citizens to run Connecticut's schools. In Pennsylvania, despite political tensions, there were 917 districts by 1841, run by 5,502 directors and 19,410 school committee members, and staffed with 6,470 teachers.[158] As officials took responsibility over schools, many of them served as grassroots advocates of public schooling. Many were the local representatives of the national education reform movement.

In addition to local officials, education reformers, teachers, and their political allies pressured lawmakers for free schools. Organizations like the Pennsylvania

Society for the Promotion of Public Schools, the Western Academic Institute in Cincinnati, and the Kentucky Common Schools Society provided a platform for free-school advocates. Teachers formed local and state associations to shape public opinion and to pressure lawmakers. William Russell, who was born in Scotland and moved to Georgia to teach before coming up to Massachusetts to edit the *American Journal of Education*, told a group of teachers gathered in Norfolk County to form an association that they had two purposes. First, they must engage in "mutual improvement" as professionals. Second, their scope was much larger. Ultimately, they "are assembled to partake and to extend, within our limited sphere, the present universal impulse on the improvement of education." The local association must be "one of the many waves in that onward tide of mental action."[159]

Calvin Henderson Wiley understood the importance of organizing for change. He urged teachers and "other friends of education" in North Carolina to form county and district associations. "Associated effort" would do much more than isolated individuals by fostering "connections." Reformers, through local associations, could spread the word by circulating the *North Carolina Journal of Education*, a reform mouthpiece.[160] Barnard too understood. During his first year as secretary, he met with "friends of education" around Connecticut and reported that they had joined associations "to form channels of united action in every town."[161] Racine, Wisconsin's J. C. McMynn, elected president of the state's teachers' association, believed teachers "need a more thorough organization among themselves" to fight public "apathy." "All should unite—if there is strength in union, there is *weakness* in disunion."[162]

Reformers also sought to publicize their cause through print, establishing at least twenty education journals by 1840. These journals gave reformers, teachers, and others a common language and shared goals. Finally, some reformers, like Mann and Wiley, held elected offices or were appointed to influential government positions.[163]

Thus many factors reinforced the movement for free public schools even as Americans divided over school reform. By the 1830s, communities had already invested heavily in schools and established new policies and practices; stakeholders —parents, teachers, and others—organized to advocate reform; and parents wanted their children to have access. All these factors made changing paths difficult. Yet, even with all these forces pushing for free public schools, the path was not easy.

In New York, rural and urban voters divided over whether schools should be free. In 1849 the legislature mandated free-school terms of at least four months across the state for youth between five and twenty-one years old. The law was made subject to popular ratification and passed with broad support, 249,872 to 91,571.[164] The law did not eradicate tuition since many districts kept school for terms longer than four months, but it set an important precedent.

At the time, 36.3 percent of total New York school income came from tuition, but tuition composed a much larger percentage of rural schools' annual budgets.[165] In response to rural outcry, the law was once again put out for a public vote. It passed again, but this time by a much smaller margin.[166] Both times, the majority of New Yorkers supported free schools, though rural voters were less likely to do so. New York's secretary of state sought to make amends by supporting an 1851 statewide $800,000 property tax to distribute better the costs of schools by having wealthier areas subsidize poorer areas. One-third of the tax would be based on population, the other two-thirds by the terms of the state school fund. After the state supreme court determined that the popular referenda had been unconstitutional, however, many rural districts reimposed tuition. Tuition in New York schools was ultimately abolished in 1864 for high schools and 1867 for all schools.[167]

Free schools were even more contested in Pennsylvania. In 1834, after districts were authorized to raise taxes, 485 out of 987 school districts voted against free schools or took no action. Communities were divided. A convention of citizens in Delaware County resolved in October that "it was never intended by our constitution that the education of those children whose parents are able to educate them, should be conducted at public expense."[168] Thaddeus Stevens, who would go on to Congress to become one of America's leading antislavery activists, was in 1834 a state representative. He argued, in what became a famous speech, that while it was difficult to do new things when the public is against you (something he no doubt also learned opposing slavery), the common good trumps public opinion. Politicians should "remove the honest misapprehensions of the people," not "take advantage of them."[169]

But Superintendent Francis Shunk, who grew up on a farm, served in the War of 1812, and who would later serve as governor, understood the problem: "It may not be easy to convince a man who has educated his own children in the way his father educated him, or who has abundant means to educate them, or who has no children to educate, that in opposition to the custom of the country and his fixed opinions founded on that custom, he has a deep and abiding concern in the education of all the children around him, and should cheerfully submit to taxation for the purpose of accomplishing this great object."[170]

Over the next few decades, Pennsylvanians' division continued, especially in more rural areas. A school tax collector in 1859 recalled that "many guns were leveled at me, and threats made. At one house I was badly scalded by a woman throwing boiling water over me; at another a woman struck me on the back of the head with a heavy iron poker; and at another I was knocked down with stone and assaulted with pitchforks and clubs but," the collector heroically noted, "I succeeded in getting away with three cows." Wealthy farmers, in particular, refused to pay "until I had taken some of their stock."[171]

Yet overall momentum was in favor of free schools. As more communities established common schools and funding improved, more Pennsylvanians came on board. As early as 1837, 742 of the state's 987 districts chose to tax themselves for education. There was a dip during the financial crises of the 1840s, but by 1848, legislators felt confident enough to require district taxation to support free public schools. By 1868, only 23 hard-core resisting districts remained.[172]

Taxation below the Mason-Dixon Line

Southern taxes were lower than northern taxes. In 1830 northerners paid about nine cents per capita in taxes, which rose to fifteen cents per capita in 1840 and thirty-six cents per capita in 1850, compared to southern rates of five cents per free person in 1830, eleven cents in 1840, and twenty-six cents in 1850. If enslaved people are included, the southern rate falls to three cents per capita in 1830, seven cents per capita in 1840, and thirteen cents per capita in 1850. Even more important, southern property tax rates were much lower than the North's.

While statewide taxes are more redistributive—shifting money from wealthier to poorer areas—citizens are more likely to support local taxes because they either benefit directly or can see the benefits in their communities. As a result, areas that relied on local taxes expanded public support for education more quickly. Nationally in 1850, 49 percent of school costs were paid by local taxes, but in the North it was 61 percent compared to the South's 18 percent. In both regions, income from state funds offered about 27 percent and endowments 2 percent. Yet tuition in the South covered 54 percent of school costs compared to 10 percent in the North and 22 percent nationally.[173]

In the antebellum South, poorer whites paid almost no taxes, while the wealthiest southerners paid two-thirds of all taxes. Southerners also tended to tax luxury goods but not the farming and mechanical tools used by ordinary farmers.[174] This made elites less willing to consider higher taxes; it also meant that poorer southerners were not in the habit of paying taxes and thus resisted them when they came.

Because of their political power and the way the tax burden fell largely upon them, slaveholding elites spread an antitax gospel to convince ordinary whites that taxes were a bad thing.[175] As University of North Carolina's president Joseph Caldwell wrote in 1832, the biggest challenge facing public education was that "the methods proposed for effecting it have depended upon taxation."[176] A Virginian writing to Horace Mann in 1846 complained that opposition to public schools came "principally from property-holders who have educated their children or have none to send to school."[177]

Race also factored in southern hostility to public education. To justify slavery, southern elites argued that black people were inferior to white people. Southern elites consistently praised the intelligence of ordinary whites, who, they argued, were better suited for freedom than blacks, despite the South's high rates of illiteracy and poverty. Public education threatened this racial order by suggesting that white southerners needed more education to be good citizens. If the reformers were right, then would the same not also apply to blacks? Could black people, if educated, also be eligible for citizenship? If all people needed education to be capable citizens, then access to education, not the color of one's skin, mattered most.[178]

Yet middle-class southerners used the ballot box and public meetings to demand public education, and their efforts paid off. Slaveholding elites may not have wanted to raise taxes (their children had private tutors and could go to Europe), but in response to pressure from middle-class voters, they agreed to raise taxes so long as the bulk of the burden did not fall on them. As a result, state revenue rose dramatically in the two decades before the Civil War, but it also meant that many southerners found themselves paying taxes for the first time, and some resented it.[179]

Yet the results were substantial. In most southern states between 1850 and 1860, the proportion of school funding derived from taxes and other public sources rose dramatically. While the South lagged the North, and slavery, which created inequalities both between black and white and between whites themselves, made raising taxes more challenging, the South by the Civil War had significantly increased both public and private spending and enrollment.[180]

Democratic Education Meets Education in a Democracy

Education reformers argued that schools should do more than the basics. They should offer every child a liberal education, not just so Americans would be effective citizens but also to encourage self-culture. The reformers' vision required expanding tax support, increasing the amount of time young people spent in school, and, as the next chapter argues, preparing professional teachers. Reformers also argued that a democracy must recognize expert authority because common sense was not enough to decide what ought to be or ought not to be taught.

Many Americans did not embrace nor wish to pay for the reformers' expanded understanding of democratic education. They did not necessarily believe that citizens should defer to expertise. They distrusted educated people. And it did not help that Horace Mann and his allies showed little patience, and at times little respect, for the work ordinary Americans had done. There would have been no possibility for education *reform* had there not been schools in the first place. Americans had built the schools and shared, with Thomas Jefferson and Orestes Brownson, the belief that citizens and parents must have a say in the places where their children are educated.

Reformers, hurried as they were to make American schools better, sometimes seemed impatient with local citizens. Reformers promoted public schools as sites to prepare citizens, but it was ordinary Americans who ensured that public school districts would be forums for practicing citizenship as well. Finally, reformers did not seem aware that public support for public institutions depended on the citizens' owning them—that localism was a source of strength because it mediated between voters and the emergent state. If schools were seen as embodying the aspiration of distant elites, public support for them would be at risk.[181]

Yet, ultimately, the reformers would never have been successful if their vision did not appeal to enough Americans. In districts across the nation, many parents and citizens embraced the aspirations of democratic education and strove to make it happen through the local workings of democracy—in school district meetings, in town halls, and in elections. These Americans were frustrated by their neighbors' resistance and stinginess. Americans thus divided over education reform not just nationally but locally, and education became a central issue in American politics—as, in a democracy, it should be.

4 Teachers and Students

The World's Teachers

JOHN CHADWICK OF MARBLEHEAD, MASSACHUSETTS, had been apprenticed to a shoemaker but then made the decision to become a teacher. He enrolled in a new kind of institution—a normal school, or what would become a teacher's college—in Bridgewater, Massachusetts, in 1857. A few years later, he was called to the ministry and graduated from Harvard's Divinity School during the Civil War. He moved to Brooklyn to become pastor of Second Unitarian Church.

Chadwick was asked in 1859 to present a poem to that year's graduating class. Before a new crop of students and other community members, he bravely asserted

> But the dark age of school-time ends at last;
> The dame becomes a memory of the past;
> Teachers more worthy, bless their onward ways
> And make them bright with learning's fairest rays.[1]

Nothing better encapsulates the aspirations of the era's teachers and education reformers. For too long the "dame"—the harsh disciplinarian, who expected children to obey her, to sit still for hours on uncomfortable benches in unheated schoolrooms, and made young people recite from memory long passages—would give way to teachers "more worthy" of a democratic era.

What could be more heroic? Rev. R. C. Waterston, speaking at the 1848 graduation of the West Newton State Normal School, called teaching the most noble profession, one that emulated God, the first teacher. The teacher's role was to help each young child develop herself or himself in relation to God's teachings. "Look around upon this marvellous creation," Rev. Waterston urged. The natural world is composed of "mountains whose summits are veiled in clouds" and "valleys clothed in beauty and fertility." But nature is not "marvellous" on its own, but because we learn from it and can be inspired by it. It is "Mind which gazes upon them, and feels their influence." While the "outward universe" is a cause for wonder, "it shrinks and dwindles when compared with the undying Spirit" within each of us. God has endowed Spirit "with faculties by which it may rise ever upward to the Infinite and Eternal." "There is not a star or a stone which is not placed before us as a volume to be opened and read."

We must learn to read each star and each stone. Good teachers "help the young mind to interpret nature. They guide its thought, answer its questionings and direct its investigations. They act with God and His Providence to impart instruction and develope mind." God acts through teachers, His "human agencies."[2] As Henry Barnard put it, "every school house should be a temple, consecrated in prayer to the physical, intellectual, and moral culture of every child in the community, and be associated in every heart with the earliest and strongest impressions of truth, justice, patriotism, and religion."[3]

Electa Lincoln, who served a short term as the first female principal of a normal school, opened the first day of the spring 1849 term with a devotional reading "from the 10th of John—a striking, beautiful passage where Jesus likens himself to the door of a sheepfold & to the good Shepherd." Lincoln sought "to give the passage a practical bearing." "If we would become shepherds, true shepherds, we must enter the fold by the door, by *Christ*—our motives, our aims must be Christian," she urged her students. The only way to teach is out of "love, deep stirring love for our fellow creatures and an earnest desire to benefit them, love, soul filling love of God & a desire to work his will." While some actions affect the physical universe, teaching's impact was on the "moral universe." While "we cannot always see the effect here," might teachers' actions "vibrate throughout eternity?"[4]

Teachers were envisioned as God's democratic agents, developing in each child the capacity to interpret the world, to develop her or his inner divine potential in relation to higher laws of beauty and goodness. These lofty expectations were bound to fail. In practice, most teachers were young and unprepared. And even those with good training faced school boards that wanted just the basics and students who wanted to be somewhere else. Perhaps the hardest thing for idealistic supporters of democratic education to accept—for better or for worse—was that, for so many in the classroom, school was not a liberating experience but a necessary evil.

An Ohio Schoolmistress

Most teachers did not imagine themselves as God's "human agencies" but became teachers to pay the bills. In return, teachers were seen as "hired help"— young men in or right out of college earning a bit before becoming ministers, merchants, or lawyers, or young women barely out of common school, earning a bit before marriage. School district officials did not expect teachers to be trained, to have a deep understanding of subject matter, or to consider teaching as a career. As late as 1863, for example, two-thirds of California's teachers never taught in the same school two years in succession.[5]

Irene Hardy was born in Eaton, Ohio, in July 1841. Her father was a schoolteacher, and all of his four daughters and one son taught school. Hardy became a schoolteacher to earn money for college; she enrolled at Antioch College in fall 1861. Like many other young people, she went back and forth between school and work, usually teaching in order to pay for school. She moved west, to California, for her health, and continued to teach. In 1894 she became a professor at the new Stanford University, where she taught American literature, composition, and short story writing. She completed her memoirs in 1913, reflecting on her time as a young girl in Ohio and then out west.[6]

Among her earliest memories as a child was of her father as a teacher in a district school, where, she recalled, he was quite successful. Another memory involved a tale told by her mother, who had attended school in Virginia under a teacher who "punished with a rod or the ruler"; one day she was whipped on her hand "until her palm was blistered" for eating "some sweet birch leaves behind her book, because she was hungry."

Hardy first experienced school herself at age five in "a little, square log building of the pioneer fashion." Her first teacher was Ms. Lucy Wilkinson, "a widow with one little girl." She then moved on to "Bailey's Schoolhouse" about two miles away from home. She had both a male and female teacher, but "I remember nothing of this school except an incident or two of the playground." At home, she consumed *McGuffey's Readers*. She also attended her father's school. Recitations were still the norm in 1847. Silent study soon replaced studying aloud, and it came fast, when George W. Daly showed up to teach in 1849 or 1850.

When she was ten, her family moved to Eaton, a larger town. The new town school was much different from the rural district schools she had known with regard to "dress, shoes, desk arrangement, large classes, a sort of graded system, and good deal of stir and far more lax discipline." The town school sought to embrace new ideas proposed by school reformers. Around age eleven, after being "examined in arithmetic," Irene was moved to the "Fourth Room," which served as the high school. She there came under the guidance of a new teacher, Isaac Morris, who became a mentor.

Like many other young women, at sixteen, before she was done with her own high school education Hardy "went away to teach" and "had no more direct schooling until" she went to college, at age twenty. She took the train in late summer 1857 to Richmond, Indiana, sixteen miles away, to take a teacher's examination and to apply for a position. After serving "three purgatorial weeks" as a substitute, she was appointed to a secondary school, where she taught a four-month term "and went home at the end." Because of what her father called "an ignorant Democratic legislature," there would be no more free schooling that year. The next year, Hardy taught district school "in the backwoods of Lanier Township," Ohio. She moved around between schools over the coming years.

Hardy was an exception—most young women did not teach for a long time, much less go to college and become Stanford professors.[7] But her youthful experience was typical. Across America, young women in their teens, many of whom were barely out of common school themselves, took teacher's examinations, were assigned to schools, and taught on and off without any special training or advanced education, nor with any expectation of a career.[8]

It was something to do until marriage, as eleven-year-old Caroline Cowles Richards of Canandaigua, New York, knew well. One day she confessed to her diary, "A gentleman visited our school to-day whom we had never seen. Miss Clark introduced him to us. . . . He is very nice looking, but we don't know where he lives. . . . I hope he does not plan to get married to Miss Clark and take her away and break up the school, but I presume he does, for that is usually the way."[9] The school reformers hoped to change all that.

From Submission to Democracy

According to the reformers, if every child was formed in God's image, then each child deserved to have her or his faculties cultivated. Most American schoolrooms failed to meet this high standard, or so thought reformers. Amateur teachers armed with a ruler or a switch to punish wrongdoers, with barely a common school education, reigned. They taught the rudiments—reading, writing, arithmetic—but not much more since they themselves knew little more.

It was not just the formal curriculum, but the way it was taught, that concerned reformers. For them, democratic education should make every American "a responsible free agent, each individual accountable for his own life and opinions, to the One Divine Master of all."[10] But teachers taught dependence, not independence. They asked students to listen, to accept, to memorize, and rarely to think for themselves and to be "accountable" for their choices.

William McGuffey was downright hostile to traditional teaching: "Nothing can be more fatiguing for the teacher, nor irksome to the pupil, than a recitation conducted on the plan of 'verbatim answers.' "[11] His *Readers* were intended to develop students' faculties—their reason, imagination, and moral sense—but this could happen only if teachers knew what to do with them. The problem was, as Abraham Lincoln remembered of his childhood days in Indiana, "there were some schools so called; but no qualification was ever required of a teacher beyond 'readin, writin and cipherin,' to the Rule of Three. If a straggler supposed to understand latin happened to sojourn in the neighborhood, he was looked upon as a wizzard." The real problem in such a place, Lincoln reflected, was that "there was absolutely nothing to excite ambition for education."[12]

Everywhere one turned, traditional forms of teaching came under attack, as reformers sought to encourage a new democratic pedagogy for an age of self-making. At the first convention of normal school principals, held in Trenton, New Jersey, in 1859, speaker after speaker appealed for better trained teachers. "The great want of our schools is that of truly qualified teachers," lamented the convention's opening speaker, William F. Phelps, president of the American Normal School Association.[13] Rev. George B. Emerson, himself president of the American Institute of Instruction, challenged the "common impression . . . that any person of tolerable character, who has been through a school . . . is qualified to teach it." Teaching was more than "pouring into the mind of another what has been poured into ours." Teachers must act upon each child's "mind," form her "habits," and develop "character."[14]

Hiram Orcutt recalled that the teachers in one New Hampshire district—"a young man in the winter and a young woman in the summer"—were both "incompetent." They had had "no opportunity for culture and professional training." The district parents wanted "cheap teachers" rather than good teachers, and that is what they got.[15]

Poet John Greenleaf Whittier recalled the "master of the district school" the "brisk wielder of the birch and rule." Earning just a "subsistence scant," he would "doff at ease his scholar's gown / To peddle wares from town to town."[16] But the district schoolmaster deserved respect and gratitude. Whittier appreciated the "birchen arguments" that, through sheer force of will, helped young people learn "the mysteries / of those weary A B Cs."[17]

Playwright Richard Penn Smith told a story of returning to his hometown, only to discover his childhood friend was the current schoolmaster. He learns that the previous schoolmaster died of a cold "by exposing himself, when overheated by the labour of a severe flagellation inflicted upon the broad shoulders of a dull urchin," what the current schoolmaster referred to as "the ancient system of imparting knowledge."[18]

Teachers had long been expected to maintain order and to teach children to sit still, be silent, and do their work. As the school committee for one of the Groton, Massachusetts, school districts put it, teachers must ensure "due subordination . . . Lenient measures will be preferred to coercive and severe; but if the former do not avail, the latter must be adopted."[19] Susan Francis Lewis recalled her own days as a student in Groton's School District No. 2. The schoolroom was heated by a central fireplace "in the middle of the side opposite the door." Boys sat on one side of the room, girls on the other, with "a large space between them," used for students to come forward "in a line to read, spell, etc." A word was given to spell, and "if not spelled correctly by the one to whom given, was passed on" down the line, with the best speller wearing "a medal home at night."[20]

For reformers, this approach, students reciting from memory in competition with each other and in fear of corporal punishment, was no way to cultivate human potential.[21] It focused on external performance rather than what was happening inside a child's heart and mind. It did not encourage reflection but repetition. For Thomas Palmer, author of *The Teacher's Manual* (1840), the way schools taught morality was "trash" (he didn't mince words) because "the moral sense of the pupil is seldom, if ever, appealed to. Every regulation is grounded on mere authority."[22]

Edward Mansfield, in *American Education, Its Principles and Elements* (1851), concluded that most teachers taught students "to *imitate*, or *repeat*, rather than to *think*." Others bent too far the other way, allowing students to learn everything "by observation or experiment." A good teacher balanced authority with freedom. One could not substitute "machinery" (by which he meant "flimsy, parti-colored, cheap" textbooks) for the real work of teaching: engaging a young person's mind and guiding it.[23]

To George Emerson, "the object of education, in its highest sense, is to draw out, naturally and fully, every faculty of the body, mind, and soul." To be effective, teachers "must know what are the faculties, and what are the laws of their action." Character is not developed by "discourse upon morals"; rather, "moral education consists in leading one to *act* from conscientious motives," not simply in learning to obey.[24] Thomas Palmer agreed that the best education would help students "converse with Moses, Socrates, Seneca, Cicero, or Jesus." A good teacher did not just impart knowledge but also cultivated "intellectual faculties."[25]

To do so, teachers must understand the "science of learning." They needed "a comprehensive knowledge of the nature, value, and appropriateness of the educational forces or instrumentality best adapted to reach man's educational capacity," and how best to match "educational supply to the educational want," so that "throughout the several periods of man's growth" teachers consistently encouraged the cultivation of their students' "physical, intellectual, and moral nature," argued Ohio's John Ogden, author of the 1859 *Science of Education and the Art of Teaching*.[26]

To develop students' faculties, teachers needed to understand how best to engage them. To develop insight, teachers had to have real knowledge of the arts and sciences. To foster character, teachers had to embody the virtues of a good person and help students learn to act morally from within. Traditional teaching did none of these things. Only a democratic pedagogy in which educated teachers served as mentors to young people could do it.

Spare the Rod?

In the winter term of 1848–49, Artemas Longley was schoolmaster of Groton's School District No. 2. One day, according to the later memories of one student, he "called up an unruly boy, took him and threw him out of the window into a large snow bank, saying 'When you think you can behave yourself you come in and do so.'"[27] That young student was lucky. He landed in a soft snowbank. Other students would face whippings. While teaching school in Bradford during winter

1855, Frank C. Morse, who would go on to serve as a chaplain to the Thirty-Seventh Massachusetts Infantry Regiment during the Civil War, wrote that he "punished John L. Otis severely for misconduct."[28]

Many children thought this kind of treatment was excessive. Teenager Leavitt Thornton, who lived on a farm on Martha's Vineyard, one day observed in his diary that his schoolmate and the schoolmaster "had some difficulty." In response, the teacher "feruled him quite badly and I think for nearly nothing." After missing school for a week because of more pressing concerns, Thornton returned and noted in his diary that the schoolmaster was having "a dreadful" time with the kids and that "[I] rather pity the man." By mid-November, however, the master seemed to have found his feet for, Thornton wrote, "the school gets along first rate." About a week later, however, he described the school day as "uneasy." After missing another few days, he returned to discover that "the master was rather savage" and threatened to "lick some of them pretty soon."[29]

Such severe discipline was not teaching students to respect their teachers, nor was it encouraging them to love learning, but rather to obey out of fear of punishment. Punishment also became, for Thornton at least, the primary source of anxiety and memory of school. Forget becoming good citizens or self-culture. The goal was to avoid being hit. This would never do, reformers believed. Children would learn to conform but not to be moral agents. They would obey but not act freely. They would respond to external forces but not internal ones.

Morse realized this. He felt "discouraged," calling District No. 2 an "unpleasant school." Too much of his energy was spent managing the classroom, trying and failing to gain the students' confidence. He knew he was failing and hoped that the next teacher would be "some one who will reach the hearts of the scholars better than I can."[30] He cared deeply. By the end of January, as his control over his classroom seemed to slip away, he "almost gave up to sobs and tears."[31] By February 1, it was all over. Morse "built the fire at the School house intending to teach school" that morning "but found things in such a condition that I took my books and left. Went to Mr. Brockway's, got my pay[.] Packed up and went home."[32]

Both teachers and students saw the schoolroom as a battlefield.[33] In one case, an 1850 schoolteacher rapped one of the larger boys in his class, the boy turned on him and fought. The teacher won by holding the boy on the floor by his neck while the girls ran out of the room.[34] Violence was used not just to discipline but to motivate. An Indiana farmer recalled his schoolmaster of the 1840s: "The master would open the book and listen." If the student did not get the lesson right, the master would respond by addressing the cheek, ear, or bottom, but not the understanding.[35]

It was impossible to reach the "hearts of scholars," reformers argued, if the schoolroom was a place of violent contest. It fostered antagonism and fear rather than love and made teachers authoritarians rather than mentors. Moreover, by relying on violence, teachers taught students to express their basest passions rather than the self-control of a responsible moral agent. Overuse of the rod spoiled the child.[36] "The doctrine of mere compulsion," believed A. S. Welch of Michigan's normal school, "has long since exploded." "The rod as an incentive to study" forced students "to labor through fear" and produced "mere verbal recitations" rather than deep learning.[37]

That was a lesson West Newton State Normal School assistant teacher Electa Lincoln learned while observing Dana Colburn. "I liked Mr. Colburn's teaching much," she wrote in her diary. "'Twasn't the teacher that struck me, as much as manner." He treated his students "like gentlemen and ladies." Rather than ordering them around, he "spiced a request, now & then, with an 'if you please.'" The lesson was not lost on Lincoln. "I wish teachers of small scholars would, in this particular, follow his example," she wrote in her diary. Politeness and respect for students "might enforce just as strict an obedience" as force and threats. A teacher "would gain more respect and love & at the same time, by example" teach young people "an observance of the rules of politeness."[38]

Lincoln captured privately (and it was intended to be private; the cover of her diary states: "If this journal should be in existence when I am dead, I wish it to be burned unread") what Horace Mann and others were stating publicly. It was no accident that Colburn was modeling what he hoped teachers in training would do in their own classrooms, or that Lincoln, a teacher in the normal school, recognized it.

New Ideas Cross the Atlantic

American educators were inspired by what they observed in Europe, where education seemed much more advanced than in the United States.[39] Reports circulated around the United States about the innovations Europeans were making. As early as 1817, North Carolina's Archibald Murphey was telling his state's legislature about new approaches to teaching in Europe, and two years later New York schoolteacher John Griscom published *A Year in Europe*. Both men spoke highly of Prussia and of Swiss educator Johann Pestalozzi.[40]

Pestalozzi reframed the relationship between psychology and education. If the end of education was the full development of human beings, this meant nurturing students' innate faculties over time. This required teachers who understood the psychology of education, who could tap into students' reason, moral sense, and imagination.[41] Pestalozzi's ideas gained widespread attention following the translation into English of French education minister Victor Cousin's report on Prussian school laws. Calvin Stowe, a professor of biblical literature at Lane Theological Seminary, and Harriet Beecher Stowe's husband, was charged by the Ohio legislature during his visit to Europe to find "such facts and information as he may deem useful to the state in relation to the various systems of public instruction and education."

Stowe was amazed by Prussian schools. They paid good salaries to well-trained teachers. They had abandoned rote learning to tap into children's innate curiosity. "I will say from the outset, that the industry, skill and energy of the teachers regularly trained to their business, and depending entirely upon it; the modes of teaching; the habit of always finishing whatever is begun; the perfect method which is preserved; the entire punctuality and regularity of attendance on the part of the scholars; and other things of this kind, facilitate a rapidity and exactness of acquisition and discipline, which may well seem incredible to those who have never witnessed it."

Moreover, the teachers knew how to teach. "What faculty of mind is there that is not developed in the scheme of instruction sketched above? I know of none. The perceptive and reflective faculties, the memory and the judgment, the imagination and the taste, the moral and religious faculty, and even the various kinds of physical and manual dexterity, all have opportunity for development and exercise."

Stowe worried that the United States was falling behind Europe. A republic, he reminded Ohio's legislature, depends on an educated citizenry. Education mattered more in America than it did in Europe. Yet Americans invested less in their schools and teachers. But Stowe had hope: "If it can be done in Europe, I believe it can be done in the United States; if it can be done in Prussia, I know it can be done in Ohio."[42]

In early 1843, Secretary Mann decided that he should tour Europe himself to get a firsthand look at its schools. Around the same time, in a move that surprised many of his friends, he proposed to Mary Peabody. They were married in May, and the planned European vacation doubled as Horace and Mary's honeymoon. Mann's tour took him across Europe, visiting schools and talking to officials, and he offered the lessons he learned in his *Seventh Annual Report* to the Massachusetts Board of Education.[43]

Like others, Mann was enamored by what he saw in Prussia. He recognized that the goals of democratic education were different from those of Prussian education because democracies should not promote "passive obedience to government, or of blind adherence to the articles of a church." But, he responded, "the human faculties are substantially the same all over the world," so the principles, if not the ends, of education would be as well.[44]

Massachusetts led the world in one important way—the principle that schooling should be premised "upon a footing of equality before God." But the Prussians knew how to organize education better. First, the state oversaw education, not to serve "rulers" but "for the welfare of the subject." Second, schools were divided into age-based grades to encourage students' social, moral, and intellectual development. But most of all, the teachers were better. "About twenty years ago, teachers in Prussia made the important discovery, that children have five senses, together with various muscles and mental faculties, all of which, must be kept in a state of activity, and which, if not usefully, are liable to be mischievously employed." To engage students' hearts and minds required effective teachers, not teachers who "stand over them with a rod and stifle their workings" or rely on "fear" to encourage obedience. Moreover, rather than have children recite from memory or repeat what a teacher said, Prussian teachers helped students gain "precision in the expression of ideas" and encouraged them to "exercise their intellect."

In Massachusetts, "not a single faculty of the mind is occupied," Mann averred. "A parrot or an idiot could do the same thing." In arithmetic, Massachusetts students spent a lot of time memorizing abstract rules, but Prussian students engaged in more "analysis of all questions, and in not separating the processes, or rules, so much as we do from each other." The result was that students "proceed less by rule, more by an understanding of the subject."

In other words, Prussian teachers encouraged students to be more intellectually independent than did American teachers. This was clearly backward since it was the United States, not Prussia, that claimed to be a free democracy.

While America might take pride in providing access to education, Mann urged his fellow Bay Staters to improve the status of the teaching profession and, by doing so, to transform lifeless classrooms into lively places where "children are delighted." In the best classrooms, students' "perceptive powers are exercised. Their reflective faculties are developed. Their moral sentiments are cultivated. All the attributes of the mind within find answering qualities in the world without."

In other words, in the best classrooms, children should feel alive.

Lancasterianism

The most prominent alternative to Pestalozzi was proposed by Joseph Lancaster.[45] Whereas Mann and others thought a democratic pedagogy ought to appeal to children's innate sensibilities, Lancasterianism, or the monitorial system, was a system of industrial efficiency.

Joseph Lancaster was born to a London sieve maker, and he worked at two different schools before, in 1798, opening his own. Deeply committed to access, Lancaster admitted, and even clothed, many poor students. As the number of students grew, he lacked the resources to teach all of them. He thus decided that, to save money, older students should teach younger ones. He was neither the first nor the last to do this. What distinguished his system was what Carl Kaestle calls its "elaborate set of rules, routines, and pedagogical inventions."

This approach had several advantages. First, it was cheap because Lancaster relied on older students to teach. Second, some considered Lancaster's emphasis on repetition and competition to be effective. In groups of ten or twelve, led by a monitor, students drilled in reading, spelling, or arithmetic. Each day, every student was ranked publicly, motivating students to excel or, at least, to avoid embarrassment. Students received "merit tickets" for behavior and performance.

Lancaster's model was popular in New York City and Pennsylvania. The New York Free School Society operated eleven monitorial schools in 1825 and stayed true to the model into the 1840s. The first Lancasterian school in Philadelphia opened in 1808. In 1818 Pennsylvanians mandated the Lancasterian approach to educate the poor in the city and, later, throughout the state. New York's governor DeWitt Clinton considered the Lancasterian model the best way to expand access with less dollars. Lancasterianism was for education "what the neat finished machines for abridging labor and expense are in the mechanic arts."[46] Mann wanted public schools to correct for the degrading, dehumanizing experience of industrial forms of labor. Clinton wanted schools to emulate them.

And for those in the schools, it was like working in a factory. To one student of a Lancasterian school in frontier Detroit, the school was a model of harmoniously moving parts. Because students could advance whenever they stood "at the head of the class three nights in succession," students progressed at their own rate without being held back by their peers.[47] But not everyone saw harmony in the model. One writer, who recalled being in school in 1820s New York City, described his teacher as "the Monarch of the school, with ferule, cat-o'-nine-tails, and other instruments of torture, to uphold his government." Under the teacher was the "dictator" to announce the lessons. And then came "the monitors." Both dictator and monitors were "selected from the larger boys," who took turns. "The schoolmaster seldom or never came in contact with the scholars under the monitors, except with the ferule." Every monitor every morning would start "drilling his own company." This was indeed a factory floor or a plantation, with the master teacher overseeing everything but engaging little, except to punish, and each team of students being led by a monitor. Looking back, this writer, who recognized that his teachers were doing their duty, could only say, "I forgive them."[48]

Horace Mann was less forgiving. "The idea that there are two antagonistic powers in the schoolroom, each struggling for mastery over the other,—like the rival houses of York and Lancaster, contending for the English throne,—will be as fatal to the prosperity of a school as is a civil war to the prosperity of a country," Mann wrote in 1845.[49] He worried that Lancasterianism would teach students to compete for external rewards and glory instead of developing appropriate moral character. He also argued that it denied students access to qualified, well-prepared teachers. "One must see the difference between the hampering, blinding, misleading instruction given by an inexperienced child, and the developing, transforming, and almost creative power of an accomplished teacher," Mann wrote.[50]

The Revolt of the Boston Schoolmasters

Why would anyone oppose Mann's wonderful vision of schooling? Because, responded thirty-one Boston schoolmasters, in what became a major pamphlet and political war between Horace Mann and the most respected teachers in Massachusetts, children did not want to go to school. True love is tough love. Young people must be educated. Their minds and hearts must be addressed. Teachers must make them knowledgeable and have good moral character. And this would never happen, Boston's master teachers argued, if we coddled them. Mann and his allies, many of whom had never stepped into a classroom, had no idea what they were talking about.

The conflict began after Mann, in his *Seventh Annual Report*, waxed poetic about the inspiring, engaging, loving classrooms he observed in Prussia. In response, Boston's schoolmasters published in 1844 a long, thoughtful reply. They acknowledged that education "amateurs" like Mann rarely cared about what actual teachers might think, but they hoped the public might.[51] The teachers felt insulted by Mann's tone, which suggested that Prussia's teachers were doing great things, while back at home every teacher was incompetent. They, in turn, mocked Mann's embrace of every new intellectual fad that came along, while honest teachers had to work with real children using tried and true methods. Why did Mann seek to undermine confidence in teachers, they wondered, especially when Mann had no teaching experience?

More was at stake than dignity and pride. The schoolmasters questioned whether the teaching Mann saw in Prussia was really able to create thoughtful, moral adults. "The path of the public teacher of youth is one beset with many and peculiar difficulties," they wrote. Despite Mann's hopes, and despite a teacher's best efforts, students "seldom appreciate his exertions." Far from it, the teacher is obliged to serve "indolent and disobedient pupils."[52] Real children were not sweet, intellectually curious, and eager to please their beloved teachers. They were preoccupied with their immediate interests and inclined to laziness; they saw school as a burden and disliked it. Teachers, out of love for their students, must force them to get an education that few students actually wanted.

Mann argued that teachers must appeal to students' "curiosity." Boston's masters disagreed. Appeals to curiosity would not lead to autonomy but instead would encourage students to follow their own impulses, pell-mell, without their being able to sit still and actually learn anything. Yes, teachers should interest their students in the subject of study, but "we do object to the exercise of that ability to such extent, and in such manner, that the pupils become accustomed to depend, for their motive to mental effort, upon that excitement alone which is furnished by their teacher."

That was the nub. Reformers believed that tapping into children's curiosity and interest would make them more independent learners. Boston teachers, adding a dose of realism, reminded them that few children really wanted to work hard on intellectual tasks. If young people were taught that all learning must be pleasing, they would only do things that were fun, not those things that were worth doing. Students had to gain the discipline to study hard if they were to get a good education, and if they were to be able to do hard intellectual work all their lives.

The same was true for moral education. So long as people are people, "school order, like that of the family and society, must be established upon the basis of acknowledged authority, as a starting-point." It was nice to imagine appealing to every child's moral sense, but Massachusetts was not some prelapsarian Eden. It was composed of real, flesh and blood, fallen beings. The reason Prussia could get away with less discipline was because it had an authoritarian government. Young people were taught to obey. Teachers did not need to use force because of "the coercive power of school law." "We must take human nature as it is," the reformers reminded Mann.[53]

Certainly, Mann never aspired to give up authority. Mann and his allies were not Pestalozzian purists who believed that children must be allowed to follow their natural inclinations. Instead, they believed that Pestalozzi's insights on child psychology would foster better teachers, who could use psychology to aid them in their efforts. Their aspiration remained tied to a larger vision of the good citizen and person. But the Boston teachers were correct that Mann's approach favored the internal to the external. Mann rejected corporal punishment and competition because he wanted young people to see the goods of education as worthy on their own terms.

The temerity of Boston's schoolmasters unleashed the wrath of Mann's Boston allies. In the face of Mann's and the teachers' public, and not very becoming, pamphlet war, Mann's friends looked for a way to embarrass and discredit his critics.[54] While the masters' reputation insulated them from criticism, parents increasingly worried that the teachers protected themselves and were too violent. The time was ripe to bring them down to size. But how to do so?

The answer, Mann's friends realized, was testing. By forcing all Boston's grammar school students to take a written test, on subject matter that they had supposedly mastered, reformers could translate students' failures into a condemnation of the masters' pedagogy. In 1845 Boston mayor Josiah Quincy Jr. appointed three members to the Boston School Committee's reading and writing committee. These were not just any people; Quincy had stacked the deck with Mann's allies.

Mann and his friends on the Boston School Committee met after hours, wrote back and forth, and came up with a plan. As the press wars raged and newspapers filled with stories of violent Boston teachers beating children, the reading and writing committee decided to evaluate schools on the basis of student performance. They would visit the schools and ask questions in each major subject area. The big innovation was that instead of providing oral answers, students would have to write their answers down on a test that none of the teachers or students had yet seen.

And the results were, as might be predicted in such a context, disastrous. Students performed terribly. They could not answer the most basic questions nor do the most basic math. Clearly, the Boston teachers had no idea how to teach. Clearly, Massachusetts needed new schools to prepare a new generation of teachers. And, clearly, Massachusetts needed to embrace educational reform.

There are two points to be taken here. First, the Boston schoolmasters did not believe that education would ever be, for students, an intrinsic good. Second, the reformers responded in a way that has become endemic to American history—by finding tools to embarrass and discredit teachers without stopping to listen to their ideas or to learn from their experience.[55] And, as we will see, as hopeful as reformers were, the realities of teaching were much different on the ground, and, for better or for worse, the Boston masters had some basis for their resistance.

The Rise of Professional Teaching Schools

There were two types of schools, Professor Alpheas Crosby of Salem Normal School argued: general schools such as common schools, academies, and colleges, and professional schools, which teach theology, law, medicine, military science, or agriculture. Normal schools were among the latter group. Their goal was not "the general discipline or culture" of students but "their special preparation to meet the demands of a particular profession, that of the Teacher."

Normal schools were fine and good, but they would never make a difference if ordinary Americans did not grant teaching the same respect that they granted law, medicine, and the ministry. And the evidence, Crosby admitted, was not promising. Not only did Americans overwhelmingly rely on females—thus demonstrating the low prestige of teaching—but even then, few women teachers could make a career when schools were haphazard, pay was low, and employment was always temporary.[56]

Crosby's perspective was shared widely.[57] North Carolina's Braxton Craven, who would become president of his state's normal school, believed that without normal schools "we can never reach any eminence."[58] A teacher must "not only possess the knowledge he is required to impart," argued another North Carolinian, but "must also know the best methods, taught us by experience, of conveying that information to young and reluctant minds."[59] Henry Barnard praised Connecticut for establishing a normal school, proof that legislators understood "the necessity and importance of specific preparation for the business of teaching."[60]

The first state to open a normal school was Massachusetts, when Edmund Dwight donated ten thousand dollars to improve teacher training on the condition that the state match his grant. The legislature authorized the new board of education to act. Three sites were chosen.[61] The school in Lexington (which moved to West Newton in 1844 and Framingham in 1853) was for women only and opened in 1839. The other schools were coeducational. A fourth school for women opened in Salem in 1854. New York authorized a normal school in Albany in 1844; Connecticut and Michigan authorized normal schools in 1849. By the Civil War, four more states had followed: New Jersey (1855), Illinois (1857), Pennsylvania (1859), and Minnesota (1860). By the end of the 1860s, there were thirty-five public normal schools in sixteen states.[62]

Cities and counties also offered normal school programs. Boston started one in 1852. In 1868, Worcester too sought to run its own normal program. In fact, high schools prepared more common school teachers than normal schools during the nineteenth century. Philadelphia established the Philadelphia Model School, and in 1848 the school became the Philadelphia girls' high school, which offered teacher training. Chicago's first high school opened in the mid-1850s with a two-year normal program among its offerings. By 1885, a normal program existed in twenty-one cities, largely for female students.[63]

Many academies also offered teacher preparation programs, and some, like Emma Willard's Troy Seminar in New York (established in 1821), Catharine Beecher's Hartford Seminary in Connecticut (1832), and Mary Lyon's Mt. Holyoke seminary in Massachusetts (1837) provided young women with a college-level education in academics and teacher training.[64] New York provided state funding to academies to offer normal programs.[65] Academies often added on a teaching course here and there, as did some universities before the Civil War. Brown University established the first university education professor in 1850, but the post lasted only four years. Others followed—with normal departments emerging at Indiana University in shifts and starts and in the universities of Iowa (1855), Missouri (1868), and Kansas (1876).[66]

Reformers advocated teachers' institutes in communities where normal school preparation was limited. Some were state funded, others informal. They lasted a few weeks, but were popular with teachers seeking community and professional development. They were also cheaper than normal schools or other programs for taxpayers and teachers.

The first teachers' institute may have been held by Henry Barnard in October 1839. As secretary of the Connecticut Board of Education, he brought together twenty-six young men, who received professional training for six weeks and observed teachers in Hartford's public schools. A few years later, J. S. Denman, county superintendent in Tompkins County, New York, put together a two-week teachers' institute for twenty-eight teachers. By 1845, half of New York's counties and the states of New Hampshire, Massachusetts, Ohio, and Pennsylvania all offered teachers' institutes. By the 1850s, teachers' institutes had spread from Maine to California, and some states made them mandatory. After the Civil War, teachers' institutes spread widely, offering many common school teachers a basic introduction to new, better ideas about how to teach. By the 1886–87 school year, the U.S. commissioner of education estimated that 2,003 institutes served 138,946 teachers, about half the teaching force.[67]

The challenge was that even reformers disagreed on the qualities of a professional teacher. Some, like Professor Crosby, were purists. They believed that teachers should master education's underlying principles, just as doctors understood medicine and lawyers law. Crosby advocated not an advanced understanding of academic subjects but instead "the principles and best methods of instruction in all those branches of learning which he may be called upon to teach."[68]

Others promoted higher education in the liberal arts and sciences; teachers could not teach subjects that they did not understand. Charles Hovey, principal of the Illinois State Normal University (which would become Illinois State University), commented during an intense discussion at the 1859 convention that it was not enough for normal schools to teach students how to teach. They had to know "what to teach and why such a thing is taught in a particular way." He claimed that "those schools that teach the subjects as well as the way to teach them, turn out the best teachers."[69]

Frederick Augustus Sawyer, who moved from Massachusetts to South Carolina in 1859 to become principal of the state normal school there, and who would later serve as South Carolina's Republican senator after the Civil War, tried to split the difference. Normal schools differed from high schools in their relationship to the arts and sciences. "In the High Schools they are taught as an end, but in the Normal Schools they are used as an instrument to gain an end." You cannot teach someone to weave without understanding "the warp and woof." The same was true for "arithmetic or geography."[70]

Normal school advocates never resolved what has become a lasting challenge to the teaching profession. Normal schools, and later education schools, claimed professional dominion over knowledge about how to teach, but they did not have the same claim to the knowledge of the arts and sciences that teachers were responsible for imparting. Could education be separated from the arts and sciences that were its foundation? Are teachers masters of teaching as a technique or the knowledge to be taught?[71]

Added to this was a more practical problem. Students came to normal schools ill-prepared in the arts and sciences and needed remedial academic work. Normal school educators had hoped to provide a professional education to teacher candidates who had already learned academic subjects but found instead that they had to teach elementary academics.[72]

The ideal normal school graduate was envisioned as someone with knowledge of the subjects to be taught, expertise in how to teach them, and good moral character. At Bridgewater, the course of study combined academic subjects ("Reading, Spelling, Enunciation, Writing, Geography, Physiology, Composition, Grammar, and Arithmetic" during the first term, with more advanced subjects being taken up in the second and third terms) with education in the theory and practice of teaching. The latter included studying "the School and the Schoolmaster" and attending "lectures delivered every week before the whole school, upon the duties and employments of teachers." Thus, all three elements—academic knowledge, the theory and practice of teaching, and character—were required of Bridgewater's graduates.[73]

Students learned through daily lectures on different subjects.[74] Normal student Caroline Goodale's schedule revolved around individual work during study hours, lectures to provide knowledge, and students' written abstracts or oral recitations on assigned subjects or questions. The recitations did not excite all students. Bridgewater Normal student Henry Pierce wrote to his brother in April 1845, "I recite my lessons to Mr Green and I do not like it much."[75] But Goodale reflected a more varied experience. On February 11, 1845, for example, she recorded in her diary:

> We had an exercise in globes this morning. . . . We had next an exercise in grammar we had a very good lesson in this. I am glad to hear that Mr Mason is going to favor us with his presence tuesdays and fridays to instruct us in singing. . . . I don't think that I am any farther advanced [in singing] than I was several years ago. . . . We had an exercise in Pedagogies. We were requested to write how we would treat those that are connected with our school but not under our care. These exercises were read before the class.

Here we see multiple forms of learning. There were some "exercises" in which, presumably, students were assigned work to do, but also lectures. There was a break in the middle to learn singing. And then they learned about teaching. Instead of passively listening to a lecture, they thought about a question, wrote their own ideas, and read them to each other. This encouraged each student to think seriously about the craft of teaching.

In Goodale's second term, learning to teach became a more prominent feature of her experience. She recalled in her diary for November 21, 1845, her "fluttering heart" as she waited with anticipation to offer a model lesson. Miss Ware was called first, and she "succeeded admirably." Goodale was more critical about her own presentation. Her lesson plan was to "write sentences upon the board and then call upon some one to correct them." So far so good but, she lamented, "I thought I could make this interesting but I entirely failed to do this."[76] Her sentiment helps us see how, at least at one normal school, students trained by offering each other model lessons. She would have to "do better next time."[77]

Normal School Life

Normal schools were not just about the formal curriculum; they were missionary in their aspirations. Rather than simply impart knowledge, they tried to foster the deeper commitments that defined the character of a good teacher. Teaching was, as Electa Lincoln had said, God's work. Well-educated, well-trained teachers would help develop the image of God in each child. If they were shepherds, she told the normalites gathered before her, they must always reach out with love, "for the sheep will either not follow us, or following us, will be led astray."[78]

Lincoln cared deeply about her students. "I am discouraged. Everything seems to go wrong," she lamented in fall 1848. "I do not teach to suit myself. I do not inspire others with zeal, with the deep, lively interest which they should have in their studies." She wanted to help her students to develop a real love of learning and to foster their curiosity. Instead, she worried, "It seems to me as if I had lost my faculties for teaching, if I ever had them."[79]

But her commitment never waned, and she remained a tough but caring mentor. During study hours, there was to be no "communication." Each must do her work. Lincoln's strictness reflected her aspiration that women prove their abilities not just to themselves but to the world. A young woman who has "learned to depend on <u>herself</u>," she wrote in her journal, "has made a long, a very long stride towards the attainments necessary as a teacher." While she wanted each graduate "to learn to walk intellectually" on her own, she also asked them to leave the study room quietly, without "moving the chairs or scuffing the feet (which seems to me quite unladylike)."[80]

There can be no doubt that Lincoln saw herself as an exemplar of what women might become. As the first female principal of a normal school, she felt the eyes of the world upon her. "It has been said that women cannot do much in the way of conducting a school like this," she confessed to her journal. "If there is such strong feeling in the community on the subject, I am all the more anxious to succeed." "Woman is regarded as beneath, in many respects, man, & 'tis woman's place to raise herself in others estimation."

For this reason, she was "particularly anxious in regard to order." She knew that "orderly habits in school are the standard by which we judge of the intellectual advancement of its inmates as much as orderly habits in an individual are the criterion by which we judge the ordering of the mind. And it is right that a school should be so judged." But this meant that any disorder on the part of her students had broader implications—about whether women could be as effective teachers and principals as men.[81]

Being away from home for school was a formative experience for many women. Goodale, in her third and final term at West Newton, wrote in her journal that "this term is nearly half gone and my Normal life is fast coming to a close. I dislike to think of it, as being so. Would that I continue here longer." Lydia Stow, who graduated with the first class at Lexington Normal, went back to visit the school and her professor Cyrus Peirce. As she left, she reminisced: "I shall have the happiness of looking upon the hours spent here as being the most profitable and pleasant of any that have gone by."[82] And many of her fellow alumnae did too. Starting in 1850, they met annually for many years to renew memories and friendships and their commitment to the idea of professional teaching.[83]

The Education of Catharine Beecher

As the number of schools expanded, so did the need for teachers. Simultaneously, immigration, westward expansion, and urbanization transformed American society, making it more mobile and diverse. Everything was in motion. With the downfall of the established churches—Massachusetts being the last to disestablish public religion in 1833—there were no common institutions to socialize young people into their roles as adult citizens. Men seemed preoccupied with surviving or getting rich, but the standards of the market were not appropriate

Figure 4.1. Catharine Beecher. Schlesinger Library, Radcliffe Institute, Harvard University

for home life or for citizens. Here, sacrifice was demanded, and duty must trump self-interest. Women, Catharine Beecher believed, could and must step in to save the nation, to offer all young people a good education, one that would bring them together as Americans and teach them to serve the larger community.

Beecher was born in 1800, the eldest child of Rev. Lyman Beecher, who would become one of the country's most influential evangelical ministers. Her sister Harriet Beecher Stowe was author of *Uncle Tom's Cabin*, and her brother, Rev. Henry Ward Beecher, was also a major public figure, remembered for encouraging antislavery activists to send rifles to Kansas to combat proslavery forces. The rifles, because they purportedly were shipped in crates labeled "Bibles," became known as "Beecher's Bibles."[84] As her father's influence grew, he moved the family in 1809 from East Hampton, on Long Island, to Litchfield, Connecticut. There, Beecher entered Sarah Pierce's Litchfield Academy, founded in 1792, one of the most famous, and elite, female academies of the era. Pierce believed not only in the intellectual equality of women but also in a role for women in civic affairs.[85]

Pierce was not alone. Across the nation, female academies offered young women serious education, similar to what men might receive in college.[86] Educator Emma Willard, for example, in 1814, as her family faced financial hardship, opened up a boarding school in Middlebury, Vermont. Over the next few years, she worked on a plan to create a female college chartered by a state legislature. She earned New York governor DeWitt Clinton's support, who invoked her ideas in an annual address and urged Willard to come to New York. In 1819 the legislature chartered the "Waterford Academy for Young Ladies," one of the first higher educational institutions for women in the country. It would receive a share of the state's public funds. That spring, Willard moved from Vermont to Waterford. In 1821, thanks to a generous offer of financial support, Willard moved her academy to Troy, New York, where it flourished.[87]

Willard argued that the country's future depended on the higher education of both sexes. In her 1819 *Plan for Improving Female Education*, Willard lamented that many women's schools focus on "showy accomplishments, rather than those, which are solid and useful." Female education must "seek to bring its subjects to the perfection of their moral, intellectual, and physical nature."[88] Beecher certainly learned these lessons at Pierce's academy and, with them, the tension faced by educated woman in a society that limited civic and professional opportunities to men.[89] Pierce inspired Beecher to treat womanhood as a blessing rather than a curse. But while Beecher recognized the importance of the home to society, her ambitions went beyond the household. Teaching was one of the few places to turn.

Beecher thus opened her own school, the Hartford Female Seminary, in 1823 and began her life's work. The school was successful. For the next eight years, before moving to Cincinnati with her father, the school was the primary focus of Beecher's energy. But one should not idealize. She found it extremely hard. The daily grind of teaching was not immediately fulfilling, although, over time, she came to appreciate it. In 1826 she sought an endowment for her school and better facilities. Tapping into Hartford's leadership, she raised five thousand dollars in subscriptions. In the fall of 1827, the seminary opened in a new classical building.

"Knowledge, when it can be obtained without the sacrifice of higher duties, is as valuable to woman as to man," Beecher believed.[90]

Beecher's commitment to women's influence on society, especially as educators, was premised on her belief that women were equal in intellect but better suited than men to be teachers because of their commitment to serving others. She challenged those, like antislavery activists Angelina and Sarah Grimké, who sought equal rights for women. Instead, Beecher believed that women, while equal, had a special, distinct role to play in society, one in which the important virtues of womanhood would serve to transcend existing social divisions.[91]

Women were not to be timid or inferior but different. Because American society was fragmented, competitive, and selfish, it was the particular task of women teachers to offer a countervailing moral force capable of holding people together and inspiring them to live good lives. America was falling apart—race riots, class distinctions, partisan bickering, economic crises—and women, as teachers, must step into the breach.

American schools needed good teachers, but teaching was not like other professions that bring "wealth, influence, or honour," Beecher wrote in 1829. In fact, teachers were looked down upon by society. Teaching would never attract the best people, yet the quality of America's schools depended on the quality of America's teachers. Americans understood that it took years of training to make a shoe, but they believed that any person could teach. Amateur teachers who did not understand psychology were ill-equipped to shape the "mental and moral habits of children." In contrast, educated women too often had little that challenged them in daily life. They were prevented from using their minds. But, as teachers, educated women could take charge of the "cultivation and development of the immortal mind."[92]

Women needed an education of equal academic quality to men but oriented to their particular social roles and duties, Beecher believed. Men would not step up to be teachers when the "claims of the learned professions, the excitement and profits of commerce, manufacture, agriculture, and the arts" beckoned them. Instead, it was to America's women, "fitted by disposition, and habits, and circumstances, for such duties," to whom we must now turn.[93]

A democracy demanded an educated citizenry. Young people must learn about "their high duties." They needed an education sufficient to ensure that "they cannot be duped and excited by demagogues." All Americans "must be trained to read, and think, and decide *intelligently* on all matters." Rather than give in to "the heats and passion of political strife," American citizens "must be trained to rule their passions and to control themselves by reason, religion, and law." It was up to "the young daughters of this nation" therefore "to become the educators of all the future statesmen, legislators, judges, juries, and magistrates of this land."[94]

Feminization of Teaching

Beecher was not the only reformer who considered women particularly suited to teaching. Horace Mann agreed. "Is there not an obvious, constitutional difference of temperament between the sexes, indicative of a pre-arranged fitness and adaptation, and making known to us, as by a heaven-imparted sign, that woman, by her livelier sensibility and her quicker sympathies, is the fore-chosen guide and guardian of children of a tender age?" he asked, wondering why women would ever seek to get jobs and "barter away that divine and acknowledged superiority in sentiment which belongs to her own sex."[95] Many educators believed that the violent nature of classrooms would be tempered by women's presence. Boys felt challenged by male teachers and sought dominance, but would defer to women, or so it was said.[96]

Over the middle decades of the nineteenth century, the teaching profession shifted from predominantly male to female. In Massachusetts, for example, the percentage of female teachers went from 60.2 percent in 1837 (out of a total of 5,961 teachers) to 81.5 percent on the eve of the Civil War (out of a total of 10,311 teachers).[97] By 1850, 60 percent of American teachers were female—the number reached 80 percent in the Northeast and 82 percent in the Midwest, but only 35 percent in the South.[98]

Critics have noted that the ideal of the affectionate female teacher reinforced rather than challenged traditional gender ideas.[99] It is true that many supporters of female teachers did not advocate equal rights and female suffrage. Instead, they challenged Americans to think of duty and devotion as virtues that were necessary for a free society to survive and for all children to flourish.[100] Yet, perhaps it is worth noting, the feminization of America's teaching force may have had less to do with the purported virtues of women than with the simple fact that they could be paid less. As common schools expanded, and as more parents paid tuition and more citizens taxes, female teachers were much cheaper than their male counterparts. Concord, Massachusetts, school committee members concluded that female teachers not only were more effective but "can be obtained for two-thirds or three-fourths of the expense."[101] Cincinnati's school board argued in 1840 that because they did not wish to reduce salaries, hiring more female teachers would help them make ends meet.[102] In Boxford, Massachusetts, female teachers received in 1841 on average 41 percent of the wages of men.[103]

As demand for teachers skyrocketed thanks to an expanding public system, it was met by an increasing number of educated women with few career choices.[104] This complicated efforts to raise teachers' status. The first volume of the *North Carolina Journal of Education* simultaneously stated that "a woman who delights in teaching, is infinitely better fitted for the government and training of small children than a man" and that "if any one knows why a woman should teach, or do any other good work, for half of what a man would receive for the same service, let him give the world the benefit of his knowledge."[105]

Thus, while some like Beecher and Mann sought to elevate women for having specific virtues vital for teaching, for many Americans, female teachers' primary virtues were that they were cheap and plentiful. Far from elevating the teaching profession, the feminization of teaching eroded respect. Efforts to professionalize teachers, therefore, did not have the same success as nineteenth-century efforts to professionalize such male professions as law, medicine, and academics.

Age Grading and Longer Terms

Education reformers sought not just new teachers but new kinds of schools, organized into grades with longer annual terms. To achieve these goals, they urged combining local district schools into larger schools with more students and resources. It has often been thought that the primary impetus for creating larger schools organized by grades, rather than mixed-ability one-room schoolhouses, was efficiency. Like a factory, a graded school allowed for the division of labor.[106] School reformers did indeed argue that age-graded schools were more cost effective, but efficiency is not just about cost. It is about maximizing outcomes with finite resources. Age grading was connected with reformers' higher purposes. "The first element of superiority in a Prussian school, and one whose influence extends throughout the whole subsequent course of instruction, consists in the proper classification of the scholars," Mann wrote. When "children are divided according to ages and attainments" and each "teacher has the charge only of a single class," teachers could devote themselves to promoting deeper learning.[107]

Reformers' understanding of human psychology convinced them that people developed progressively. It made little sense, they believed, for a child to do something before she was ready for it. Education must be age appropriate. Educators worried that having teenaged boys in the same room with young children would affect children's moral and intellectual development, especially because childhood was supposed to be sheltered from adult concerns. This concept was something new. It was in the same decades that some public schools started to organize themselves by grade level that Americans started to think of childhood as a series of discrete developmental stages.[108]

But that was not how most Americans went to school. Schooling was not the kind of systematic, uniform experience that Americans take for granted today. Academy students often attended for short spurts followed by long absences. In district schools, attendance varied not only between terms but often from day to day. Children went to school as their or their parents' schedule permitted.[109] Today, we expect students to start in kindergarten and move forward through twelfth grade as a matter of course, but this was the outcome of school reformers' desire to redesign schools around a sequence of grades.

H. H. Barney, principal of Cincinnati's Central High School, who would later become the first elected state superintendent in Ohio, wrote in 1851 of "a new and noble system" that had emerged in the past fifteen years, what he called the "Republican System of Union or Graded Free Schools." The key word for Barney was "republican." The aspiration of reformers in bringing small districts together was to create a republican system, one that better served the public goals of education for all Americans.

The first step Barney celebrated was the division of schools into primary, secondary or intermediate, grammar, and central high schools. To achieve this goal, small districts would have to be unified. Compared to small districts, in unified districts with more children, students could be classified by grade levels. Smaller towns might add a high school department to lower schools; larger cities could build their own self-standing high schools.

Graded schools relied on the same "division of labor" as new "business corporations." They allowed teachers to focus on the particular psychological, curricular, and moral needs of children of different ages. In traditional one-room schools with mixed ages, all the time is "frittered away in hurried recitations" and "no opportunity is afforded for explanation and illustration" or for "indirect, collateral, and oral instruction." Teachers did not have the time "for pointing out the practical bearings and utility of the subject taught" much less "for awakening and disciplining the mind of the pupil, by a searching and skillful examination into the amount of his knowledge, and the processes by which he acquires it."

For students, this meant that learning was reduced to "the mere act of remembering" and, for teachers, instruction reduced to that of listening to students "repeat by rote." In short, to advocates of democratic education, graded schools were vital to achieving their aspirations because a graded school system, "like the rains and dews of heaven, confers its benefits and its blessings equally upon all." It would "take the industrious, talented and worthy children of the humblest as well as the richest parent, and lead them along and upward by simple and beautiful gradations, developing in harmonious proportion their intellectual and moral nature, till they step forth American citizens complete." It would allow more students to move beyond "merely reading, writing and cyphering" to an education that "cultivates and invigorates the whole man, sharpens every faculty, multiplies his resources, and makes him a man of all work, and fit for all work."[110]

William Harvey Wells agreed. He designed his 1862 volume, *The Graded School*, as a "practical" guide for teachers. By dividing children into grades, Wells argued, teachers could offer more, better, and deeper instruction in every subject, suited to each child's academic and psychological level. In reading, for example, "no reading lesson is to be left until the pupils understand the meaning of every word, and are able to express that meaning in their own language." Ideally, students would engage in "intellectual reading," making sense not just of words but passages, and thus really exploring a text. This kind of teaching, Wells implied, was not possible when teachers were rushed in order to attend to the multiple and diverse needs of a mixed one-room schoolhouse.[111]

The Ohio Teachers Association argued in 1876 that the one-room school, designed to bring together all the students of any age from a neighborhood into a single building, made little sense. By 1840, Cincinnati had come up with a graded course in which students would progress academically. Cleveland in 1846 classified students by grade—"primary, secondary, intermediate, grammar, high." By the 1850s, most large districts had instituted graded schools, with final examinations to qualify students to move up from one level to the next.[112]

If to reformers the impetus for graded schools was moral and pedagogical, for parents it allowed a clear credentialing system. Although reformers opposed excessive competition in schools because they worried that it taught students the wrong lessons (to favor external prizes over their inner character), parents wanted some way to distinguish children's accomplishments. Graded schools achieved a nice balance. Students' achievements could be measured by the last grade they completed. Some children would get into and out of high school; others would not. Yet, by ensuring that the average student, if he or she met the grade's expectations, could continue to the next year, grades balanced equality and distinction. One could distinguish the worthy from the unworthy without unleashing a dangerously competitive spirit among children (or their parents).[113]

Age grading had made little sense when children started and stopped school according to the vagaries of their lives. In such a context, age and academic ability were only loosely coupled. By the antebellum era, however, more children began school around the same age and attended regularly and in large numbers, enabling teachers to assume some correlation between grade and ability. Educators could now design coherent courses of study to develop students' capabilities, skills, and knowledge. Because they could draw from more students, graded schools first emerged in cities and larger towns. In rural areas, one-room schoolhouses remained popular and practical. In fact, as late as 1960, one-room schoolhouses may have composed almost half of American school districts, although not of students.[114]

In addition to graded schools, reformers sought longer school years. In Pennsylvania, for example, the average school term increased from 3 months and 12 days in 1835 to 5 months and 5.5 days on the eve of the Civil War.[115] In 1829, Ohio required a 3-month term for districts receiving state funds; 1849 and 1850 laws required that schools operate for at least 36 weeks and no more than 44 weeks annually.[116] In Massachusetts in 1826, small towns (1,249 residents or less) had an average school term of 127 days compared to 172 days for towns with 2,500 to 4,999 residents and 204 days for cities with more than 5,000 residents. Between 1840 and 1860, the statewide average increased from a term of 145.8 days to 158.8 days, reaching an average of 176.5 days by 1875.[117] In Lima, New York, the median term in which schools were in session increased from 8.25 months in 1825 to 9.5 months by 1840.[118]

Better teachers, graded schools, and longer terms led to what historians call "an intensification" of the educational experience. This would be one enduring legacy of the common schools movement—students would go to school longer and receive a more coherent academic curriculum from professional teachers.[119]

From Exhibitions to Tests

Schools—teachers and students—were traditionally evaluated in two ways: through final school exhibitions open to community members and through examinations conducted by district officials.[120] Exhibitions were formal events. Elizabeth Clapp recounts:

At ten minutes of eight I started to go to the exhibition. . . . Mother, Mary, and David went too among spectators. . . . The first class girls were reciting. . . . About 10 o'clock we had a recess. Before recess I was very much crowded. When we first came up into the hall there were but 3 in our setee, but other girls came and so made 7. At last a little boy, whom Emily Russell is acquainted with, came into our setee, and so there were 8. A great many people were constantly coming in, who could not get a seat, and so they stood up side of where I sat, and I could see hardly anything. . . . After recess the dialogues were spoken. The first one was "The hard name." The second "It never rains but pours." The third one we had last year so as "Taking Boarders." I could not hear hardly anything, but I could see a little, although Mr. Crafts would not let us stand up. After that the diplomas, and 6 medals were given out. Two girls were disappointed in not getting a medal. Eunice Wheeler was not quite old enough (being 14) although she deserved it. Cherrington also deserved it as much as any girl but she was but 13.[121]

Similar events took place throughout America's schools, especially in smaller towns and rural areas, during the nineteenth century. Exhibitions emphasized memory and public oratory and were seen by students and their parents as important rites of passage.

Cambridge teenager Henry Lunt spent a longer than usual day at school in the fall of 1856 "because we had to stop and rehearse pieces for examination." The next week, students recited and declaimed the various subjects over Tuesday and Wednesday. Tuesday night, Henry went to a lyceum lecture on "the Culture of the Love of Reading," which he enjoyed (at the time, he was reading *The Life of Washington*). Once exams were over, Henry "played backgammon" and then, on Friday "morning, kicked foot-ball, and loafed."[122]

School district officials would also visit schools to make sure all was well. Students' and teachers' diaries refer consistently to these visits. Formal examinations were designed to assess a teacher's effectiveness. District officials would orally examine students on subjects and evaluate the answers. Teacher Frank Morse approached examination day "with considerable anxiety" and spent the last two weeks of the term preparing his pupils: "Drilled the scholars upon rigid reviews and examinations preparatory to the examination."[123] On March 6, 1856, Morse was relieved that his students had a "very good examination indeed" before "Mr. Adams," presumably a member of the local school board.[124]

Increasingly, reformers raised concerns about oral examinations. Students could be prepped, and often the examiners themselves had little sense of the material. The process seemed too arbitrary, too impressionistic. Educators thus turned to written tests. Horace Mann, when he went after Boston's masters, relied on written tests. According to the Ohio Teachers Association, "in every well regulated graded school, the progress of the pupils in their studies is ascertained by examination tests, either oral or written, or both."[125]

The shift to tests reflected a broader shift from oral to written culture. Increasingly, teachers asked students to read quietly instead of aloud; writing became the preferred form of expression, both because Americans lived in a world of print and because educators considered writing important for self-culture. Pencil-based exams came to be seen as superior to oral presentations and exhibitions.

Advocates believed that tests measured something objective and scientific. The development of graded schools, moreover, made it possible to establish standards for promotion. By the 1850s, the Cincinnati school board had a "Committee on Printed Questions" to give written exams for every student. After the Civil War, testing spread like wildfire across the nation. By the 1870s, recalled one educator, "all the city schools of the United States were running wild on the subject of written examinations."[126] Some teachers worried that they were being judged on tests taken by students who rarely came to class or on material that students had never covered. But tests had come to stay, for both students and teachers.

Life as a Teacher

Ultimately, no matter how good the exhortations and speeches, no matter how inspiring the normal school and academy instructors, teaching came down to entering a classroom with particular boys and girls within particular communities. Sometimes that was hard. Nothing was more challenging for teachers trained in America's normal schools and academies than to realize that their courses in democratic education had not accounted for the realities of education in a democracy. This was striking for the young women who attended normal school, embraced the reformers' ideals, and set off to become professional teachers, only to learn that many American school districts did not want what they offered.

This was difficult for Lydia Stow.[127] After graduating from the normal school in Lexington, Massachusetts, she went home to Dedham to live with her grandmother and aunt. Following a bout with scarlet fever during Christmas 1840, she accepted a summer session position teaching in a one-room schoolhouse.

She had twenty students, and while she found her patience tested at times, she remained true to her normal school mentor Cyrus Peirce's teaching against corporal punishment.

She took the winter term off and went to visit her classmate Louisa Harris in Roxbury. In Harris's class, Stow noticed "antinormalism." Harris, faced with unruly students that were a far cry from the idealized children that she had imagined, had resorted to "using the stick on the hands on one of the pupils." "Too bad," Stow wrote in her diary.[128] But Stow also discovered that reality had a way of interfering with her ideals when she took a position in a South Dedham school the following year. No matter how much her professors at the normal school had told her that teachers were moral saviors—democracy's agents—she realized that all that she had learned went out the door once cheap taxpayers placed her in a summer school with sixty-plus students and expected her to accomplish something.

Stow felt that the community did not support her work. Given the number of students, the school committee agreed to give her an assistant, but other community members considered this to be a wasteful expense. They circulated a petition to shut down the school. Some argued that Stow's teaching was flawed. The committee voted eight to six to keep the school open. This was an inauspicious way to start a teaching career.

And the students were no better. They were not willing to be educated, and Stow, like her friend, turned to the rod. She hated doing so. But, as she wrote in June 1842 of an eleven-year-old boy, "he was so angry and furious that it was as much as Miss B [her assistant] and myself could do to master him." Her mentor Cyrus Peirce, upon learning that she had turned to corporal punishment, scolded her in a three-page letter, urging her to "try faithfully all other methods first or at least such as reasoning, persuasion and the like." But while these were nice words, Stow had five dozen unruly students to control and a school board—not to mention the community beyond it—against her. She had barely survived an effort to shut down the school. They wanted her to impose discipline, to prove that she could control the students. She learned through letters that her normal school friends had done the same.[129]

The National Board of Popular Education, organized by Catharine Beecher to send single eastern Protestant women to needy western schools, sent almost six hundred women west to bring knowledge to the frontier. These women, many of whom were trained in the normal schools or academies of the East, left their families and familiar places to be missionaries to the American West. Many needed the money. A good number had taught for several years and wanted higher salaries or new venues. All were inspired by Protestantism and believed that teaching would change the world for the better.

Before heading west, they attended the National Board's institute in Hartford, which had close ties to Ipswich Female Seminary and Mount Holyoke. The candidates were taught by "strong female models" and inspiring speakers, who sought to instruct the recruits in democratic pedagogy. Candidates also reviewed academic subjects, as they would have done in normal schools. They were told that their work would save the world. But like Lydia Stow and Louisa Harris, these teachers soon found themselves moving from a world in which they were celebrated as saviors to the realities of actual students and school boards.

Arozina Perkins was born in Johnson, Vermont, in March 1826, the youngest of twelve siblings. As a teacher in New Haven, she realized that it was hard work. "Have been toiling hard," she wrote in her diary on October 6, 1849, "with sixty restless, unquiet spirits, and trying to lay for them a stone or two in the foundation of their fabric of life." It was no easy task. In April 1850, she left for Hartford to attend the National Board institute, and by October she was heading west.

After rocking train rides and boats running aground, she found herself in rugged Fort Des Moines, Iowa, in November: "I had been sped in the swift moving car, tossed upon the heaving, tumultuous bosom of Erie, threaded the windings of the Ohio and ascended awhile the broad stream of the Mississippi; I had been racked and *churned* nearly 200 miles in mud wagons and hacks, and *now*, as I was at the end of the race there were obligations of gratitude in my heart for my safe preservation."

It was not easy being so far from home. She "felt *lonely*, extremely so," she confided to her diary. She also discovered that there was already a school taught by a Mrs. Bird and a district school three months each year. She decided to take on teaching anyway, and her first day keeping school, in a Methodist church, nine scholars came. Having discovered that there were already several schools in various states of success and failure, she wondered what to do, but determined to teach in winter and opened her own school. She was quite successful, perhaps at Mrs. Bird's expense, and soon had thirty-two students.[130]

Augusta Hubbell, originally from Genesee County, New York, was less successful. Writing Miss Swift, she admitted that she "has already returned East." She had been hired to teach school in Tipton, Iowa, and commenced in May 1853. She had bad luck, however. First, as a single woman, she had many suitors. She almost moved to a local hotel when the proprietor offered her cheap boarding, but she soon discovered that this was because the single male boarders had offered to "make up the difference from their own pockets for the sake of my company." While she "accepted invitations a number of times to ride out Saturday afternoons," she never "passed the bounds of prudence," but rumors circulated nonetheless. She then became very sick and could not teach. The school directors used the occasion of her sickness to ask her to leave the school. The directors stated that "complaints had been made." They agreed that the students "had never learned better but some thought me imprudent." While this was "mere rumor," it was enough for her to lose her job.[131]

Mary Augusta Roper found herself in the middle of a similar local storm, this one having to do with ethnicity and religion in Mill Point, Michigan, in the early 1850s. Roper herself felt isolated, noting that, of four hundred inhabitants, "there are only four families in the place of intelligence." The school director, one Mr. Smith, desired a pious teacher like Roper, but it was clear that many of the other families did not approve. Slowly, the number of students was reduced by half. She believed that the problem was " 'that my scholars love me' too much" because she refused to use violence. "An old Irish woman" evidently believed that Roper's "no Teacher, she don't *lick* them at all, she ought'er at'em with the broomstick."

"I never used the rod," she wrote Miss Swift, "unless when a scholar refused to obey me," in about "three instances." Her students' parents seemed happy, but Smith was forced out, and ultimately the effort to teach in an unfriendly community left her with a "depression of spirit."[132] Roper's language reflects not only her prejudice against other members of her community but also the incompatibility of her teaching style with community expectations. That was certainly true for Mary Chase, who was hired to teach a district school with seventy students in Savanna, Illinois, only to discover that the new school directors wished her to leave because they were dissatisfied by her "method of conducting the school."[133]

In sum, frontier teachers discovered that real students and school boards had values and needs much different from Catharine Beecher's. At the same time, many made connections with students and parents and felt that they were doing good work. Board teacher Martha Rogers, sent out to Missouri, wrote back that while she longed for a better schoolhouse, her students were "happy in school & loved to come" and that she had "gained the respect & confidence of the people generally & the warm esteem of the religious part of the Community."[134]

And the same was true of other teachers. There were always some students who were inspired, and some communities that were supportive. There was often just enough to make it all worthwhile. For all the big talk, a teacher's life came down to whether he or she was successful with students, and whether those students wanted to be there. It was the classroom that mattered, and it was a complex space.

Embattled, and Embattling, Schoolmasters

Most teachers in America had not been trained in academies or normal schools. As late as 1896, only one in five or six of the teachers filling fifty thousand teaching openings would be normal school graduates.[135] Rather, they were young people who taught for a couple seasons in the thousands of rural and small-town schools that dotted the American landscape. Men were generally hired for the winter term (in which older boys attended) and women for the summer term. Teaching was neither a career nor a calling, but teachers took their jobs seriously. In fact, despite being temporary, those hired to teach cared quite a bit about whether they were successful, and whether their students appreciated them.

Frank Morse realized how dependent he was on his students. "Love of teaching varies as the conduct of the scholars," he wrote in his diary.[136] After running from his first job, he returned to teaching in Chelmsford District No. 2. He could not help but feel, despite the rhetoric that he may have heard from reformers and education leaders, that "a Teacher's life is one of toil and hardship" at times and "pleasantness" at others.[137]

Because most teachers were not trained in the new way, and because, as Lydia Stow learned, most school boards wanted schools that demonstrated student success through oral recitations and examinations, most teachers continued to rely on traditional teaching methods. Students demonstrated mastery through recitation and an end-of-year oral examination by school board members. And parents wanted teachers they could trust.[138]

Rarely was time made for intellectual exploration on its own terms or for the kind of creative insights that Mann and other educators celebrated. Most teachers lacked the time and the capacity to do that. As a result, most teachers could not tap into their students' hearts and minds and were forced to find ways to compel obedience and study. This often meant relying on coercion from without rather than encouraging the development of the child from within.[139]

Teachers cared, but the way that they showed it was shaped by community expectations and their own experiences. Disciplining students was no fun. Rebellious classrooms were taxing and unnerving and ultimately left teachers disheartened. Most teachers aspired to keep the respect of their students and the school committee. Their own sense of self-worth depended on how students treated them.

John Dean Caton, who would go on to become Illinois's chief justice in the 1850s, recalled teaching in a New York district school in the 1820s, when he was seventeen. He had been hired to teach a three-month term, and some of his students were older than he was. Because he was devoted to his students, he would "spare no pains or labor to impart instruction to all." He aspired to treat every child "with the greatest respect and kindness" and in return was satisfied that he was respected by students and parents alike.

An exception was "one larger fellow older than myself." In Caton's memory, this boy was "ugly and profane and delighted in abusing the smaller boys." After repeated "admonitions," Caton decided he needed to assert his rule. On the way to school one morning he "cut several birch whips about five feet long and as large as my thumb at the butt." That morning at school he "applied the birch about ten blows as hard as I could lay it on." When the boy looked like he might "attack," Caton "struck him over the head and face with my whip." As the boy "quailed to humble submission," Caton made him take off his coat and then "took a fresh whip and laid on perhaps fifteen lashes with my best efforts" as "the cotton from his shirt sleeves actually flew across the house in bits." The boy left school never to return. While his exertions "made some talk in the district," the community and school board seemed to believe that Caton had acted reasonably.[140]

Although Caton's source of pride was his success with other students, his need to discipline is a reminder that American classrooms were sites of struggle. Hiram Orcutt, hired to teach in Andover, Massachusetts, was determined to appeal to his students' better nature, but he had hardly started talking when he "observed half a dozen boys jumping out of their seats without permission." Rather than resorting to the rod, Orcutt reminded them that he "needed their assistance." He wanted to teach them, but to do so he needed the school to be "orderly, studious, and obedient," and he preferred to avoid "*force.*" They voted to support him and cooperate and, he believed, he had achieved "complete moral power over them." While Orcutt did not deny that the rod was sometimes necessary, he was proud that he avoided using it.[141]

The mainstream American classroom remained a fairly traditional place, where obedience to external demands and outward performance was the coin of the realm. Take Charles Frederick Bosworth's 1852 depiction of a schoolroom. Here we have a caring motherly teacher using her pointer to help a young boy recite his lessons properly. Around her, however, students are focused on anything but learning. An older boy is sneaking a kiss with one of the older girls. The boys in the benches are supposed to be quietly learning but are in fact doing anything but. One student, sitting under the desk, has probably been relegated there to be shamed for failing to recite his lessons properly. He appears quite grumpy but at least has his book open before him.

Locke Amsden

Another schoolmaster's story is that of Locke Amsden. Young Locke was part of a loving, caring farm family, but his father could not help but find him useless, especially when compared to his hard-working brother; all Locke seemed good at was reading and math. His family agreed to save up to send him to an academy, after which Locke sought a teaching job. He walked to a nearby town to present himself for the opening.

After a thorough examination by the committeeman, Locke undertook a winter school for fourteen dollars. He was aware that the previous schoolmasters had struggled to subdue the eldest boys, two of whom sneered at Locke's assumption that he could do better. Locke understood that in this community "a false standard of honor had . . . sprung up among the scholars." "Instead of intellectual attainments, physical prowess, or mere brute force, had unfortunately been made the subject of predominating applause."

Only Locke's pride kept him from backing out, although he was scared to face the schoolboys. He hoped "to break down this false standard, and set up the true one." Locke's brother Ben had his own plan and accompanied him to the new town to warn the older students that Locke was known for his violent temper. The first few days of school were quiet. Locke was a bit troubled that the younger children were so afraid of him, while the older boys, it was clear, were deciding whether Ben's stories were credible or whether they should test their new schoolmaster.

In the meantime, Locke determined to treat all the scholars with respect, the result being that, in time, all the students' "mingled feelings of hatred, fear, and suspicion . . . rapidly melted into an affectionate reverence." Locke used their respect for him to encourage them to learn something. Like a good teacher, Locke studied each student and found ways to tap into each's unique "dispositions." Locke admirably embodied the ideals of a well-trained teacher, who understood human nature and respected every child.

And the result was amazing. Where once the students thought of nothing but

Figure 4.2. Charles Frederick Bosworth, *The New England School* (ca. 1852), oil on wood. Collection of the Massachusetts Historical Society

"rough athletics," they now filled their days, and their nights, with "talk of studies, anecdotes of the school, or the discussion of the arithmetical puzzles, and the various interesting and curious questions relative to the phenomena of nature."

Locke had been so successful that the students came down with what a doctor referred to as "brain fever" from too much mental excitement and exertion. The parents were upset, and called a district meeting. The students it seemed were becoming too intellectual, wanting so much to learn that it was making them sick. It was an epidemic for a community that did not embrace book learning to see their children being consumed by it. But just as Locke was about to lose his job and see his school shut down, his local ally, a doctor, confirmed that the sickness was caused by faulty ventilation and not, as many in the community seemed to think, from the black magic of mathematics.

A powerful story, but alas, a work of fiction written by a Vermont reformer and writer.[142] In real life few teachers taught in a manner that would inspire such transformation and even those who did were, it seems, fighting an uphill battle against communities that cared little for serious learning and students who rarely felt amazement and wonder, filling their time instead with aspirations to pass examinations and get out of school.

Life as a Student

The only thing that may have been harder than being a teacher was being a student. Students did not experience the classroom as a site for the cultivation of their reason, moral sense, and imagination, or as a place where curiosity and wonder reigned. Instead, almost every recollection of pre–Civil War classrooms emphasized children's effort to satisfy teachers' expectations through memorization and recitation—a series of hoops to pass through rather than a place to marvel at the world.[143]

While not all children disliked school, their experience did not approximate the world that education reformers had painted with their words. As a result, students found themselves confronting teachers, school board members, and parents, whose primary goal was to force them to perform rather than to incite them to learn.

Warren Burton offered his reflections, *The District School as It Was*, in 1833. He had started school when he was just three and a half under his first summer teacher Mary Smith. He was excited to go. He remembered getting "arrayed in my new jacket and trowsers" and "Sunday hat." He also remembered, as did many students, his "little new basket" to carry his dinner back and forth. His teacher governed with love and affection, had "a cheerful smile," and helped young Burton master his ABCs—"no small achievement." Students were required to sit still but it was made easier because of Ms. Smith's "goodness"; she offered "sympathy rather than reproof."

Yet Burton still looked forward to the winter school under the male master, even though he had heard that the master ruled through "frowns and ferulings." Burton arrived the first day with a "hoping yet fearing heart." But his fears, he discovered, were overdone. Instead, he recited regularly, as did the other students, and the real problem was that school was "monotonous." His lessons "conveyed no ideas, excited no interest, and, of course, occupied but little of my time." Burton was thus relieved when, the following summer, he returned to Ms. Smith.

Burton goes on to discuss his other teachers and experiences. What is striking, however, is how much difference a teacher can make. Ms. Smith clearly had an impact on him. She became a mentor, even if her teaching was traditional. But for most of the time, Burton experienced education in a district school much differently. His memories emphasized fear of, and actual, punishments, and when it came to learning, he focused largely on what was required of him, and rarely spoke of joy or excitement. It was instead, as he described the recitation of his grammar lesson, a "rigmarole."[144]

School was not remembered as a place where students could be themselves; it was only during noon hour, when children were let loose to play, that many students—including Burton—came alive. For boys in particular, snowball fights come up often. Something was clearly wrong if time in school was monotonous at best, alienating at worst. For students, teachers may have been caring mentors, but school was rarely described as an intellectually rich, creative place.

But it was part of growing up. Young people recognized its importance and felt important when they were old enough to go. Young Julia Hieronymus looked forward to school—something the big kids did—or at least that is how she remembered her four-year-old self when she looked back from an older age. She was excited to be sent to "a country school" in early 1800s Clarke County, Kentucky, particularly because her mother had packed her and her brother's basket with "a square black bottle of milk, two or three nicely baked waffles, two fried eggs, slices of ham, two apple turn-overs, and buttered bread, rendered luscious by being thickly overspread with maple-sugar." Halfway to the schoolhouse two miles away, she and her brother stopped under a tree and took advantage of some of the "good things" in the basket.

Her brother, two years older, found the idea of going to school "not half so pleasing as to myself" and urged Julia to head home and ask permission to skip school, which she did. Her mother responded, after "gathering a switch" and "applying the rod freely" to her brother "to quicken his indolent faculties," by walking them to school where she "handed us over to 'the master.'" She was seated beside "one of the larger pupils" who was then charged with teaching her the ABCs.

While her brother may not have enjoyed school, Julia did. It was held in a simple "square room, with a fireplace" and boasted "hard, rough, wooden benches, without backs." The students watched for noon, when they could escape with "shouts of merriment" and "ringing laughter" from their imprisonment. Whether fun or not, Hieronymus was thankful for "Mr. Pettichord, my Clarke County teacher," for she "learned to read," which "has been a passion with me all my life."[145]

John Ball, born in a log cabin in rural New Hampshire in 1794, reflected, looking back from his eightieth birthday, that "our opportunity for education was very
limited." The district offered a school term of "but six or seven weeks in the year."
His father, moreover, "did not seem to think any further education than an ability
to read, write, and cipher in the simple rules to be needful." At the same time,
young Ball seemed to know that education mattered. He appealed to his father
to let him take lessons from a clergyman in the next town over. He also "taught
a small school" to help pay for his lessons, which he continued to do for several
seasons, ultimately qualifying himself for admission to Dartmouth.[146]

Girls worried about letting down their teachers. Elizabeth Clapp received a
diary for her thirteenth birthday on April 9, 1852. She was, by her diary at least,
a very good student. On April 30, for example, she received "9 credits" for her
composition assignment. It was a good month. "I have not had a single error, or
any thing of that sort; and it is the first month I have kept without having one
since I have been in Miss Baxter's class, (which is since last September.)." In her
spare time, Elizabeth played piano, attended Sunday school, and read. School was
not always easy, however. On Saturday, May 8, she "failed in Geography, and as
the errors were doubled, it counted 2 errors. I am very sorry indeed." The next
day she finished *Uncle Tom's Cabin*, which she and her friends had found fascinat-
ing. Even as she struggled, and once in a while got into trouble with her teachers,
when the students "were placed according to our rank" on Tuesday, March 8,
Elizabeth proudly noted "I am no. 1."[147]

Girls, in fact, usually performed better in school than boys. The Dedham, Massachusetts, school committee worried, in 1852, that "girls of ten years old are
advanced well in their studies" while "boys of sixteen years old are advanced but
little beyond the alphabet."[148] And girls tended to stay in longer. In Lowell, about
60 percent of high school students between 1836 and 1851 were female.[149] But
this just proves the point in some ways. At a time when not much formal education was necessary for economic success, boys opted out at larger rates because
they had other options. This suggests that, to a large extent, absent an economic
motive for further education, many boys did not enjoy it enough (or have the
means) to stay longer, whereas girls, without alternative economic possibilities
other than teaching, had less to lose.[150]

For thirteen-year-old Samuel Bigelow, school was trying. He was not the best
student. His diary is full of entries like this one for January 7, 1851: "School lessons passed off not very well for I missed in geography lesson and have got to stay
after school tomorrow." What made that day tolerable was a "pretty good coast to

school" on the sled. A week later, "lessons did not pass off very well." The students "missed in Geography and this afternoon in Arithmetic." Poor Samuel once again had to return "after school for our Geography & Arithmetic" but fortunately "did not miss" any this time.

Despite his mixed relationship with school, Samuel's parents wanted him to continue, and he took the examination to enter high school in March. He continued to study geography and other subjects, waking up early in the morning to make it work. By December, he had developed a sense of humor about his struggles, noting on New Year's Eve 1851, "This morning went to school as usual, but I did not miss my Latin (which is very unusual)."[151]

For both Elizabeth and Samuel, school was about meeting external expectations. There is little evidence in their diaries that they valued their schooling on its own terms. Elizabeth valued recognition as a top student and reacted terribly when she lost points or received a demerit for poor behavior. She clearly desired her teachers' esteem. Samuel, on the other hand, seemed resigned to the fact that school was tiresome but that it had to be done. He dutifully did what was asked of him even though, as he put it, after a "hard History lesson" and an incomplete arithmetic homework, he only found joy when "at recess we had some snow balling."

In fact, for Samuel, snowballs and sledding may have mattered more than school.[152] On Friday, March 4, 1851, after studying geography in the morning before school and reciting it in the afternoon, he recounted that "before recess we had some snowballing." The next day, after he "put up the Sheep," he "went down to the house and snow balled George," his brother.

Students were all over the place—appreciative, restive, resentful, hostile, caring. School was where their parents told them to go. Those who were too poor to truly take advantage of schools, or only had a little, knew they were missing something—"my advantages for education were very poor," remembered Chauncey Jerome of his Connecticut childhood. Having to "work on the farm," the most he could get was "attending school in the winter season, and then only about three months in the year, and at a very poor school."[153]

Children and adults recognized the advantages of schooling, or at least most did, when they lacked it. In their own diaries and reminiscences, there is no sense that young Americans felt school was unimportant. What it was not was interesting. Teachers had not managed—and in many cases lacked the education to manage—to open the world of liberal education to students.

As a result, students struggled. Levi Beardsley, who was born in 1763, grew up in frontier Otsego County, New York, and would ultimately enter politics as a Democrat and serve as president of New York's senate. He realized that his early schooling lacked much and that children "were of course restless, and wanted to go out." One ingenious teacher permitted one child at a time to escape, so long as no more than one ever departed, leading the children to develop an ingenious solution—"a hole was bored in one of the logs of the house, in which a wooden peg was inserted, which any one might take as a passport out of the [school] house." Despite the conditions, "better progress was made in education than could have been expected," Beardsley reflected. "I could always read and spell as well, and I thought a little better than any in school, and when put to my arithmetic, went directly ahead of all the competitors."[154]

However much reformers wanted schools to be nurseries for youth, schools were too often experienced, as one Virginia newspaper editorial from the second quarter of the nineteenth century put it, as "prisons of the body and treadmills of the mind." Far from a "scholastic paradise," the schoolroom was a place "to be fagged, flogged, thumped, and coerced to mental labor and constrained in personal liberty." What child was not "always wishing to get out of school and to get home"?[155]

Little wonder there was a tradition of "turning out" the teacher near the end of the school term. When one South Carolina teacher left for a morning walk, the older boys barricaded the doors. The furious teacher refused to be turned out, and climbed up on the roof and started to tear it apart to regain entrance. The leaders of the rebellion, fearful of being whipped, removed the barricade in return for amnesty.[156] In Pennsylvania, a teacher might arrive at his schoolhouse door one day to discover it "fastened." With anger, the teacher would demand entrance and seek to reassert his rightful authority on the door by "pounding it with an ax until he split it in several places." When that failed, he "climbed to the roof and commenced tearing away the clapboards" before seeking entrance via the "south window."[157]

Sometimes, a master would go too far in his effort to impose discipline, and there might occur, as Warren Burton recalls happening when he was ten, a "mutiny." A particularly violent schoolmaster, whose previous job had been on a wartime privateer, and whose actions had started to concern parents, one day drew blood when he struck a child on the head with his ruler's edge. The larger students rose up, grabbed the schoolmaster, carried him out, and threw him onto an ice-encrusted hill. "Down, down he went," Burton recalls, "until he fairly came to the climax, or rather anti-climax, of his pedagogical career."[158]

Such scenes, even if ritualized, make clear that teachers and students alike saw schooling as a battle of wills and wits, not a place where, in the words of North Carolinian Joseph Caldwell, one was "humanized."[159] To use another framework, school was a form of work—it was obligatory, imposed, had purposes foreign to itself, and was not joyful; in contrast, the world of play brought immediate joy, had no purpose other than itself, and was shaped by the students themselves.[160] But within these parameters, boys and girls made friends, were mentored by teachers, and gained some knowledge and skills necessary for effective participation in the economy and as citizens. And some may have even learned to love learning.

So It Goes

As we move from exhortations of teachers to the more mundane realities of teaching and being a student, we see that the idealized aspiration for democratic education faltered in schoolrooms across the nation. Teachers, especially those from the new normal schools, with new ideas about what to teach and how to teach it, faced immense challenges: local school boards that preferred the older methods and did not support reform; students who were not interested in learning; and, perhaps most ironically, education reformers who simultaneously advocated better teacher training and demonstrated a lack of respect for teachers.

Schools may have effectively taught the basics, the three 'Rs and a bit more, but they were less effective at inspiring young people to be citizens and to engage in self-culture. Instead, students saw schooling as something to get through. While in some cases this led to actual violence between teachers and students, in most cases there was tacit agreement that teachers had the authority to demand students' compliance, and that students, with the support or pressure of their parents, would have to perform. There is little evidence that students left school wanting more.

Even Caroline Goodale, a thoughtful, caring, and committed normal school student, noted in her journal: "Was late this afternoon and could not persuade Miss L to admit us, was sorry, but must confess I spent my time very agreeably." Even for this teacher in training, time outside of school was more agreeable than time in class.[161]

To this extent, the Boston masters and local school boards had a point: perhaps true love meant requiring young people do what they ought to do whether they wanted to or not. Adults had responsibilities to children who often do not know what will best serve their long-term happiness. The Boston masters asked Horace Mann to grow up.

Reformers had hoped that the choice would not have to be made, that children would develop their intellect and character because it was liberating to do so. But teachers and students were caught in the middle of contradictory political, social, cultural, and intellectual claims for schooling. Given that there was no consensus on education's purpose, children and teachers found themselves elevating goods external to education rather than those internal to it. Students wanted to please their parents, teachers, and community. They wanted good marks and to earn credentials. They did what they were supposed to do. And teachers continued to rely on the rod and implemented tests and grades to encourage compliance. In time, states would impose mandatory attendance laws.[162]

And then children played. Despite reformers' hopes, school was not play, perhaps because, as nine-year-old Catherine Elizabeth Havens of New York put it in her diary, "I don't think grownup people understand what children like."[163] The reformers hoped that a reformed, democratic pedagogy would help transform formal schooling from work to play, from something done out of duty or to achieve credentials, to something that one did for its own sake. They aspired for a world in which all children developed their full potential, including the development of their intellectual capacities and moral dispositions.

The challenge was, no matter how much reformers wanted to liberate the human spirit, children wanted to go sledding.

5 Containing Multitudes

Of every hue and caste am I, of every rank and religion,
A farmer, mechanic, artist, gentleman, sailor, quaker
Prisoner, fancy-man, rowdy, lawyer, physician, priest.
I resist any thing better than my own diversity.
Walt Whitman, *Song of Myself*

Common Schools for a Common Nation

"OUR PUBLIC SCHOOLS ARE THE MOST DEMOCRATIC INSTITUTIONS that this peculiarly democratic country affords," proclaimed E. Hodges, superintendent of schools in Fond du Lac, Wisconsin. The schools treat all children equally, educating them not just in the "rudiments" but with the knowledge necessary for citizenship. In a society divided by religion, ethnicity, party, and wealth, public schools would "harmonize the various discordant elements that are found in society" as students "sympathize with and for the other." Immigrants would learn Americans' "customs, assume their manners, and become homogeneous with them." "The equality upon which they would be placed at the public schools, and the discipline which they should there receive, would *Americanize* them in the shortest possible time."[1]

Ohio's Calvin Stowe told a gathering of the Western Literary Institute in 1836 "that unless we educate our immigrants, they will be our ruin." "To sustain an

extended republic like our own, there must be *national* feeling, a national assimilation."[2] Common schools, funded by taxes, free for all, and overseen by citizens,
would bring together a diverse society. The schools would in fact serve as a glue
binding Americans to each other.[3]

It was not just immigration that worried reformers. Economic inequality was
growing. If well-off parents opted out of the common schools, then the schools
would be treated as pauper schools, undermining their public purpose. Americans had a "duty" to "render the advantages of common schools . . . to all classes
and conditions of society," resolved a meeting of educators in Orange County,
New York.[4] John Pierce, the new state of Michigan's superintendent of public
instruction, celebrated public schools where "all classes are blended together;
the rich mingle with the poor, and are educated in company . . . and mutual at-
tachments are formed."[5] New York's Free School Society concurred that common
schools are places "where the rich and the poor may meet together."[6]

Horace Mann considered bringing together rich and poor to be one of the
most important functions of public schools. If rich parents "turn away from
the Common Schools" and choose to send their kids to "the private school or
the academy," then the poor will end up with a second-class education.[7] To ensure
that students, and their parents, intermingle, "there should be a free school, sufficiently safe, and sufficiently good, for all the children within its territory."[8] That
last word, "territory," mattered a lot. The children who lived together within the
same district must attend the same schools. Segregation, especially of rich and
poor, hurt all children by increasing inequality and reducing social solidarity. In
the South, where academies were most active, voters treated the public schools as
charity for poor children. Breaking the link between public and charity required
schools attended by the entire community. As an 1822 report commissioned by
the Kentucky legislature put it, public schools would succeed only if they were
for all children. To separate the poor children would turn education into welfare,
"a degradation too humiliating for the pride of freedmen."[9]

Mann believed there had to be a connection between the cultural *nation* and
the republican *state*, a nation-state. He worried that absent the ties that bound
citizens together, violence could result. His conclusions came in part from firsthand experience. On the evening of August 11, 1834, a mob of Protestants attacked the Catholic Ursuline Convent in Charlestown, Massachusetts. Rumors
had spread that nuns were held captive in the convent under terrible conditions.
Boston's leading minister, Rev. Lyman Beecher, had been preaching the dangers
of Catholicism. As the mob forced its way into the convent, the sisters helped

the school girls—most of whom were Unitarian, not Catholic—escape out the back. A bit after midnight, the school and a nearby farmhouse were burned to the ground. The nuns and the schoolgirls watched in fear from the garden.[10]

Mann was chosen as a lawyer on the committee appointed to investigate the riot. One committee member worried that Mann was biased against Catholics, but others reassured him that Mann was not. Mann threw himself into the work. He considered the riots a "horrible outrage," but after ten days of working "almost without intermission," he became too ill to complete his work, although he signed the committee's final report, which condemned the rioters as well as the authorities and citizens who stood by "while not one arm was lifted in the defence of helpless women and children, or in vindication of the violated laws of God and man. The spirit of violence, sacrilege, and plunder, reigned triumphant."[11]

Mann was confident that diversity required a deeper level of solidarity, that one could not have *pluribus* without *unum*. In a diverse society, it was the public schools' unique responsibility to encourage "a general acquaintanceship . . . between children of the same neighborhood."[12] All Americans must be prepared to work together as citizens. Immigrants who grew up in societies that favored "servility" and obedience to "some self-appointed lord or priest" would have to learn to be independent. They would also have to learn that liberty was not "an absence from restraint and an immunity from punishment." Immigrants were "unfitted" for self-government "until they have become morally acclimated to our institutions."[13]

Efforts to encourage civic solidarity through common schools posed a challenge in an increasingly diverse society. As the number of Irish immigrants expanded, Catholic leaders argued that Catholic students should attend separate schools because public schools were too Protestant. In contrast, African Americans struggled against the opposite problem. Denied access to public schools in the South and often forced to attend segregated schools in free states, African Americans argued that all Americans, black or white, must be able to attend the same schools on the same terms. Segregation presupposed and reinforced inequality. In a diverse society, exclusion was more dangerous than inclusion. By examining Catholic arguments for separate schools and African American arguments for integrated schools, this chapter interrogates the school reformers' vision to encourage social solidarity through public education.

A Violent World

Education reformers were not unreasonable in looking for common institutions for all Americans because the Ursuline Convent riot was not an isolated incident. Throughout the country, Americans engaged in violence over party, religion, class, and race. Even homicide was increasing.

In the early days of the War of 1812, a partisan group of thirty to forty men, surrounded by a larger group of spectators, mobbed the offices of the Baltimore newspaper *Federal-Republican*. That summer, white Baltimoreans threatened the city's black community. In July, when the *Federal-Republican*'s editor determined to continue publication, things got worse. Garrisoned in their new offices, the Federalist editor and his supporters fired blanks into the hostile crowd gathered outside. The crowd rushed the building, and the Federalists responded with live ammunition. Republicans returned fire and rolled up a cannon. The Federalists were led to jail, in part for their own safety, but that night the crowd returned and beat the Federalists until they were bloody and dropped hot candle grease into their eyes.[14]

If you lived in Philadelphia, you might have thought the world was falling apart. In 1828, the same year as Andrew Jackson's election, Irish weavers and native-born Americans fought in Kensington, followed by race riots in the summers of 1834 and 1835 in Southwark. Three years later a mob hostile to abolitionists (advocates of the immediate abolition of slavery) burned down downtown's Pennsylvania Hall. Later that night, a crowd descended on the Friend's Shelter for Colored Orphans. In summer 1842, an Irish mob attacked black temperance activists in Moyamensing. In 1844, during the so-called Philadelphia "Bible Riots," anti-Catholic Protestant mobs and Irish Catholics went at each other in May and July, leading to at least twenty dead and more than one hundred injured. The riot's cause was Protestants' fear that Catholics wanted to remove the Bible from public schools, but the riots reflected deeper tensions between working-class Protestants and new immigrants. Five years later, a race riot left several white and black citizens dead.[15]

Anti-Catholic violence seemed to be everywhere. In 1829 a group of Bostonians attacked Irish Catholic homes. Four years later, in retaliation for drunken Irish immigrants beating to death a native-born American in Charlestown, five-hundred people marched through the Irish part of town and burned homes.[16] In 1853, after the Ellsworth, Maine, school board decided that all children must read from the Protestant Bible or be expelled, the local priest opened a Catholic school. In response, a mob attacked the church and school and tarred and feathered the priest. An expelled student's father went to court, but the Maine Supreme Court held that students could not opt out of reading the Bible.[17] The following year, a St. Louis mob destroyed fifty to sixty homes in an Irish part of town, leaving eight to ten dead, while in Baltimore, rioters supporting the anti-Catholic Know-Nothing Party fought with their Democratic Party rivals in 1856, 1857, and 1858, resulting in 8 to 17 deaths and up to 150 wounded.[18]

Catholics in March 1834 attacked a nativist speaker addressing Baptists in Baltimore, and another group of Catholics attacked Broadway Hall in New York a year later.[19] Irish Catholics in New York City attacked black New Yorkers during the Civil War's draft riots. In 1833, when Prudence Crandall refused to shut down her boarding school for black girls in Canterbury, Connecticut, citizens clogged her well with manure, broke the school's windows, and even tried to burn down the school.[20] In August 1835, a mob of one hundred white inhabitants of Canaan, New Hampshire, used ninety-five oxen to tear the one-year old racially integrated Noyes Academy from its foundation and deposit it in a swamp a half mile away.[21] In the 1830s, Connecticut mobs disrupted antislavery meetings in Canterbury, Norwich, Hartford, Middletown, Plainfield, Danbury, Meriden, Brookfield, and New Haven.[22]

Working-class Americans mobbed the elite Astor Place Opera House in New York City in 1849. The state militia responded by firing into the crowd, leaving eighteen dead.[23] Violence erupted during upstate New York's "Anti-Rent wars" between tenants and their rich landlords.[24] In the West, settlers relied on "frontier justice" rather than the law and attacked Native Americans. Anti-Mormon settlers in 1830s Missouri burned crops and houses, horsewhipped men, and even raped women. Ultimately, Mormons fled for Illinois, where their founder, Joseph Smith, was lynched.[25]

In Ohio, whites burned black schoolhouses.[26] In Boston in 1851, black advocates of school integration attacked and almost killed a black opponent two nights in a row, but white violence against black Americans was more common, including an antiblack riot in Providence in 1824. Five years later, whites in Cincinnati drove hundreds of blacks from their homes.[27] In 1859 white workers attacked free blacks competing for jobs in Fell's Point shipyard in Baltimore.[28] Enslaved people rose up against their masters, most famously during Nat Turner's 1831 Virginia rebellion. Masters in turn relied on violence to subdue enslaved Americans. Northern antislavery leaders worried about the intensity of southern racial violence and the antisocial passions that it unleashed.[29]

Sometimes we think that violence is exceptional, but it is sadly more common to human history than we like to admit. After the French Revolution, Americans were all too aware how easy it was for democratic societies to resort to violence. Something had to hold Americans together, to protect them from the anger and hatred that could divide them. As the incidences of violence piled up, it became clear, in the words of one historian, that "Americans could kill each other because they did not identify with each other."[30]

Religion, Nationhood, and Nonsectarian Schools

Religion united and divided Americans. After the American Revolution, the United States was a "roof without walls."[31] Americans built the walls of their nation by forming common institutions—parties, churches, voluntary associations, and reform groups. Through these institutions, more and more Americans became connected to others across the country.[32] While these new institutions forged common ties, they also excluded those that did not belong. Racial and religious minorities—especially blacks and Catholics—did not see themselves in the new national imaginary. In fact, to a certain extent, it was against minorities that Americans came to define themselves as a white Protestant republic.[33]

Yet Americans were also committed to the separation of church and state and to religious liberty. They understood that efforts to coerce religious uniformity had led to "centuries of struggle and of suffering, and the shedding of rivers of blood."[34] Americans had lived with religious pluralism since the earliest days of colonial settlement. By the time of the Revolution, they had moved "beyond toleration," in the words of one historian, to embrace a common culture that favored Christian "fundamentals above particulars" and recognized the equality of every confession.[35] Thus, most states did away with tax-supported religion after independence, the last being Connecticut in 1818, New Hampshire in 1819, the new state of Maine in 1820, and Massachusetts in 1833. Yet, even as tax support declined, more and more Americans joined churches, reinforcing the link between Protestantism and American nationalism.[36]

Americans wanted their public schools to be for all children and wanted religion to unify rather than divide.[37] They thus advocated nonsectarian schools. Nonsectarian public schools were not secular. American culture was, and remains, deeply defined by religious faith. Yet a heavy emphasis on particular doctrines would divide Americans and threaten public schools' ability to forge a common nation. Instead, reformers argued, schools should emphasize only those aspects of Christianity that were widely shared and leave the particulars to churches and parents.

Thus, at a time when Massachusetts was roiled in conflict between orthodox and liberal Congregationalists, the legislature prohibited using public funds for schoolbooks that "favor any religious sect or tenet."[38] In New York, legislators in 1838 received a petition asking them to ban Bible reading in public schools. Daniel Dewey Barnard, who sat on the state assembly's Committee on Colleges, Academies, and Common Schools, authored a report denying the request. Barnard, a Massachusetts native, had attended common schools and Williams College and would go on to serve as a Whig in the U.S. Congress and, later, as minister to Prussia.[39]

He disagreed with the petitioners that Bible reading led to "a union of church and state." First, education was a "public necessity" that could not be achieved by "voluntary contributions." All taxpayers must thus pay their share. No parent could opt out of this public obligation, although religious freedom permitted parents to remove their children from the schools if they felt it necessary. Second, the state did not mandate Bible reading. Such decisions were left to local communities. In a democracy, the minority must show some deference to the majority. Third, the Bible was taught for its moral lessons, not for religion. Children's "moral powers . . . must be informed and cultivated" somehow. If the Bible could be banned, could the minority prohibit "Plato or Aristotle, or Seneca, or Mahomet"? Ultimately, Barnard believed that "to teach Christian morals . . . is a widely different thing from teaching what is understood to be a Christian religion."[40]

Nonsectarianism was a reasonable compromise, a way to respect the public's faith while encouraging common institutions for a diverse society. Yet, for Catholics, Jews, and others, nonsectarianism was not neutral. Even evangelical Protestants were unsatisfied, seeing in nonsectarianism a public commitment to religion removed of all its defining features. As one historian has aptly put it, advocates of nonsectarianism sought " 'religion' rooted in no community of faith," but religion is always specific, based in tradition and interpretation, and never generic.[41]

Thus, to Bishop Benedict Joseph Fenwick, S.J., of Boston, Catholic children were "obliged to use books compiled by Protestants by which their minds are poisoned as it were from their infancy."[42] Even if the Bible was avoided, American schoolbooks, whether they taught history, geography, or morality, assumed a link between Protestantism and freedom and were filled with explicit and implicit biases against Catholicism.[43] Far from encouraging assimilation, Catholic students were taught that they were not welcome in America.

Yet, advocates of nonsectarianism like Mann countered that, without character education and religious influence, children would grow up "deformed and monstrous."[44] To Mann, nonsectarianism was to religion what nonpartisanship was to politics. Schools must not embrace one political party over another, even as it would be absurd to suggest that schools should not prepare young people to participate in political life. If schools could teach citizenship while "avoiding the tempest of political strife," they could also teach religion "upon the most broad and general grounds."[45]

A Plea for the West

Catharine Beecher, who advocated the professionalization of teaching, gained her appreciation for education's centrality to the republic from her father Lyman. Lyman Beecher was born in New Haven in 1775. He was raised by his aunt and uncle on a farm in North Guilford, Connecticut. After attending Yale, Beecher was called to the Presbyterian church of East Hampton, Long Island, and later to the Congregational church in Litchfield, Connecticut. Rev. Beecher was a lifelong advocate of public religion and education. He also believed that in a democracy, ordinary citizens, not just elites, were responsible for both.[46]

Beecher urged Americans to come together to promote Christian values. He was a leader in mobilizing Americans to support Sabbatarianism (the protection of Sunday as a holy day) and temperance (limiting alcohol consumption). At first, he distrusted ordinary people's involvement, but he soon came to believe that America's future depended on it. He had, for example, opposed the disestablishment of Connecticut's public religious system, only to discover that in a voluntary church, ministers "exert a deeper influence." Citizens organized at the grassroots could shape public culture through their own efforts.[47]

After he was called west to lead Cincinnati's new Lane Seminary, he found himself in a new frontier society with growing numbers of immigrants but not the schools, churches, and other institutions that he took for granted back east. Rather than turn to the state, he reached out to the people themselves to raise money for seminaries like his own, which would in turn prepare Protestant ministers and teachers for the frontier.

The American West's future depended on "universal education, and moral culture," which required "schools, and colleges, and seminaries, and pastors, and churches." Inaction threatened America's future (it is worth remembering that he was a college president engaged in fundraising) because of the "rapid influx of foreign emigrants, unacquainted with our institutions, unaccustomed to self-government." European tyrants sent to American shores "floods of pauper immigrants" to undermine America's republican experiment. Catholic immigrants, "through the medium of religion and priesthood," were "accessible to the control of the potentates of Europe" and would threaten liberty.

The problem was not Catholicism "as a religious denomination" but its alliance with Europe's kings and priests. The only way to make Catholicism safe for American democracy was to bring Catholics and Protestants together in common institutions. "Let the Catholics mingle with us as Americans, and come with their children under the full action of our common schools and republican institutions, and the various powers of assimilation." As Catholics "mingled in our schools, the republican atmosphere would impregnate their minds."

Beecher condemned violence against Catholics, but he also considered it "folly" to pretend that unreformed Catholicism did not threaten the republic. The Catholic Church must be "liberalized, and assimilated to our institutions." Beecher expressed grave fear about what he called "masses of dark mind." "Can Jesuits and nuns, educated in Europe, and sustained by the patronage of Catholic powers in arduous conflict for the destruction of liberty, be safely trusted to form the minds and opinions of the young hopes of this great nation?" Beecher wondered.[48]

Nativism

Growing numbers of Americans in the 1830s and 1840s were foreign born, becoming, according to the 1850 U.S. Census, 9.7 percent of the total population. Reformers like Mann aspired for public schools to be sites for civic unity in an increasingly diverse society. Yet, as Beecher's words demonstrate, there was a fine line between promoting unity amid diversity and giving in to ethnic and religious prejudice, and even violence.

Anti-Catholicism had deep roots in Anglo-American history. Religious warfare had been a constant of the sixteenth and seventeenth centuries. To many Americans, Protestantism and republican liberty were deeply connected, as were political slavery and Catholicism because, Protestants believed, both monarchs and the pope demanded obedience and subjection.[49] Catholic doctrine opposed democracy well into the twentieth century, reinforcing Protestant Americans' conclusions.[50] As one author put it in 1849, "No place in the world progresses towards liberty without Protestant Christianity."[51]

Anti-Catholicism led to street violence and to nativist politics in response to immigration, especially as many of the new arrivals were poor and found themselves on the streets or making use of public welfare or private charity.[52] Nativists formed the New York Protestant Association in 1832 "to promote the principles of the Reformation" and "illustrate the history and character of Popery."[53] While many Americans expressed shock at the burning of the Ursuline Convent, some nativists celebrated the rioters in speeches, sermons, and pamphlets.

The man who invented the telegraph, Samuel F. B. Morse, led the charge against Catholic immigrants. Growing up in Massachusetts, Morse distrusted Catholicism from an early age. His beliefs were affirmed when visiting Rome in 1830, and he decided to share his concerns through a series of anonymous letters published in fall 1834.[54] Native American (meaning native-born Protestant American) organizations formed throughout the nation, and by the time of Morse's letters, these local efforts were congealing into a national movement under the American Party. The American Party sought to limit immigration and naturalization and to challenge the Whig and Democratic parties, which they believed were too corrupt to protect American liberties.[55] In New York's 1844 elections, American Party candidates won office at the Whigs' expense. The new party elected some members to Philadelphia County offices in spring 1844 and that fall won some congressional seats in Pennsylvania and New York.[56]

The Know-Nothing Party was more successful by appealing not just to nativists but also to antislavery northerners frustrated with the two national parties after the Compromise of 1850. Many Know-Nothing voters considered Catholicism a form of religious slavery akin to the South's chattel slavery.[57] The Know-Nothings emerged out of the Order of the Star Spangled Banner, formed in 1850 in New York City. Why they were called Know-Nothings is not clear. Many believe it was because of their secrecy. They gained spectacular, if short-lived, success. In addition to winning many local offices, in 1854 they gained the state house and almost every seat in Massachusetts's legislature, while showing strength in Pennsylvania and New York. The following year, they gained control of New England, with the exception of Vermont. They displaced the Whig Party as the Democrats' primary opposition in other parts of the nation and elected seventy-five representatives to Congress. Some even thought that the Know-Nothings would elect the next president.[58] Ultimately, however, they faded quickly, their members moving back to the Democrats or joining the new Republican Party.

Catholicism in America

Even as the Know-Nothings spoke out against immigrants, immigrants sought to find a place for themselves in their new home. Before 1855, immigrants arriving in New York City would disembark directly onto the city streets. One can only imagine the "fear, uncertainty, excitement, and deception" they experienced as they stepped onto American shores.[59] Starting over in a new world and becoming part of the larger society were challenges faced by every American immigrant then as today.

Immigrants arrived in America because they were poor and needed opportunities. In the case of the Irish after 1845, they were literally starving. Between 1820 and 1840, more than 260,000 Irish came to America; in the six years between 1846 and 1851, that number reached 1 million after a fungus destroyed Ireland's potato crops.[60] In the fifteen years following the outbreak of the potato blight in 1845, nearly 1.7 million Irish immigrated to the United States.[61] The Irish composed 45.6 percent of all immigrants in the 1840s and 35.2 percent in the 1850s, by which time two-fifths of all foreign-born Americans were originally Irish.[62]

Germans also came to America in large numbers. Before the Civil War, about 1.5 million Germans migrated. German immigrants tended to be middle-class farmers and artisans who migrated as families and had more resources than most Irish immigrants.[63] While the Irish tended to move to the nation's growing cities, where there were more jobs, Germans moved west in large numbers to seek land.

Irish immigrants were largely Catholic, as were about 25 to 30 percent of German immigrants. By 1850, Catholicism was the largest Christian denomination in America.[64] The Catholic Church responded by organizing parishes, sending priests, and opening cathedrals and schools. As the church expanded its presence in America, American Catholicism was shaped by European Catholicism's effort to promote a vision of Christian community that set itself against modern individualism.

The European church's resistance to modern individualism stemmed from experience. During the French Revolution, the Catholic Church had been attacked, many priests were assassinated, and the pope taken prisoner by Napoleon. By the 1830s, the church found itself at odds with European and American reformers. European nationalists sought a liberal order premised on individual civil and economic rights, including the separation of church and state, and national unity. Yet liberal nationalism elevated the individual and nation over the church,

Catholic leaders argued. Moreover, liberal reformers were openly anticlerical. In response, the church sought to affirm its teachings and unity, but the result was that the church often allied with monarchs against democracy. In 1832 Pope Gregory XVI condemned the separation of church and state, angering reformers on both sides of the Atlantic.[65]

American bishops had to negotiate between Europe and the United States. In America, church was separated from state, but the culture and the schools remained largely Protestant in outlook. In an 1840 pastoral letter, bishops worried about Catholic children in public schools concluded that "we are always better pleased to have a separate system of education for the children of our communion" because they learned "by painful experience" that their faith was not respected and instead treated as "error."[66] At the First Plenary Council of American Catholics in 1852, church leaders condemned the idea of education without religion, admitted that most public schools were Protestant or secular in their practices, and thus recommended establishing Catholic schools.[67]

Catholic leaders were thus questioning individualism and nationalism at the very moment that the common schools were being asked to promote both. This led to a serious culture clash.[68] During the European revolutions of 1848, as democratic reformers cracked down on and even expelled Catholics, American Catholics condemned Italian revolutionaries who had "broken and burned the carriages of the Cardinals" and "plundered the churches."[69]

For many Protestant Americans, the renewed vigor of the Catholic Church in Europe and its resistance to democracy and the separation of church and state confirmed what they had long thought. The result was that two communities, each with its own ideas and historical experiences, met at a time when American reformers, like their European counterparts, were trying to create a united nation-state.[70]

The Great School Wars

Efforts to foster a shared culture must always confront the fact that people in a diverse society have "stubborn particularities of loyalty and conviction" that form the "'mediating structures' and world views by which people actually live." In other words, while the common schools sought to bring people together, children did not arrive as blank slates but with personal histories.[71]

In New York City, two historical communities confronted each other in what has been termed the Great School Wars.[72] The first was the Free School Society, a private association that had received public funding to run the city's schools. The second was the growing group of Catholic residents who saw the society's schools as sectarian. Both communities had tradition and history on their side. Both were trying to do the right thing.

In 1825, after a conflict over whether public funds should go to the Bethel Baptist Church, the city determined that no public funds would go to religious institutions. The society—now renamed the Public School Society—thus gained a near monopoly on public education funds.[73] In 1834 New York City bishop John DuBois asked the society to appoint a Catholic teacher to one of the schools. DuBois was born in Paris but fled during the French Revolution, arriving in Norfolk, Virginia, in 1791. He remained in the church's service and, in 1826, was consecrated third bishop for New York, a diocese that included the entire state and parts of New Jersey.[74] The Public School Society denied his request because choosing a Catholic teacher violated their commitment to nonsectarianism. They could not or refused to see that to Catholics, the society's schools promoted "sect-less Protestantism."[75]

Tensions intensified with the arrival in New York City of Bishop John Hughes. Born to poor farmers in Ireland, Hughes emigrated in 1817, when he was twenty years old. After attending seminary in Maryland, he was ordained in 1826. In a series of debates in Philadelphia in 1836, Hughes had made clear his commitment to his new home. "I am," he noted, "an American citizen—not by *chance*—but by *choice*." In 1838 he came to New York City to assist the long-serving Bishop DuBois. Hughes tried to work with the leadership of the city's schools; he was adamant, however, that Catholic children could not attend schools biased against their faith and that, in America, they should not have to.[76]

In the middle of the dispute was the state's Whig governor, William Henry Seward, born in Florida, New York, in 1801, and a Union College graduate. Seward was elected to the state senate in 1830 and became governor in 1838. He would go on to the U.S. Senate, where he would become known for his opposition to slavery, and would serve as President Abraham Lincoln's secretary of state during the Civil War. Like Horace Mann, Governor Seward was committed to educating all Americans and was concerned that many Catholic children did not go to school. He recognized that they were uncomfortable with the society's schools and sought a compromise by recommending that public funds subsidize Catholic schools.[77]

"The children of foreigners . . . are too often deprived of the advantages of our system of public education" Seward told state legislators in 1840. He blamed

Figure 5.1. Reverend John Hughes. Library of Congress LC-USZ62-96710

"prejudices arising from difference of language or religion." The governor recommended "the establishment of schools, in which they may be instructed by teachers speaking the same language with themselves, and professing the same faith." Americans "have opened our country . . . to the oppressed of every nation" and now had the obligation of "qualifying their children for the high responsibilities of citizenship."[78]

Seward miscalculated. His party was appalled at the idea of using tax dollars for religious schools. Nativists condemned the idea of public support for Catholicism. Catholic leaders, on the other hand, welcomed the proposal and asked New York City's board of assistant aldermen for city funding. Petitions also came in from a Scotch Presbyterian church and a Hebrew congregation. The Board reaffirmed its commitment to nonsectarianism but urged removing books offensive to Catholics.

That was not enough, Catholic leaders responded. They reminded city leaders that "the rights of conscience, in this country, are held . . . to be sacred and inviolate." They then argued that the Public School Society expressed a "*sectarian principle*" with deleterious impact on children. Textbooks consistently condemned "popery." As New York "citizens," they sought a share of public funds. In turn, they would abide by state laws prohibiting religious education "during school hours."[79] In short, they made a case for the protection of their religious freedom and for minority rights.

Seward was in a bind. In 1841 the governor's secretary proposed replacing the Public School Society with a publicly run common school system like in the rest of the state. In the legislature, Democrat John L. O'Sullivan (who popularized the phrase "Manifest Destiny") proposed a voucher system instead. Reform stalled until Democrats were swept into office in 1841, thanks in large part to Catholic votes from New York City. A new bill was introduced creating public schools in the city, but in deference to Whigs in the senate, it prohibited funds for religious schools. Senate Whigs voted en masse against the bill, but it passed, and Seward signed.[80]

For Bishop Hughes, this was no solution at all. He had not sought secular public schools but public support for Catholic schools. "The time is almost come," Hughes wrote in an 1850 pastoral letter, "when it will necessary to build a schoolhouse first and a church afterwards." In 1840 the diocese had nine schools, but under Hughes, the number grew to thirty-three parochial schools and seventeen high schools.[81] Nonsectarian education was unacceptable, Hughes believed. To read the Bible without comment ignored the fact that, to Catholics, the Protestant Bible was "not a complete copy" and was not considered "given by the inspiration of the Holy Spirit." Secularism was even worse "because on religious principle alone can conscience find a resting place." Secular schools promoted "infidelity."[82]

Protestantism, Hughes argued, was false because of the doctrine of individualism, which taught people to elevate themselves above their duties to God, which the Catholic Church contrasted with the idea of community.[83] Protestantism "casts off all authority," Hughes believed. It had begun as a rebellion against the church and would ultimately lead to chaos. Since "God is invariable," Hughes claimed, you must choose to "follow His light or yours." Looking around at America, he noticed that everyone was demanding rights but forgetting duties and obligations. Women sought the vote, "forgetting their own dignity." Millenarians proclaimed the final judgment. "Imposters" like Mormons promoted false idols. Without authority, all was reduced to a "base human standard," leaving each individual isolated, alone, and unable to live up to her or his true dignity as one of God's children.[84]

What kind of society would exist when everyone could do whatever they wanted? In his sermon, "The Church and the World," Bishop Hughes argued that the church was appropriately suspicious of revolution because, too often, revolutionaries substituted their needs for God's authority. In contrast, the Catholic "church teaches that man is, by his nature, a being of society," that "society is an institution of God," and that "society is impossible without power and authority." The church did not choose forms of government, so long as the ends of government were upheld. Recent European events made clear that, without authority, "anarchy" erupts. The Reformation stripped the church of its "moral power" and "isolated man, to a certain extent, from his fellow beings, and made him think of and for himself, in such a sense that he was something to the world, but the world was nothing, or but little, to him, except so far as he could use it for his own advantage."[85]

Horace Mann also recognized the dangers of individualism and had argued that all things, including property, come to us through society and ultimately from God (see chapter 1). He had criticized employers for putting self-interest ahead of the common good. His support for public schools was based on his belief that true human flourishing could happen only in a community. Yet Mann and other Protestants celebrated a form of autonomy that could mask the community's role in making individual flourishing possible. Increasingly, Americans would come to think of the individual as existing prior to her or his socialization by the community. Hughes asked Americans to pause and consider the costs of individualism, especially when it was unanchored to sources of meaning beyond the self.

Ordinary Catholic Americans

Ordinary Catholics tried to make sense of how to live in a nation with a Protestant culture. To what extent ordinary parishioners shared the hierarchy's concerns is hard to know. It is worth remembering that history is not philosophy and that people can and do embrace contradictory ideas and aspirations. To begin, immigration transformed American Catholicism. Before the influx of the Irish, Catholics in America had been made up of a few elite families, Native American Indians, and Francophone Louisianans. In time, Irish priests would become the majority within the hierarchy, and by 1860 1.6 million of the nation's 2.2 million Catholics would be Irish.[86] As new priests with new ideas transformed American Catholicism, many native-born Catholics, especially in Louisiana, resisted. For native-born Catholics, the tension between being Catholic and being American was not felt as deeply. They had not experienced firsthand the violence that affected the church in Europe. In fact, some Louisiana Catholics joined the nativist Know-Nothing Party.[87]

New Catholic immigrants, like all immigrants since, sought to become American while retaining aspects of their religious and ethnic identities. Before the Civil War there was no widespread celebration of pluralism, of the idea that America is composed of diverse groups, all different but also sharing a common civic and cultural core, but Americans had long lived in diverse societies, and they had long thought about how to live with political and religious difference.

The question many native-born Americans were asking, and many Irish immigrants were as well, was whether it was possible to assimilate while retaining one's religious and ethnic commitments.[88] Assimilation requires becoming part of a shared culture by participating in common institutions, rituals, and practices.[89] And immigrants, even as they sought to sustain their own traditions, did participate in shared institutions. They comingled with other immigrants and native-born Americans in the workplace and, like their fellow citizens, formed and joined fire companies and fraternal clubs.[90] The Democratic Party reached out to Catholic immigrants and helped them integrate into American politics.[91]

The labor movement also brought together diverse Americans. Immigrants arriving during the famine were poor and took bottom-rung jobs as day laborers, dock workers, and domestics. Over time, many immigrants managed to save money and achieve economic security.[92] By participating in the labor movement, immigrants built bridges with other immigrant and native-born communities. The Irish were active in the labor movement, and in turn early union organizers and activists sought to build a coalition of workers and, as a newspaper supporting the Working Men's Party put it in 1828, "Let the Subject of Religion Alone."[93] The Irish also made up about a quarter of American troops in the Mexican-American War and fought on both sides of the Civil War. While poor people often make up a disproportionate percent of the nation's soldiers, by participating in war, immigrants become part of the larger nation.[94] And as Irish immigrants gained a place and a stake in politics and the economy, they came to share other American ideas good and bad, including racism.[95]

Even as Irish Americans integrated into American society, they did not leave behind the Catholic Church. The church provided economic relief and support networks.[96] And faith mattered. More immigrants were joining the church in the two decades before the Civil War than ever before as Catholics promoted parish revivals around the country.[97] And with growing numbers, the church sought to provide young people a Catholic education. Some Catholic leaders questioned whether parents should be allowed to send their children to public schools. Some pastors even denied the sacraments to parents whose children went to public schools, but practical considerations and parental resistance prevented the excommunication of public school families. That this question was on the table makes clear the depth of concern among both Catholic leaders and parishioners.[98]

Catholics had good reasons to be suspicious of public education. The British had sought to expand education in Ireland, but Catholic leaders recognized the Protestant agenda of this effort and brought these memories with them to America.[99] Many Catholic parents chose to keep their children out of public schools. In the 1870s, most of the 25 percent of Boston children who did not go to school were Irish Catholic.[100] Where Catholic schools were available, parents opted for them. In Detroit in 1852, about thirteen hundred Catholic children were in parochial schools, compared with about twenty-nine hundred in the public schools.[101] In St. Louis before 1850, Catholic schools educated more children than public schools; by 1860 that number remained 36.5 percent.[102] After New York City's decision to deny public funds for denominational schools in 1825, Catholic education struggled. By 1830 there were only five schools for the city's seven thousand Catholic children.[103] Hughes was determined to change this. By 1865, three-fourths of the city's parishes had their own schools, which educated sixteen thousand children, or about one-third of Catholic schoolchildren.[104]

Ethnicity and region shaped parents' choices. Most Massachusetts Catholic children went to public schools, whereas in New York and Philadelphia parish leaders and parents sought Catholic alternatives and clashed with public leaders over access to public funds. In the Midwest cities of Chicago and Cincinnati, Catholics split their energies between building public and parochial systems. Local demand mattered. Where local bishops and parents felt that Catholic schools were needed, they tended to get funding and support. Ethnicity also mattered.

Italian immigrants were significantly less committed to parochial education than were German Catholics, with the Irish in the middle.[105]

Catholic leaders continued to seek public support for parochial education. In Detroit, Catholic leaders in 1852 urged the state legislature to allow Catholic schools to access public funding. The result was a debate much like that in New York, in which Protestants protested permitting "parents to choose the teachers for their children," and Catholics responded that public schools were unfit for Catholics. Protestants invoked Michigan's constitutional prohibition against using public funds to support religious teachers; Catholics invoked the same constitution's protection of equal rights for all religions. Legislators overwhelmingly opposed public funding. Detroit Catholics then turned to the upcoming city council and school board elections, working hard to elect sympathetic members, but in both 1853 and 1854 the "school question" mobilized voters to come out in favor of the common schools. After the Civil War, Detroit's Catholic leaders turned instead to expanding their own separate system.[106]

Similar stories, with their own local dynamics and timelines, can be told for Philadelphia, Cincinnati, St. Louis, Chicago, and elsewhere. San Francisco, expanding rapidly thanks to the Gold Rush, offered public funds for denominational schools in 1851 but reversed its position the following year. The California state superintendent disagreed, and in 1853 three Catholic schools received public funds. In 1855 the Know-Nothings gained half the seats on the city's board of education and demanded that Catholic teachers pass an exam and attend a Saturday normal (teacher education) class. The teachers, who were nuns, responded that they were cloistered. Public funding of Catholic schools ended, although private Catholic schooling continued to expand.[107]

While it is hard to know what shaped parents' decisions about where to send their children to school, there is evidence that many Catholic families found public schools alienating and, sometimes, even worse. In Boston's Eliot School in 1859, young Thomas Wall, at the urging of his priest, refused to repeat the Protestant version of the Ten Commandments. Other young boys followed his example, and as many as three hundred students were dismissed. Blaming Wall for all the chaos, his schoolmaster beat Thomas's hands until they bled. After twenty to thirty minutes of violence, Wall gave in and recited the Commandments. His parents turned to the courts, and the schoolteacher was acquitted. A few months later, however, the Boston School Committee determined that Catholic students were not required to recite something that violated their beliefs.[108]

Because many families did not feel comfortable in the public schools, they opted for Catholic schools instead. By the 1870s in New York, 17 to 33 percent of Catholic children went to parochial schools.[109] Nationally, after the Civil War, as much as a third of Catholic children went to Catholic schools in the nineteenth century.[110] By the mid-1960s, 12 percent of America's children were being educated in Catholic schools.[111] This could not have happened without lay support.

Yet the opposite is equally true: most Catholic families sent their children to public schools, where they learned alongside other Americans. The questions Catholic Americans raised did not go away, however. If, as Orestes Brownson and John Hughes argued, religion and education could not be pried apart, and if the common schools favored one faith or no faith, how could schools ever truly be common? And what would this mean for those who believed, with Horace Mann, that public schools must promote a common civic culture?

Leave Us Alone

The public schools encouraged a national culture, which generated tension with those Americans who wished to maintain the distinctiveness of their own cultures. Many immigrant communities moved west, where they could settle together to maintain their autonomy. Some Americans worried that the "separations of people into classes, using even different languages, must materially impede the formation of a national character, and the spread of useful knowledge."[112] Yet, for many immigrants, American freedom included the freedom to be left alone to practice their own religion, to speak their own language, and nonetheless to be able to participate in the broader economy and civic life. This is not to say that America did not change people; the very fact that being left alone was considered a right reflected the influence of American ideals. Immigrant communities helped make a case for pluralism and minority rights that has continued to shape not only American politics but also the conversation over the limits and legitimacy of public schools.[113]

European migrants often came west via chain migration—in fact, in some cases, entire communities moved together. More often, these connections linked new arrivals to those already here, leading to new, coherent ethnic and religious communities of Germans, Irish, Norwegians, Swedes, and others throughout the Midwest.[114] Small school districts and local control allowed communities to make their own choices about teachers and curricula. Baptists, Methodists, and others who lived near each other could choose teachers who shared their values.[115] Yet local control was consistently challenged by reformers seeking to improve quality and to foster a national culture.

The debate was particularly intense in Pennsylvania, whose residents considered their state especially diverse when compared to "other states having one language, one people, one origin, and one soil," as Superintendent Thomas Henry Burrowes put it in 1836.[116] At the time of the Revolution, perhaps about a third of Pennsylvanians were ethnic Germans. German migrants had emigrated as whole families or even as entire villages and settled in rural Pennsylvania, western Maryland, and parts of backcountry Virginia and North Carolina. They left their southwestern German wine-growing lands because of overcrowding and sought new land in the New World. These "Pennsylvania Deutsch" settlers, unlike later German immigrants, were Protestants in the Lutheran or Reformed (Calvinist) confessions. They lived together in cohesive German-speaking communities; until the 1850s, Pennsylvania printed laws and other official documents in both English and German.[117]

German Pennsylvanians educated their children in church-based schools or by pooling resources to hire teachers. They preferred their own schools to the new public schools which, they felt, did not reflect their culture, language, and religion.[118] By 1820 Lutheran congregations operated 256 schools, and by 1825 Reformed congregations operated 118.[119] Through their schools, they could pass on their language, traditions, and faith to their children. German schools used German-language texts that also reinforced their communities' religious commitments.

The expansion of the common school system was thus seen as a threat to their local culture and religious freedom, especially after 1854, when county superintendents were required to ensure that common schools be taught in English. School districts with large numbers of German Pennsylvanians refused to join the common school system. Pennsylvania law required each district to vote annually on whether to fund public schools, and 80 percent of predominantly-German districts resisted into the 1850s.[120] For these Americans, the costs of participating in the common schools seemed too high a price to pay.

The right to be left alone meant something very different for Native Americans. Indians did not ask to be part of the American nation and were not migrants. They were instead forced to engage with an expansive American nation-state determined to assimilate them and to expropriate their lands as Americans moved west.[121]

A committee of the U.S. House of Representatives declared in 1818 that Native American "sons of the forest should be moralized or exterminated. Humanity would rejoice at the former, but shrink with horror from the latter." Americans should place "into the hands of their [Native American] children the primer and the hoe." Native Americans would become settled farmers, and "as their minds become enlightened and expand, the Bible will be their book." The following year Congress passed the Indian Civilization Act, which offered financial aid to religious missionaries and others to settle among and teach Native Americans "the habits and arts of civilization." By the late 1820s, congressional funding aided 21 schools with eight hundred students; by 1861, the number of schools had grown to 147.[122]

While some missionaries learned Native languages and customs, the goal of both policymakers and missionaries was to transform or "civilize." President James K. Polk's commissioner of Indian affairs, William Medill, thus reported in 1845 that "the mere teaching of letters to the savage mind is not sufficient to give new direction to his pursuits." Instead, educators would have to resort to "combining with letters such studies as call forth the energies of the body, and inspire a taste for the arts of civilized life."[123]

After the Civil War and the Indian wars that followed, the federal government sought to educate Indians on reservations. Treaties required tribes to support schools funded by the U.S. government. Teachers in agency schools, often inspired by Christian faith, worked hard to educate Native American children, and they were both appreciated and resisted by their tribal hosts. By the latter nineteenth century, however, American leaders were convinced that their efforts were failing and that the only solution was to remove Indian youth from their homes and cultures and transport them to English-only government-run boarding schools or to incorporate Native Americans into local American public schools. For Native Americans, the U.S. government's efforts to transform, coercively if necessary, Indian societies challenged their efforts to sustain their political autonomy and cultural traditions.[124]

Like the German Pennsylvanians and Native Americans, many evangelicals also worried about the public schools' impact on their faith. They disagreed with critics who argued that the public schools were too Protestant. If anything, they responded, the public schools were not Protestant enough. Efforts to be nonsectarian, they argued, led to secularism and reduced religion to "moral education." A good education required shaping character, and this required religion. Efforts to accommodate every faith meant removing the particulars of any faith.

In response, evangelical Protestants established Sunday schools around the country. These schools met in churches and emphasized character education. By 1832, 8,268 schools were associated with the American Sunday School Union. Sunday schools had originated after the Revolution to help working people, children as well as adults, black as well as white, gain basic literacy. By the 1830s, however, they shifted focus as the common schools took over responsibility for teaching Americans to read and write. Instead, they now focused on counteracting the secular tendencies of nonsectarianism.

The American Sunday School Union questioned the public schools' determination "To Diffuse Knowledge without Religion." Horace Mann's effort to teach the basics of Christianity for moral purposes was rejected because a good education required orienting people toward God. In 1838 Frederick Packard, who served as the American Sunday School Union's corresponding secretary, proposed a series of books for common school libraries, but the Massachusetts Board of Education—invoking the 1827 law prohibiting sectarian texts—rejected them. Packard and Mann got into a heated debate, during which Mann upheld the principles of nonsectarianism, while Packard responded that Mann's nonsectarianism reflected the sectarian principles of Unitarianism and Universalism.

The Sunday school movement emerged in order to ensure that young Americans would receive the religious education that they did not get in common schools. For some, this was a partnership, a way to balance the needs of faith with those of serving all young people in a diverse society. But for others, this was a sign of the public schools' failure to teach character. For them, the public schools did not embrace Protestantism and in fact might threaten it.[125]

The Quest for Inclusion

Catholics and German Pennsylvanians worried that reformers' efforts to foster a shared culture were premised on eradicating their own minority cultures and faiths. Evangelicals worried that school reformers, seeking to include everyone, had watered down their Protestantism until it was meaningless. School reformers insisted, in response, that all Americans needed to be part of a common culture. Only then would all Americans see themselves as responsible to and for one another.

Indeed, if public schools prepared people to be citizens, access to them was a sign that one was considered a citizen.[126] To be treated as a people apart was to be treated as unequal, to be denied recognition by one's civic community, to be sent into exile.[127] This was something that African Americans understood. Race was the largest factor dividing Americans from each other. Even many white Americans who opposed slavery could not imagine an egalitarian mixed-race society. Some embraced colonization, the idea that black Americans would leave their homes in the United States and return to Africa.[128] To these white Americans, black Americans must truly be sent into exile.

For northern African Americans, the barriers to full citizenship rose during the first half of the nineteenth century. Although northern states had abolished slavery after the Revolution and granted blacks basic civil liberties, in the decades before the Civil War they also imposed new restrictions on voting. As property qualifications disappeared for white men, new restrictions landed on black men. Some midwestern states even prohibited free African Americans from settling and restricted their civil liberties.[129] In this context, African Americans debated whether to embrace separate schools or to demand integration. Most northern blacks believed that access to common schools, like access to voting, was a prerequisite to being recognized as fellow citizens. They sought inclusion rather than exclusion.

The trend was against them. Delaware in 1831 excluded black Americans from public schools. In 1823 New York authorized separate schools, which legislation confirmed in 1841, although rural areas often permitted black children to attend the same schools as white children. In New York City, the free African schools merged with the Public School Society's schools and ultimately joined the common system. Rochester and Syracuse had integrated schools but Albany and Buffalo did not. In 1864 the legislature authorized separate schools for white and black students. In Connecticut, an 1833 law, in response to southern pressure, prohibited schools and academies from enrolling out-of-state students. Ohio's supreme court upheld segregation in 1849. Pennsylvania authorized it in 1854.

Rhode Island, for the purposes of school taxes, counted black children as five-fourteenths of a white child. Segregation remained legal until the legislature, after much effort, abolished separate schools in 1866. Indiana in 1837 determined that public schools would be limited to whites and, in 1853, agreed to refund black taxpayers their school taxes. Illinois counted only white students for school tax purposes; in 1855 the state also agreed to refund black taxpayers. Wisconsin, on the other hand, did not distinguish between black and white children, and the same was true in Iowa after 1857.[130]

Without public support, northern blacks started their own schools. Like white Americans, northern blacks relied on social capital, pooling resources from their communities, often through churches, to hire teachers.[131] Some of these "free African" schools gained public support: in Detroit, black schools joined the public system in 1842; in Poughkeepsie, in 1843; and in Schenectady, in 1854. Cities responded differently to the issue of segregation or integration. New Haven, for example, funded separate elementary schools, but Baltimore refused to use public funds for black education.[132]

In 1812 Boston agreed to subsidize black schools and, by the 1830s, the Boston School Committee was operating black elementary schools. Yet in 1845, when Massachusetts law authorized damages to any children denied admission to their neighborhood schools, the School Committee denied that this required integration. In 1849 a group of black Bostonians met "to contend for equal school rights." Lowell, Nantucket, New Bedford, Salem, and Worcester had already integrated. Salem's city attorney celebrated "perfect equality" as the bedrock principle of common schooling. Boston's School Committee was not convinced. Blacks, they contended, had a different "physical, mental, and moral structure" from whites. Boston's African Americans were also divided, some calling for separate schools, others demanding that the city recognize them as fellow citizens.

Benjamin Roberts, who was trained as a shoemaker and became an antislavery journalist, took the effort to desegregate all the way to the Massachusetts Supreme Court. Roberts had a four-year old daughter. As he watched her walk by white-only schools to the local black school, he recalled how he had felt when he had to do the same as a child. "The pupils of the several schools, as we passed, took particular notice of our situation: and we were looked upon, by them, as unworthy to be instructed in common with others." He did not want his daughter to experience the same social exile.

Other black Bostonians remained committed to the African American Smith School, so much so that in September 1849, black supporters of the separate school hurled stones and other projectiles at integrationists who had blocked entrance to the school earlier in the day. The supreme court upheld segregation but, thanks to grassroots efforts by black and white citizens, the legislature overturned the decision five years later.[133] White Americans understood that access to common schools meant access to membership in the nation. "Now the niggers are really just as good as white folks," commented a skeptical editorial in the *New York Herald*.[134]

Horace Mann recognized that segregation threatened the common school ideal. In private he condemned racism but was accused of acquiescing with it in his public statements and actions. He denied the accusations, claiming that he purposefully visited white and black schools and believed that Massachusetts law required "equal school privileges" for all children. When he was later elected to the U.S. House of Representatives, he was a strong antislavery advocate. While he personally opposed both slavery and segregation, he did not make racial integration a priority at a time when other Massachusetts citizens were working hard to desegregate the state's schools.[135]

The situation for African Americans was much worse in the South. Planters understood the connection between literacy and resistance. As early as 1739, following South Carolina's Stono Rebellion, which led to the death of more than twenty white southerners, South Carolinians prohibited enslaved people from reading and writing. David Walker, who was born to a free mother in North Carolina and ultimately settled in Boston, urged African Americans to rebel in his 1829 *Appeal to the Colored Citizens of the World* and linked learning to read with power.

Southerners responded to Walker's *Appeal* by cracking down. In December, officials in Savannah, Georgia, seized sixty copies of the *Appeal*. Soon after the Georgia legislature outlawed teaching black people, free or enslaved, to read and prohibited the circulation of material that could provoke rebellion. Louisiana responded in kind the next year, prescribing death or hard labor for any person writing anything that would "produce discontent among" free blacks or "insubordination among the slaves." North Carolina also prohibited teaching enslaved people to read or write. Arithmetic was permitted because skilled enslaved artisans needed to cypher. Virginia in 1831 prohibited free blacks from learning to read or write.

Southerners saw their fears confirmed in 1831 when the literate Bible-reading slave Nat Turner and his coconspirators rose up. Fifty-five whites lost their lives. In turn, Virginia, Alabama, and South Carolina passed even stricter literacy restrictions. Ultimately, Alabama, Georgia, Louisiana, Mississippi, Missouri, North and South Carolina, and Virginia all set strict limits on teaching black people to read and write.[136]

All these fears, all these laws, all these limits suggest that white southerners knew that at least some black southerners could read. A Virginia legislator, commenting on his state's decision to prohibit black education, claimed that it would shut down "every avenue by which light may enter their minds."[137] But enslaved and free African Americans knew that learning to read would empower them to challenge slavery. As Booker T. Washington, who would go on to become one of America's most important educators after the Civil War, recalled of his slavery days, "I had the feeling that to get into a schoolhouse and study . . . would be about the same as getting into paradise."[138] Washington did just that, in 1872, as a free man, by enrolling in Virginia's Hampton Institute. He went on to become the first president of Tuskegee Institute in Alabama.

Despite white southerners' best efforts, a few enslaved people did learn to read and write. Sometimes masters or mistresses would provide a basic education. Sometimes enslaved people would learn from white children. More often, enslaved people would study on their own. Mandy Jones recalled "pit schools" near her Mississippi plantation, where enslaved people had dug a hole in the ground and covered it with brush. "Slaves would slip out of the Quarter at night, and go to dese [sic] pits," where a teacher with "some learning would have a school." Sometimes enslaved people learned on their own at night, one person teaching another. The risks were great. One former slave recalled that his master "hung the best slave he had for trying to teach the others how to spell."[139]

Susie King, who was born in 1848 on the Isle of Wight, reported how she and her brother were sent to Savannah, Georgia, to live with and study under a free black woman, Mrs. Woodhouse. She and the other children had to be very careful. They would keep their "books wrapped in paper to prevent the police or white persons from seeing them." They entered the teacher's kitchen "one at a time" to avoid arousing suspicion. And they "left the same way." Evidently, Woodhouse taught about thirty students at a time.[140]

That even a small number of enslaved people learned to read and write is significant. Black communities had their own networks to draw from. They would protect each other and devote time and resources to each other, in order to ensure that some had access to knowledge. With the Civil War, these clandestine networks emerged into the open as enslaved people and northern armies undermined slavery's hold on the south. Freed African Americans not only demanded access to education but, like their white counterparts, pooled time and money to build schoolhouses and to hire teachers. Neighbors taught each other. Working with, and at times in tension with, well-intentioned northern white philanthropists, black Americans sought to provide themselves and their children the education that, under slavery, they had been denied.[141]

Education, black southerners recognized, was vital for effective citizenship. Echoing Thomas Jefferson, the Colored People's Convention of the State of South Carolina stated in 1865, "Knowledge is power, and an educated and intelligent people can neither be held in, nor reduced to slavery." Freed African Americans became some of the most vocal, and influential, advocates of tax-supported public education. In response, many white southerners, some as members of the Ku Klux Klan, used violence to try to intimidate black teachers and northern white teachers in order to maintain the racial hierarchy.[142]

Because public schools did not just educate citizens but determined who was considered worthy of being a citizen, gaining access to them was vital for African Americans. The stakes became higher after the Supreme Court, in its 1857 *Dred Scott* decision, determined that black people were not entitled to American citizenship. For African Americans, exile was involuntary. They saw the costs of exclusion as higher than the challenges of inclusion.

What to the Slave Is the Fourth of July?

Frederick Douglass recognized that being educated was essential for freedom. Douglass was born enslaved in Maryland, as he put it in his 1845 autobiography, in "Tuckahoe, near Hillsborough, and about twelve miles from Easton, in Talbot County." He did not even know his birth date. "The white children could tell their ages. I could not tell why I ought to be deprived of the same privilege." Because slave property was a major source of wealth, owners kept good records, and Douglass's owner recorded his birth in his ledger as February 1818. The day was not noted.[143]

After a failed first attempt at freedom, Douglass ultimately escaped from Baltimore on a train with papers attesting to his identity as a free African American sailor. He arrived in Wilmington, Delaware, where he took a ferry to Philadelphia, and then a train to New York City. He continued north, settling in New Bedford, Massachusetts. As he started life as a free man, he also engaged with the northern antislavery movement and became one of the movement's most well-known writers and speakers.

In 1852, at a speech in Rochester's Corinthian Hall to celebrate the Declaration of Independence, Douglass posed a very simple question: "What to the slave is the 4th of July?" What should he, a black man born into slavery, say about the Fourth? He recognized that America's founders were "great men." But was he not part of the "nation." "Do you mean, citizens, to mock me, by asking me to speak to-day?" he wondered. While white Americans celebrated, Douglass could only hear "the mournful wail of millions." For African Americans, the Fourth of July was "a sham."

But, of course, it was not. Douglass knew that. The fact that he was speaking to the people before him proved it.[144] He was invited to speak as a member, a citi-

Figure 5.2. Frederick Douglass (1870). Library of Congress LC-USZ62-15887

zen, of a nation that rejected him. Social exile, exclusion from the nation, was to Douglass a denial of his basic humanity. Slavery denied people's humanity. Only this could explain why Douglass, as a child, was "awakened at the dawn of day by the most heart-rending shrieks of an aunt of mine," who his master "used to tie up to a joist, and whip upon her naked back till she was literally covered with blood."[145]

When Douglass was sent as a child to a new home in Baltimore, his new mistress "commenced to teach me the A, B, C" and "to spell words of three or four letters." His early instruction ended when her husband found out. "A nigger should know nothing but to obey his master," he told her. Education would "forever unfit him to be a slave."[146] Douglass was determined to become unfit for slavery. Through perseverance, he "learned to read and write." He had to do so covertly. Douglass turned to "all the little white boys whom I met in the street," from whom he took lessons. He happened upon *The Columbian Orator*, one of the most prominent early schoolbooks, which emphasized the value of liberty. It had its effect. The idea of remaining enslaved was too much for him. His master was right, Douglass concluded. "Learning to read had been a curse rather than a blessing." He wanted freedom.[147]

Freedom was more than a legal status; it was about being considered a man by others. While being let—rented out—to a Mr. Covey, Douglass reached his limit and "resolved to fight." The battle lasted "nearly two hours," but Douglass had won. Although still enslaved, Covey "never laid the weight of his finger upon me in anger."[148] The struggle between master and slave forced Douglass's master to recognize Douglass as a fellow man. It was, in Douglass's telling, his first step in his transition from slave to free person. Importantly, the change was not on his part alone. It required change from both sides. That, he made clear to his Rochester audience, was true in Rochester as well. Both sides had to recognize each other as fellow human beings and citizens. Shared membership in the nation was necessary. Only then would the Fourth of July mean something to all Americans.

Civil War and Beyond

Ultimately, it was not immigration but slavery that led Americans down the path to civil war. Education reformers were right. Democracy depends on underlying social bonds. Those bonds fractured in the decades leading up to the firing of guns on Fort Sumter in the Charleston harbor. Northern and southern Americans who had participated in common institutions—not just schools, but also churches, voluntary associations, and political parties—divided along sectional lines.[149]

Yet, despite slavery being the cause of the war, the war encouraged anti-Catholicism. Many northern Americans linked Catholics to slavery, not only because of the pope's authority but because most northern Catholics voted for the Democratic Party against Lincoln's Republicans.[150] And, after the Civil War, the question of how to hold the nation together was not an abstract one.

For its part, the Catholic Church continued to link nationalism to the division of Europe into confessional states during the Reformation, which had broken up Christendom's unity. The church condemned Italian republican nationalists who had tried to limit the Vatican's authority over the Papal States in the name of nationhood.[151] The Vatican emphasized the church's authority rather than the nation-state's. The result was that the "school question" became one of the hot button issues of the post–Civil War decades.[152] While southern African Americans and northern philanthropists were promoting public education in the South, northerners were wondering whether the schools could bring together a diverse nation.

The question broke again into national consciousness with the "Cincinnati Bible War" of 1869–73. Cincinnati was a rapidly growing city, and about half its population after the Civil War was foreign born. In 1869 Catholic schools educated twelve thousand to fifteen thousand children compared to nineteen thousand in the city schools. A new Catholic member of the school board proposed merging the Catholic and public schools, and Father Edward Purcell, vicar general of the archdiocese, agreed, so long as current Catholic teachers could keep their jobs; schools did not teach religious subjects; and schools could be used for religious purposes on weekends. But then a non-Catholic board member added a second resolution prohibiting "religious instruction and the reading of religious books including the Holy Bible." Even though the resolution was not introduced by a Catholic, the public was convinced that Catholics wanted to remove the Bible from America's public schools.

Both Protestants and Catholics—especially German Catholics—came out in opposition to the proposals. Ultimately, Catholic leaders backed out of the merger. Yet the Bible question remained alive. Some opponents invoked the nonsectarian principle—the Bible was a moral text and would not be taught as religion. Yet, as Rev. Amory Mayo, a Unitarian, put it, "the priesthood has always been hostile to American ideas and institutions" and was placing American children "into sectarian and Romish schools." That November, the school board adopted the resolution against Bible reading twenty-two to fifteen.[153]

Pro-Bible forces brought the question before the Ohio Superior Court. The case of *Minor v. Board of Education* has been called by one historian "the century's most comprehensive legal debate over the role of religion in public education." The arguments lasted five days. The plaintiffs' attorneys had to convince the court that the Cincinnati school board acted illegally by prohibiting Bible reading. They appealed to the Ohio Constitution's claim that "religion, morality, and knowledge, however, being essential to good government, it shall be the duty of the general assembly to pass suitable laws, to protect every religious denomination in the peaceable enjoyment of its own mode of public worship, and to encourage schools and the means of instruction." On February 15, 1870, the court sided with the plaintiffs, ruling that the school board could not prohibit Bible reading because the Ohio Constitution presumed that religion and morality served the public welfare.

The defense appealed to the Ohio Supreme Court, which sat on the case for three years, while Americans continued the debate. Ultimately, the Court over-turned the earlier decision. Justice John Welch, writing for the court, determined that the Cincinnati school board had discretion to prohibit Bible reading. But, significantly, the court went further. It denied that the Ohio Constitution re-quired public schools to promote religion. For starters, the court noted that "if Christianity is a law of the State, like every other law, it must have a sanction," but nobody imagined that Ohio would punish citizens for their faith. More im-portant, the court continued, Bible reading could never be neutral. Somebody would have to decide which Bible to teach, and which verses from it. The court thus questioned the very foundation of nonsectarianism as many Americans, in-cluding Horace Mann, had understood it. But then Justice Welch's opinion took one more step. Religion, he wrote, lay "outside the true and legitimate province of government." To use public funds to promote faith was "the very essence of tyranny."

Public reaction to the decision was limited, in part because the court per-mitted school boards to exercise discretion. Yet the case signifies that at least some Americans were considering the possibility of secular public schools.[154] In response to these trends, other Americans sought constitutional affirmation that America was a Christian nation. During the Civil War, some Protestants had floated the idea of a constitutional amendment affirming America's Christian foundations. Petitions signed by thousands came into Congress, but a House re-port rejected the idea of amending the Constitution because the Founders had "decided, after grave deliberation . . . that it was inexpedient to put anything into the constitution . . . which might be construed to be a reference to any religious creed or doctrine."[155]

But then another aspect of the question almost resulted in a constitutional amendment, thanks to Senator James G. Blaine of Maine. As part of his cam-paign for the presidency, Blaine endorsed a constitutional amendment prohibit-ing the use of public funds to support religious schools. In a fall 1875 speech, President Ulysses Grant had recommended that no tax dollars be used for "sec-tarian schools" and that religion be left "to the family altar, the Church, and the private school." Blaine himself was not anti-Catholic; his mother was Catholic, he attended mass as a child, and his daughters had attended Catholic boarding schools. But he was running for president.

In August 1875, Congress overwhelmingly passed a proposed constitutional amendment prohibiting states from using public school funds to support religious schools. When the amendment reached the Senate, however, it was expanded to include all religious institutions (such as charities) and all public funds. Ultimately, the amendment failed to achieve a two-thirds majority in a largely partisan Senate vote, Republicans in favor, Democrats against.[156]

In time, most states would pass their own constitutional amendments prohibiting public school funds going to religious schools. In the twentieth century, the U.S. Supreme Court would determine that public-school prayer violated the U.S. Constitution, opening a new chapter in the ongoing effort of Americans to figure out the relationship between public education and religion in a diverse nation.

Mystic Chords of Memory

Abraham Lincoln was a self-made man. He came from humble birth and rose to become president of the United States. His campaign biography and his biographers have made much of his rags to riches story. Born into a log cabin, Lincoln worked hard, and learned on his own by candlelight. He had little formal schooling. Importantly, however, Lincoln did not see his self-making as the act of a heroic individual. Instead, when he got involved in politics he joined the Whig Party, the party committed to using government to promote opportunities, everything from building canals to funding public schools. Self-making, the future president believed, took a village.

In his first published political speech, delivered before the Young Men's Lyceum in Springfield, Illinois, in January 1838, the twenty-eight-year-old lawyer looked around at America and saw violence everywhere. He thus focused his remarks on "the perpetuation of our political institutions." He first pointed out that American success, its prosperity, its commitment to liberty, was not something that the living generation had earned. We were not self-made. Americans then living "toiled not in the acquirement or establishment of them—they are a legacy bequeathed us" from the Founders.

But that legacy was threatened not by foreign invasion but by threats "amongst us." "Accounts of outrages committed by mobs, form the every-day news of the times" from New England to the South. The risk of violence and disorder seemed very real to the young Lincoln. The stability of democratic governments depended on "the *attachment* of the People." A society in which people "gather in bands of hundreds and thousands, and burn churches, ravage and mob provision-stores, throw printing presses into the rivers, shoot editors, and hang and burn obnoxious persons at pleasure, and with impunity" was one in which free institutions would fail.

These early themes were echoed in his First Inaugural Address in 1861, as southern states were leaving the Union and the threat of civil war loomed. Democracy, he argued, requires citizens to feel a deep emotional bond to each other. They must see themselves as members of a nation. Lincoln started with a political argument: "The central idea of secession, is the essence of anarchy." If southern states refused to acknowledge the will of the majority and left the Union, "anarchy or despotism in some form is all that is left." The very principle of democracy is that the majority, within the boundaries of the Constitution and law, can rule.

Yet Lincoln understood that arguments about political theory would not hold the nation together. Ultimately, democracy required "bonds of affection." He thus appealed to "the mystic chords of memory" that tied Americans together. By remembering the shared sacrifices of the past, when Americans united to gain liberty, he hoped that Americans would embrace "the better angels of our nature."[157]

A good nation must be a just nation, Lincoln believed. This was no small thing to say in the midst of the Civil War in which slavery, as Lincoln put it in his Second Inaugural, "was, somehow, the cause of the war." Americans, as a nation, as a people, would have to pay for this injustice. Having failed to create a nation that lived up to its founding principles, God may will for the war to "continue, until all the wealth piled by the bond-man's two hundred and fifty years of unrequited toil shall be sunk, and until every drop of blood drawn with the lash, shall be paid by another drawn with the sword." If that was what it took, so be it. "The judgments of the Lord, are true and righteous altogether."[158] Americans must love their country and each other, and in doing so must seek justice for all.

Public schools, by bringing diverse young people together in common institutions, and by bringing adults together to govern those institutions in common, were envisioned as places where Americans would forge common ties. Reformers hoped that students would learn to see themselves as fellow citizens and Americans. They aspired for a civic culture—some kind of cultural glue—at a time of increasing diversity and social tension. Americans then, as Americans now, debated what should compose that cultural glue—what in a diverse society ought to be common to everyone. Americans struggled and strove to become, as the poet Walt Whitman put it, "not merely a nation but a teeming nation of nations."[159]

Conclusion

THE TWO NARRATIVES OFFERED IN THIS BOOK are both true, even if they are in tension with each other. According to one, education reformers sought to expand access to liberal education in order to prepare young people for responsibilities as citizens and to enable them to engage in their own self-culture. Reformers argued that in an increasingly diverse society, common institutions were essential for young people to think of each other as fellow citizens. They believed that every child deserved an education equal to any other child. They met resistance from many ordinary Americans who, balking at the cost and exhibiting at times a hostility to intellectual life, resisted.

But another lesson can also be gleaned. Elite reformers aspired to impose their particular vision of education, but many Americans wanted schools that remained close to them, not just in governance but also in culture. They considered public schools to be extensions of their communities and families. They argued that, in a democracy, citizens should determine what kind of education to provide and how to do it.

If we take the ideal of democratic education seriously, reformers were right to argue that a democracy owes every child a liberal education. But if we take equally seriously the idea of education in a democracy, we must also respect the messy give-and-take among citizens competing over different visions yet finding ways to forge lives together. Questions about public education were debated within a diverse citizenry, and no reform program could have emerged, nor should have emerged, unchanged as it went through the democratic wringer. Indeed, the positive result of these two competing ideals—democratic education and education in a democracy—was that education became a staple of democratic politics. It entered the public sphere where citizens, and political parties, argued over what to do. In other words, the division between reformers and their opponents brought education to the center of American political life where, given its importance to society, it belongs.

America's public schools were designed for all Americans, regardless of wealth, religion, or background. They were intended to turn a diverse society into a single nation. In an age in which self-making depended on citizens cooperating—the public school being a key example of the benefits of pooling time and resources for a common good—reformers considered it vital that citizens think of themselves as part of a larger community with shared ideals and obligations. Tipping the scales too far one way risked imposing the public's authority over aspects of life that belonged rightly to individuals and religious communities. But tipping too far the other way threatened to fragment the new republic, making it more difficult for Americans to work together. Diversity was both America's greatest strength and one of its most pressing challenges.

Reformers and teachers hoped that public schools would liberate the human spirit, but few students remembered their experiences that way. As a result, reformers continued, and continue, to echo Mann's and McGuffey's criticisms of teaching and teachers. A study of high schools in New York in the 1930s concluded that teachers emphasized "*drill on technical skills and memorization of a kind of factual material*" that did not "produce scholarship in any real sense."[1] Perhaps we expect too much; real-life classrooms were complex places, where teachers and students were subject to competing pressures often far removed from the rhetoric of education reformers and policymakers. Still, the gap between aspiration and reality is no reason to abandon the aspiration. Nor should it hide what was accomplished. Between the American Revolution and the Civil War, education became a public good worthy of tax support, not only expanding young people's access to the liberal arts but preparing more people to attend high school and college.

One of Horace Mann's most noble hopes did not come to pass. We Americans, it turned out, did not want to intermingle. We did not want the common schools to bring all kinds of children together. By choosing where to live and supporting policies that fostered segregated neighborhoods, we divided ourselves by race and class, using schools to promote inequality rather than equality.[2] This is not to say that public schools cannot nor do not foster civic mindedness. Local schools are one of the few places where neighbors are obliged to act with strangers who over time become fellow citizens and, sometimes, friends. This is as important for parents as for children.[3]

Americans living before the Civil War understood the importance of institutions to individual flourishing. This was Abraham Lincoln's point when he connected the rise of the self-made man to a society that invested in schools and internal improvements like canals and railroads. This was the Republican vision that gained expression in the Homestead Act, which offered land in the West to hardworking Americans willing to live on it and improve it. Self-making, Lincoln understood better than anyone else, was a collective effort.

This vision always had detractors who worried that for every benefit an institution could provide, it brought new dangers. Since the 1960s, we have focused on the dangers. Scholars from the left argued that public schools imposed Protestant morality on a diverse population and sought to produce docile, conformist workers for American factories.[4] One scholar wrote that the development of public schools proved that in America "there is only one way to grow up "and "there is little freedom."[5] Carl Kaestle, in his classic and sympathetic book on the common schools movement, *The Pillars of the Republic* (1983), lamented the "cultural cost" of reformers' efforts to foster a national culture and to exert professional oversight over local schools.[6] More recently, conservatives have criticized the common school reformers for imposing a government monopoly over education.[7]

These criticisms have much truth to them, but they also reflect our loss of faith in what institutions—as flawed as they might be—can do. While the history of our public schools and school reformers has more than its share of things to criticize, we also need to treat our schools—and our other common institutions—as places where human beings are nurtured. We should watch over them, and reform them when they fail us. But we also depend on them. We cannot evade our responsibilities to and for them and, by extension, each other.

To Lincoln, the American dream was about the individual who worked hard and saved until he could buy a plot of land for his family and achieve economic independence. As a young man in 1832, in his bid for election to the Illinois State Legislature, Lincoln linked individual economic success with public support. No farmer could make it just by working the land. "That the poorest and most thinly populated countries would be greatly benefitted by the opening of good roads, and in the clearing of navigable streams within their limits, is what no person will deny."[8]

Speaking more than a quarter century later to an audience of farmers at the Wisconsin State Agricultural Society fair in Milwaukee, the soon to be president once again celebrated the virtues of hard work and self-reliance. But, he added, farming must be more than just labor. If we are truly creative beings, we must have an education that enables us to fully experience all aspects of our work. "The mind, already trained to thought, in the country school, or higher school, cannot fail to find there an exhaustless source of profitable enjoyment. Every blade of grass is a study; and to produce two, where there was but one, is both a profit and a pleasure."[9]

To Lincoln, a democratic society offered all citizens opportunities to develop their full potential, which meant not just rewarding hard work but also enabling them to see the world in a blade of grass. But self-making was a collective effort. It required Americans to invest in roads, schools, and other public goods. For this to happen, Americans had to care about the health of their communities and to think of themselves as citizens with mutual obligations to one another. These beliefs, more than anything, motivated the antebellum advocates of America's common schools.

APPENDIX

Table 1. Children between 5 and 14 Years of Age Enrolled in Public Schools

Year	Percent of Population
1830	54.6
1850	68.1
1870	77.9

Source: Peter Lindert, *Growing Public*, vol. 1: *Social Spending and Economic Growth since the Eighteenth Century* (New York: Cambridge University Press, 2004), 92.

Table 2. Ratio of Scholars to Overall Population in 1850

Maine	32%
Denmark	21%
United States (excluding enslaved people, but including the South)	20%
United States (including enslaved people and the South)	18%
Sweden	18%
Saxony	17%
Prussia	16%
Norway	14%
Great Britain	12%
France	10%

Sources: Lawrence Cremin, *American Education: The National Experience, 1783–1876* (New York, 1980), 488, table: "Ratio of Scholars of the Whole Population (1850)." © 1980 by Lawrence A. Cremin. Reprinted by permission of HarperCollins Publishers. See also Andy Green, *Education and State Formation: The Rise of Education Systems in England, France, and the USA* (New York: Palgrave Macmillan, 1990), ch. 1.

Table 3. Free Schooling, the End of the "Rate Bills," and Compulsory Education Laws in the North and West

State	Year Rate Bills Abolished	Year Compulsory School Law Passed
New Hampshire	Never existed	1871
Maine	1820	1875
Massachusetts	1826	1852
Pennsylvania	1834	1895
Wisconsin	1848	1879
Indiana	1852	1897
Ohio	1853	1877
Illinois	1855	1883
Iowa	1858	1902
Vermont	1864	1867
New York	1867	1874
Connecticut	1868	1872
Rhode Island	1868	1883
Michigan	1869	1871
New Jersey	1871	1875

Source: Claudia Goldin & Lawrence F. Katz, *The Race between Education and Technology* (Cambridge, Mass.: Belknap Press of Harvard University Press, Copyright © 2008 by the President and Fellows of Harvard College), 143, table 4.1. Free Schooling, Rate Bills, and Compulsory Education Laws in the North and Midwest.

NOTES

Introduction

1. Peter Lindert, *Growing Public: Social Spending and Economic Growth since the 18th Century* (Cambridge, 2004), 1:88–99. For the challenge of making reliable national comparisons, see Andy Green, *Education and State Formation: The Rise of Education Systems in England, France, and the USA* (New York, 1990), 13–15; Carole Shammas, "Did Democracy Give the United States an Edge in Primary Schooling?," *Social Science History* 39 (Fall 2015), 315–38.

2. Thomas D. Snyder, ed., *120 Years of American Education: A Statistical Portrait* (Washington, D.C., 1993), 14, table 2.

3. Claudia Goldin & Lawrence F. Katz, *The Race between Education and Technology* (Cambridge, Mass., 2008), 153–57. See also Carl Kaestle & Maris Vinovskis, *Education and Social Change in Nineteenth-Century Massachusetts* (Cambridge, 1980), 21; Donald H. Parkerson & Jo Ann Parkerson, *The Emergence of the Common School in the U.S. Countryside* (Lewiston, N.Y., 1998), 36–56.

4. Goldin & Katz, *Race*, 153.

5. David B. Tyack & Elisabeth Hansot, *Learning Together: A History of Coeducation in American Schools* (New Haven, Conn., 1990), ch. 5.

6. Paul Finkelman, "Laws and Legislation," in *Encyclopedia of African American History, 1619–1895: From the Colonial Period to the Age of Frederick Douglass*, ed. Finkelman (New York, 2006), 2:263; Snyder, *120 Years of American Education*, 14, table 2.

CHAPTER ONE: Citizenship and Self-Culture

1. Tiffin quoted in James W. Taylor, *The Ohio School System and School Laws in Force* (Cincinnati, 1857), 96.

2. Simeon Doggett, *A Discourse on Education, delivered at the Dedication and Opening of Bristol Academy, the 18th day of July, A.D. 1796* (New Bedford, Mass. 1797), in *Essays on Education in the Early Republic*, ed. Frederick Rudolph (Cambridge, Mass., 1965), 147–65. My discussion of the Founding Fathers and civic education draws primarily on Lorraine Smith Pangle & Thomas Pangle, *The Learning of Liberty: The Educational Ideas of the American Founders* (Lawrence, Kans., 1993); Christopher Hans Anderson, "The Rhetoric of Republican Education and the Teaching of Politics in America's Schools, 1776–1860" (PhD diss., University of Minnesota, 2002); Richard D. Brown, *The Strength of a People: The Idea of an Informed Citizenry in America, 1650–1870* (Chapel Hill, N.C., 1996); Peter S. Onuf, "State Politics and Republican Virtue: Religion, Education, and Morality in Early American Federalism," in *Toward*

a Usable Past: Liberty under State Constitutions, ed. Paul Finkelman & Stephen E. Gottlieb (Athens, Ga., 1991), 91–116; Carl Kaestle, *Pillars of the Republic: Common Schools and American Society, 1780–1860* (New York, 1983), ch. 1; Lawrence Cremin, *American Education: The National Experience, 1783–1876* (New York, 1980), pt. 2; Merle Curti, *The Social Ideas of American Educators* (New York, 1935). For a cautionary perspective, see Siobhan Moroney, "Birth of a Canon: The Historiography of Early Republican Educational Thought," *History of Education Quarterly* 39, no. 4 (Winter 1999), 476–91.

3. "Address of the Publishers," *Common School Journal* 6, no. 1 (Jan. 1, 1844).

4. For discussion of colonial education, see Lawrence Cremin, *American Education: The Colonial Experience, 1607–1783* (New York, 1970); Jon C. Teaford, "The Transformation of Massachusetts Education, 1670–1780," in *The Social History of American Education*, ed. B. Edward McClellan & William J. Reese (Urbana, Ill., 1988), 23–38; Gerald F. Moran & Maris A. Vinovskis, "Literacy, Common Schools, and High Schools in Colonial and Antebellum America," in *Rethinking the History of American Education*, ed. William J. Reese & John L. Rury (New York, 2008), 17–46.

5. Samuel Adams quoted in Pangle & Pangle, *Learning*, 29.

6. Benjamin Rush, *A Plan for the Establishment of Public Schools* (Philadelphia, 1786). A critical but informative assessment of Rush's ideas can be found in Jason Frank, *Constituent Moments: Enacting the People in Postrevolutionary America* (Durham, N.C., 2010). See also Rachel Hope Cleves, *The Reign of Terror in America: Visions of Violence from Anti-Jacobinism to Antislavery* (Cambridge, 2009), ch. 5.

7. Joel Barlow, *Letter to His Fellow Citizens* (1801), as quoted in Anderson, "Rhetoric," 72.

8. Quoted in Edgar Knight, *Public Education in the South* (Boston, 1922), 130.

9. Thomas Jefferson to John Tyler, May 26, 1810, in *Thomas Jefferson: Writings*, ed. Merrill Peterson (New York, 1984), 1225–27. For Jefferson, see Johann N. Neem, "'To diffuse knowledge more generally through the mass of the people': Thomas Jefferson on Individual Freedom and the Distribution of Knowledge," in *Light and Liberty: Thomas Jefferson and the Power of Knowledge*, ed. Robert M. S. McDonald (Charlottesville, Va., 2012), 47–74.

10. Thomas Jefferson, "A Bill for the More General Diffusion of Knowledge," in Peterson, *Thomas Jefferson: Writings*, 365–73.

11. Noah Webster, *On the Education of Youth in America* (Boston, 1790), reprinted in *Essays on Education in the Early Republic*, ed. F. Rudolph (Cambridge, Mass., 1965), 41–77. On female education in the early republic, see Caroline Winterer, *The Mirror of Antiquity: American Women and the Classical Tradition, 1750–1900* (Ithaca, N.Y., 2007); Mary Kelley, *Learning to Stand and Speak: Women, Education, and Public Life in America's Republic* (Chapel Hill, N.C., 2006); Margaret A. Nash, *Women's Education in the United States, 1780–1840* (New York, 2005); Linda Kerber, *Women of the Republic: Intellect and Ideology in Revolutionary America* (Chapel Hill, N.C., 1980).

12. Benjamin Rush, *Thoughts Upon Female Education* (Philadelphia, 1787).

13. Christopher Clark, *Social Change in America: From the Revolution through the Civil War* (Chicago, 2006).

14. Quotes from Alexis de Tocqueville, *Democracy in America*, ed. Arthur Gold-hammer (New York, 2004), 3–8, 491–92. On the influence of equality, see Gordon S. Wood, *Radicalism of the American Revolution* (New York, 1991), pt. 3. On the psychology of dependence, see Joyce O. Appleby, "Thomas Jefferson and the Psychology of Democracy," in *The Revolution of 1800: Democracy, Race, and the New Republic*, ed. James Horn, Jan Lewis, & Peter S. Onuf (Charlottesville, Va., 2002), 155–72.

15. H. M. Abrams, *Mirror and the Lamp: Romantic Theory and the Critical Tradition* (New York, 1953, 1975), 22: "A work of art is essentially the internal made external, resulting from a creative process operating under the influence of feeling, and embodying the combined product of the poet's perceptions, thoughts, and feelings." See Bruce Kuklick, *Churchmen and Philosophers: From Jonathan Edwards to John Dewey* (New Haven, Conn., 1985), pt. 2; Mary Kelley, "Crafting Subjectivities: Women, Reading, and Self-Imagining," in *Reading Women: Literacy, Authorship, and Culture in the Atlantic World, 1500–1800*, ed. Heidi Brayman Hackel & Catherine Kelly (Philadelphia, 2008), ch. 3; Margaret Nash, "A Triumph of Reason: Female Education in Academies in the New Republic," in *Chartered Schools: 200 Years of Independent Academies in the United States*, ed. Nancy Beadie & Kim Tolley (New York, 2002), 64–86; Lucia McMahon, *Mere Equals: The Paradox of Educated Women in the Early American Republic* (Ithaca, N.Y., 2012), esp. ch. 2.

16. On Channing, see Amy Kittelstrom, *The Religion of Democracy: Seven Liberals and the American Moral Tradition* (New York, 2015), ch. 3; Andrew Delbanco, *William Ellery Channing: An Essay on the Liberal Spirit in America* (Cambridge, Mass., 1981); Kuklick, *Churchmen and Philosophers*; David Turley, "Religion and Approaches to Reform: Boston Unitarians versus Evangelicals in the Context of the 1820s and 1830s," *American Nineteenth Century History* 10, no. 2 (June 2009), 187–209; David Robinson, "The Legacy of Channing: Culture as a Religious Category in New England Thought," *Harvard Theological Review* 74, no. 2 (Apr. 1981), 221–39.

17. Quotes in text are from Channing, "Self-Culture" (1838), reprinted in *William Ellery Channing: Selected Writings*, ed. David Robinson (New York, 1985), 221–66.

18. For comparisons, see Jürgen Herbst, *School Choice and School Governance: A Historical Study of the United States and Germany* (New York, 2006); Andy Green, *Education and State Formation: The Rise of Education Systems in England, France, and the USA* (New York, 1990).

19. Haddock quoted in "The Rights of Parents as to Public Schools," *Massachusetts Teacher* 3, no. 4 (Apr. 1850), 116–20.

20. On Mann's life, see Jonathan Messerli, *Horace Mann: A Biography* (New York, 1972). On the Whigs, see Daniel Walker Howe, *The Political Culture of the American Whigs* (Chicago, 1979).

21. Horace Mann, "Prospectus of the Common School Journal," in *Life and Works of Horace Mann*, ed. Mary Mann & George Mann (Boston, 1891), 2:15–17. My understanding of Horace Mann builds on the interpretation of Maris A. Vinovskis, "Horace Mann on the Economic Productivity of Education," *New England Quarterly* 43, no. 4 (Dec. 1970), 550–71. See also Merle Curti, *The Social Ideas of the American Educators*

(New York, 1935), ch. 3; Joseph Persky, "American Political Economy and the Common Schools Movement: 1820–1850," *Journal of the History of Economic Thought* 37, no. 2 (June 2015), 247–62.

22. Horace Mann, "Lecture 1: Means and Objects of Common-School Education," in Mann, *Lectures and Annual Reports on Education* (Cambridge, Mass., 1867), 1:39–87.

23. Dugald Stewart, *Elements of the Philosophy of Mind* (1792), in *The Works of Dugald Stewart* (Cambridge, 1829), 1:355–94. For a discussion of how the imagination was understood in the eighteenth and early nineteenth centuries, see James Engell, *The Creative Imagination: Enlightenment to Romanticism* (Cambridge, Mass., 1981); G. Gabrielle Starr, "Aesthetics and Taste: The Beautiful, the Sublime, and Beyond in the 18th Century," in *A Companion to British Literature*, vol. 3: *Long 18th-Century Literature, 1660–1837*, ed. R. Demaria Jr. et al. (Malden, Mass., 2014), ch. 17; Ryan Patrick Hanley, "Educational Theory and the Social Vision of the Scottish Enlightenment," *Oxford Review of Education* 37, no. 5 (Oct. 2011), 587–602; Hanley, "Social Science and Human Flourishing: The Scottish Enlightenment and Today," *Journal of Scottish Philosophy* 7, no. 1 (Spring 2009), 29–46.

24. Charles L. Griswold Jr., "Imagination: Morals, Science, and Arts," in *Cambridge Companion to Adam Smith*, ed. Knud Haakonssen (Cambridge, 2006), 22–56.

25. "Popular Education," *Princeton Review* (Oct. 1857), 609–35, at 619–20.

26. Samuel Eells, "The Moral Dignity of the Office of the Professional Teacher," *Western Academician and Journal of Education and Science*, ed. John Picket (Cincinnati, 1837–38), 570–89.

27. Gillian Avery, *Behold the Child: American Children and Their Books, 1621–1922* (Baltimore, 1994), esp. 68–69.

28. Dr. Kerry, "Effect of Habitual Emotions on Beauty and Health," *Common School Journal* 1, no. 13 (July 1, 1839).

29. Massachusetts Board of Education, *The Massachusetts System of Common Schools* (Boston, 1849), 80.

30. Horace Mann, *Second Annual Report of the Secretary of the Board of Education* (1838), in Mann & Mann, *Life and Works*, 2:544–45.

31. Horace Mann, *Third Annual Report of the Secretary of the Board of Education* (1839), in Mann & Mann, *Life and Works*, 3:22–26. See also, for example, "Novel Reading," *Pennsylvania School Journal* 8, no. 12 (June 1860).

32. "Letter from a Teacher to Her Young Female Friend, Just about Commencing to Keep School," *Common School Journal* 3, no. 6 (Mar. 15, 1841). See also "Reading," *Common School Journal* 5, no. 1 (Jan. 2, 1843); E. D. Mansfield, *American Education: Its Principles and Elements: Dedicated to the Teachers of the United States* (New York, 1851), 230–39.

33. [Louis] Agassiz, "Abstract of an Address on Natural History in Common Schools," *Pennsylvania School Journal* 8, no. 2 (Aug. 1859).

34. John Griscom, "Essay on School Discipline, read before the American Ly-

ceum, May 5, 1832," in *American Annals of Education and Instruction for the Year 1832*, ed. William C. Woodbridge (Boston, 1832), 2:482–92.

35. Frederick Douglass, "Pictures and Progress" (ca. 1864–65), reprinted in *Picturing Frederick Douglass*, ed. John Stauffer et al. (New York, 2015), 161–73.

36. "The Culture of the Imagination," *US Democratic Review* 22, no. 15 (Jan. 1848), 33–45. See also [Horace Mann], "Prospectus," *Common School Journal* 1, no. 1 (Nov. 1838).

37. J. Willis Westlake, "An Address delivered before the Eclectic Literary Society of Indiana Seminary," excerpted in *Pennsylvania School Journal* 8, no. 12 (June 1860).

38. "Modern Education," *Southern Quarterly Review* 11, no. 2 (Apr. 1855), 451–76.

39. C. Watkins Eimi, "Instinct, Reason, Imagination," *US Democratic Review* 15, no. 76 (Oct. 1844), 408–19.

40. See, for example, J. C Hope, "Genius and Industry in Their Results," *DeBow's Review* 29, no. 3 (Sept. 1860), 269–80; Joseph K. Edgerton, "Genius and Some of Its Abuses," *Ladies' Repository* 9, no. 11 (Nov. 1849), 322–25.

41. Borland's address is printed in *Proceedings of a Convention for the Promotion of Common School Education* (Newburgh, N.Y., 1837), New-York Historical Society collections, New York. On Borland, see "Borland, Charles," in *Biographical Directory of the United States Congress, 1774–Present*, http://bioguide.congress.gov/scripts/biodisplay.pl?index=B000641.

42. "The Culture of the Imagination," *Connecticut Common School Journal* 2, no. 8 (Feb. 1, 1840). The essay was reprinted in *Common School Journal* 2, no. 6 (Mar. 16, 1840). A reader of education journals would have come across references to "self-culture." See, as examples: *Common School Journal* 1, no. 5 (Mar. 1, 1839); *Connecticut Common School Journal* 1, no. 5 (Dec. 1838); *Journal of the Rhode Island Institute of Instruction* 13 (July 1, 1846); *Pennsylvania School Journal* 6, no. 4 (Oct. 1857); *District School Journal of the State of New York* 8, no. 9 (Dec. 1847); "Self-Culture," *Indiana School Journal* 5, no. 8 (Aug. 1860), 282–85; *Ohio School Journal* 4, no. 1 (Jan. 1849); *Educational Magazine* (Mar. 1839). See also Superintendent of Common Schools, *Statutes of the State of New York, Relating to Common Schools* (Albany, 1847), 188; Alonzo Potter & George B. Emerson, *The School and the Schoolmaster: A Manual for the Use of Teachers* (New York, 1842), 166; Barnard, *Report on the Condition and Improvement of the Public Schools* (Providence, R.I., 1846), 37.

43. For a discussion of these historical interpretations, see Diane Ravitch, *The Revisionists Revised: A Critique of the Radical Attack on the Schools* (New York, 1978).

44. Adam Smith, *An Inquiry into the Nature and Causes of the Wealth of Nations* (1776), ed. R. H. Campbell & A. S. Skinner (Indianapolis, Ind., 1981), 2: 781–82.

45. Horace Mann, *Fifth Annual Report* (1841), in Mann & Mann, *Life and Works*, 3:93, 128; Maris A. Vinovskis, "Horace Mann on the Economic Productivity of Education," *New England Quarterly* 43, no. 4 (Dec. 1970), 550–71; Claudia Goldin & Lawrence F. Katz, "The 'Virtues' of the Past: Education in the First Hundred Years of the

New Republic," National Bureau of Economic Research Working Paper 9958 (2003), 25–26.

46. Horace Mann, *Third Annual Report* (1839), in Mann & Mann, *Life and Works*, 3:6. Many other Americans, especially in industrializing New England, shared these concerns. See Thomas Bender, *Toward an Urban Vision: Ideas and Institutions in 19th-Century America* (Lexington, Ky., 1975), 55–69.

47. Horace Mann, *Tenth Annual Report* (1846), in Mann & Mann, *Life and Works*, 4:105–40.

48. Lee M. McAfee, *Address; delivered before the Theta Delta Chi Society, at the Annual Convention, held in Washington City, May 25, 1858* (Greensboro, N.C., 1858). Also excerpted in *North Carolina Journal of Education* 1, no. 8 (Aug. 1858).

49. Brown, *Informed Citizenry*; Joseph Kett, *The Pursuit of Knowledge under Difficulties: From Self-Improvement to Adult Education in America, 1750–1990* (Stanford, Calif., 1994); David Jaffee, "The Village Enlightenment in New England, 1760–1820," *William and Mary Quarterly* 47, no. 3 (July 1990), 327–46.

50. Quoted in Richard D. Brown, *Knowledge Is Power: The Diffusion of Information in Early America, 1700–1865* (New York, 1989), 129. Donald M. Scott, "The Popular Lecture and the Creation of a Public in 19th-Century America," *Journal of American History* 66, no. 4 (Mar. 1980), 791–809; Catherine Kelly, "'Well-Bred Country People': Sociability, Social Networks, and the Creation of a Provincial Middle Class, 1820–1860," *Journal of the Early Republic* 19, no. 3 (1999), 451–79; William J. Gilmore, *Reading Becomes a Necessity of Life: Material and Cultural Life in Rural New England, 1780–1835* (Knoxville, Tenn., 1989); Angela G. Ray, *The Lyceum and Public Culture in the Nineteenth-Century United States* (East Lansing, Mich., 2005).

51. Wood, *Radicalism of the American Revolution*, pt. 3; John Larson, *The Market Revolution in America* (New York, 2009). On the novelty of finding a career, see Joyce O. Appleby, *Inheriting the Revolution: The First Generation of Americans* (Cambridge, Mass., 2000), ch. 4; J. M. Opal, *Beyond the Farm: National Ambitions in Rural New England* (Philadelphia, 2008), 127–92. On how Americans experienced the new market economy, see Jonathan Levy, *Freaks of Fortune: The Emerging World of Capitalism and Risk in America* (Cambridge, Mass., 2012); Scott Sandage, *Born Losers: A History of Failure in America* (Cambridge, Mass., 2005); Michael Kimmel, *Manhood in America: A Cultural History* (New York, 1996), chs. 1–2.

52. Quotes from Steven Mintz & Susan Kellogg, *Domestic Revolutions: A Social History of American Family Life* (New York, 1988), 52–60. For discussion on the relationship between new ideas about childhood and the emergence of public schools, see Steven Mintz, *Huck's Raft: A History of American Childhood* (Cambridge, Mass, 2004), ch. 4. According to Mintz, *Huck's Raft*, 77: "Overall, childhood dependency was prolonged, childrearing became a more intensive and self-conscious activity, and schooling was extended." See also Jacqueline S. Reiner, *From Virtue to Character: American Childhood, 1775–1850* (New York, 1996); Sterling Fishman, "The Double-Vision of Education in the 19th Century: The Romantic and the Grotesque," in *Regulated Children, Liberated Children: Education in Psychohistorical Perspective*, ed. Barbara Finkelstein

(New York, 1979), 96–113; Bernard Wishy, *The Child and the Republic: The Dawn of Modern American Child Nurture* (Philadelphia, 1968). See also Howard P. Chudacoff, *How Old Are You? Age Consciousness in American Culture* (Princeton, N.J., 1989), ch. 2.

53. E. A Doster, "The Paternal Roof," *Southern Teacher* (May 1860), quoted in Robert Hunt, "Organizing a New South: Education Reformers in Antebellum Alabama, 1840–1860" (PhD diss., University of Missouri, 1988), 84–85.

54. Claudia Goldin & Lawrence Katz, *The Race between Education and Technology* (Cambridge, Mass., 2008); Lee Soltow & Edward Stevens, *Rise of Literacy and the Common School in the United States* (Chicago, 1981), 122–47; Brian Luskey, *On the Make: Clerks and the Quest for Capital in 19th-Century America* (New York, 2010).

55. Joseph F. Kett, *Rites of Passage: Adolescence in America, 1790 to the Present* (New York, 1977).

56. Quotes in Rush Welter, *Popular Education and Democratic Thought in America* (New York, 1962), 45, 47. My discussion is from ibid., chs. 3–4; Julie M. Walsh, *The Intellectual Origins of Mass Parties and Mass Schools in the Jacksonian Period* (New York, 1998), ch. 5. See also Alan Taylor, *William Cooper's Town: Power and Persuasion on the Frontier of the Early American Republic* (New York, 1996), 285–86.

57. I rely primarily on Jürgen Herbst, *The Once and Future School: 350 Years of American Secondary Education* (New York, 1996), ch. 4; David F. Labaree, *Making of an American High School: The Credentials Market and the Central High School of Philadelphia, 1838–1939* (New Haven, Conn., 1988), chs. 1 and 2; William Reese, *The Origins of the American High School* (New Haven, Conn., 1995). See also Ellwood Cubberley, *Public Education in the United States* (Boston, 1919), ch. 7.

58. William A. Smith, *Secondary Education in the United States* (New York, 1932), 34–35.

59. Kelley, *Learning to Stand and Speak*; Nash, "A Triumph of Reason"; Kathryn Walbert, "'Endeavor to Improve Yourself': The Education of White Women in the Antebellum South," in *Chartered Schools*, ed. Nancy Beadie & Kim Tolley (New York, 2002), 64–86, 116–36.

60. "Common Schools and Their Relation to Higher Seminaries," *New Englander* 6, 23 (1848), 313–30.

61. Quoted in John E. Stout, *Development of High School Curricula in the North Central States from 1860 to 1918* (Chicago, 1921), 5. On merit, see Joseph Kett, *Merit: The History of a Founding Ideal from the American Revolution to the 21st Century* (Ithaca, N.Y., 2012).

62. Quoted in Herbst, *Once and Future School*, 67.

63. Reese, *Origins*, 97–101.

64. Ibid., 75.

65. Statistic from Herbst, *Once and Future School*, 65.

66. Orwin B. Griffin, *The Evolution of the Connecticut State School System* (New York, 1928), 72–73.

67. Quoted in Elmer Ellsworth Brown, *The Making of Our Middle Schools* (New York, 1969), 315–17.

68. Herbst, *Once and Future School*, 62–64, 75–76.

69. Michael B. Katz, *The Irony of Early School Reform: Educational Innovation in Mid-19th Century Massachusetts* (Cambridge, Mass., 1968). For statistics, see ibid. 38–40. See also Soltow & Stevens, *Rise of Literacy.*

70. The *Awl* (Mar. 8, 1845), quoted in Carl Kaestle & Maris Vinovskis, *Education and Social Change in Nineteenth-Century Massachusetts* (Cambridge, 1980), 172–73.

71. Maris A. Vinovskis, "Have We Seriously Underestimated the Extent of Antebellum High School Attendance?," *History of Education Quarterly* 28, no. 4 (Winter 1999), 551–67.

72. Wood, *Radicalism of the American Revolution*, ch. 18, and "The Enemy Is Us: Democratic Capitalism in the Early Republic," *Journal of the Early Republic* 16, no. 2 *(Summer 1996), 293–308;* Richard Bushman, *The Refinement of America: Persons, Houses, Cities* (New York, 1992); John Kasson, *Rudeness and Civility: Manners in Nineteenth-Century Urban America* (New York, 1990).

73. Kett, *Merit*, ch. 4.

74. On distinction, see Pierre Bourdieu, *Distinction: A Social Critique of the Judgment of Taste*, trans. Richard Nice (Cambridge, Mass., 1984); Thorstein Veblen, *The Theory of the Leisure Class: An Economic Study of Institutions* (New York, 1902), esp. ch. 14. For a discussion of distinction in relation to female education, see Kelley, *Learning to Stand and Speak.* The argument that education serves largely to credential people, and thus to distinguish the few from the many, is made forcefully in the work of David Labaree. See *Making of an American High School; How to Succeed in School without Really Learning: The Credentials Race in American Education* (New Haven, Conn., 1997); *Education, Markets, and the Public Good* (London and New York, 2007); *Someone Has to Fail: The Zero Sum Game of Public Schooling* (Cambridge, Mass., 2010).

CHAPTER TWO: Democratic Education

1. It was in schools, in other words, that Americans experienced what Daniel Walker Howe has referred to as the "democratization of self-construction." It might also be said that the schools helped popularize the idea of American individualism and the "social imaginary" necessary to make it a social reality. See Daniel Walker Howe, *Making the American Self: Jonathan Edwards to Abraham Lincoln* (Cambridge, Mass., 1997); Charles Taylor, *Modern Social Imaginaries* (Durham, N.C., 2004) and *The Ethics of Authenticity* (Cambridge, Mass., 1991).

2. James Henry Jr., *An Address upon Education and Common Schools* (Albany, N.Y., 1843).

3. 1835 quote from Margaret Nash, *Women's Education in the United States, 1780–1840* (New York, 2005), 84.

4. Horace Mann, *Twelfth Annual Report* (1848), in *Life and Works of Horace Mann*, ed. Mary Mann & George Mann (Boston, 1891), 4:228. On Mann, see Howe, *Making the American Self*, 158–67; Merle Curti, *Human Nature in American Thought: A History* (Madison, Wis., 1980), 181–83. Mann echoes the German idea of *Bildung*, as do many American educators. See Rebekka Horlacher, *The Educated Subject and the German*

Concept of Bildung: *A Comparative Cultural History* (New York, 2016); Ari Sutinen, "Horace Mann on Growth, the Pedagogical Method, and Public School," in *Theories of* Bildung *and Growth: Connections and Controversies between Continental Educational Thinking and American Pragmatism*, ed. Paul Siljander, Ari Kivelä, and Ari Sutinen (Rotterdam, 2012), 199–211; David Sorkin, "Wilhelm Von Humboldt: The Theory and Practice of Self-Formation (*Bildung*), 1791–1810," *Journal of the History of Ideas* 44, no. 1 (Jan.–Mar. 1983), 55–73.

5. For Jackson's transformation from an aristocrat to a man of the people, see Reeve Huston, "Rethinking 1828: The Emergence of Competing Democracies in the United States," in *Democracy, Contestation, and Participation: Civil Society, Governance, and the Future of Liberal Democracy*, ed. Emmanuelle Avril & Johann N. Neem (New York, 2015), ch. 1.

6. Quotes from Daniel Walker Howe, *What Hath God Wrought* (New York, 2007), 331. See also Richard R. John, *Spreading the News: The American Postal System from Franklin to Morse* (Cambridge, Mass., 1995), 211–14.

7. Margaret Bayard Smith, *Forty Years of Washington Society*, ed. Gaillard Hunt (London, 1906), 290–98.

8. Sophia Rosenfeld, *Common Sense: A Political History* (Cambridge, Mass., 2011).

9. "Joseph Caldwell on Public Education," in *A Documentary History of Education in the South before 1860*, ed. Edgar W. Knight (Chapel Hill, N.C., 1950), 2:357–409.

10. Caroline Winterer, *The Culture of Classicism: Ancient Greece and Rome in American Intellectual Life, 1780–1910* (Baltimore, 2002); Daniel Walker Howe, "Classical Education in America," *Wilson Quarterly* 35 (Spring 2011), 31–36; Siobhan Moroney, "Latin, Greek, and the American Schoolboy: Ancient Languages and Class Determinism in the Early Republic," *Classical Journal* 96, no. 3 (Feb.–Mar. 2001), 295–307.

11. My discussion of the *Yale Reports* relies on David Potts, *Liberal Education for a Land of Colleges: Yale's Reports of 1828* (New York, 2010), 1–73. Among many examples, see also T. M. Post, "The Classics," *Transactions of the Fourth Annual Meeting of the Western Literary Institute and College of Professional Teachers* (Cincinnati, 1835), 63–96.

12. "faculty, n.," *Oxford English Dictionary Online*, December 2015, http://www.oed.com/view/Entry/67547?redirectedFrom=faculty.

13. Francis Hutcheson, *A System of Moral Philosophy* (1755; repr., Hildesheim, Germany, 1969), 1:1–2. For discussion, see Ryan Patrick Hanley, "Social Science and Human Flourishing: The Scottish Enlightenment and Today," *Journal of Scottish Philosophy* 7, no. 1 (Spring 2009), 29–46.

14. Henry Home, Lord Kames, *Essays on the Principles of Morality and Natural Religion*, in two parts (Edinburgh, 1751), 40–41.

15. Dugald Stewart, *The Philosophy of the Active and Moral Powers of Man*, rev. ed. (Boston, 1859), 5.

16. On faculty psychology, see Howe, *Making the American Self*; Daniel Walker Howe, *Political Culture of the American Whigs* (Chicago, 1979), 29–32, 36–37; Mark Noll, *America's God: From Jonathan Edwards to Abraham Lincoln* (New York, 2002);

James Kloppenberg, *Virtues of Liberalism* (New York, 1998); D. H. Meyer, *The Instructed Conscience: The Shaping of the American National Ethic* (Philadelphia, 1972); Julie Walsh, *The Intellectual Origins of Mass Parties and Mass Schools in the Jacksonian Period* (New York, 1998), 145–203. See also David Hogan, "Modes of Discipline: Affective Individualism and Pedagogical Reform in New England, 1820–1850," *American Journal of Education* 99, no. 1 (Nov. 1990), 1–56; James Block, *The Crucible of Consent: American Child Rearing and the Forging of Liberal Society* (Cambridge, Mass., 2012), chs. 8–9.

17. *Reports on the Course of Instruction in Yale College; by a Committee of the Corporation and the Academical Faculty* (New Haven, Conn., 1828), 7. For discussion, see Potts, *Liberal Education*; Herbert M. Kliebard, "The Decline of Humanistic Studies in the American School Curriculum," in *Forging the American Curriculum: Essays in Curriculum History and Theory* (New York, 1992), ch. 1. See also William Reese, *The Origins of the American High School* (New Haven, Conn., 1995), 100–101; Jürgen Herbst, *Once and Future School: 350 Years of American Secondary Education* (New York, 1996), 143.

18. All quotes from *Reports on the Course of Instruction in Yale College.*

19. William Ellery Channing, "Likeness to God," (1828), in *William Ellery Channing: Selected Writings*, ed. David Robinson (New York, 1985), 146–65.

20. Ibid., 155–56.

21. May quoted in Paul Mattingly, *The Classless Profession: American Schoolmen in the 19th Century* (New York, 1975), 5. Bruce Kuklick, *Churchmen and Philosophers: From Jonathan Edwards to John Dewey* (New Haven, Conn., 1985), chs. 8–9; Meyer, *Instructed Conscience*; Margaret Nash, *Women's Education in the United States, 1780–1840* (New York, 2005), ch. 5; Howe, *Making the American Self*; J. B. Schneewind, *The Invention of Autonomy: A History of Modern Moral Philosophy* (Cambridge, 1998); Knud Haakonssen, *Natural Law and Moral Philosophy: From Grotius to the Scottish Enlightenment* (New York, 1996).

22. E. D. Mansfield, *American Education: Its Principles and Elements: Dedicated to the Teachers of the United States* (New York, 1851), 55–59.

23. Ibid., 60.

24. Ibid.

25. Horace Mann, *Third Annual Report* (1839), in Mann & Mann, *Life and Works*, 3:29–30.

26. Alonzo Potter & George B. Emerson, *The School and the Schoolmaster: A Manual for the Use of Teachers* (New York, 1842), 19, 23, 25.

27. Calvin Henderson Wiley, *First Annual Report of the General Superintendent of Common Schools* (Raleigh, N.C., 1854), 23–24. Another North Carolina example is Archibald Murphey's "Report on Education" (1817), in *The Beginnings of Public Education in North Carolina: A Documentary History, 1790–1840*, ed. Charles Coon (Raleigh, N.C., 1908), 1:140–41.

28. Horace Mann, "Prospectus of the Common School Journal" (1838), in Mann & Mann, *Life and Works*, 2:5–6.

29. Horace Mann, *Ninth Annual Report* (1845), in Mann & Mann, *Life and Works*, 4:3.

30. George Combe, *The Constitution of Man* (Hartford, Conn., 1850); Stephen Tomlinson, *Head Masters: Phrenology, Secular Education, and Nineteenth-Century Social Thought* (Tuscaloosa, Ala., 2005).

31. Britt Rusert, "The Science of Freedom: Counterarchives of Racial Science on the Antebellum Stage," *African American Review* 45, no. 3 (Fall 2012), 291–308.

32. *Second Annual Report of the School Commissioner, for the Year 1855* (Columbus, Ohio, 1856), 59–60. See also in H. H. Barney, *Report on the American System of Graded Free Schools* (Cincinnati, 1851), 46.

33. Francis Wayland, *Elements of Moral Science* (New York, 1835), 9.

34. Louis P. Masur, "'Age of the First Person Singular': The Vocabulary of the Self in New England, 1780–1850," *Journal of American Studies* 25, no. 2 (Aug. 1991), 189–211.

35. Most of the details of McGuffey's life are taken from Quentin Skrabec, *William McGuffey: Mentor to American Industry* (New York, 2009). See also Elliott Gorn, *The McGuffey Readers: Selections from the 1879 Edition* (Boston, 1998); John H. Westerhoff III, *McGuffey and His Readers: Piety, Morality, and Education in 19th-Century America* (Milford, Mich., 1982).

36. Number from Jean Carr, Stephen Carr, & Lucille Schultz, *Archives of Instruction: 19th-Century Rhetorics, Readers, and Composition Books in the United States* (Carbondale, Ill., 2005), 124.

37. Richard Mosier, *Making the American Mind: Social and Moral Ideas in the McGuffey Readers* (New York, 1947); Gorn, *The McGuffey Readers*, 2. The readers were even more popular after the Civil War when revisions were made without McGuffey's involvement. The readers are often seen as intended for Midwestern and Northern students, but Edgar Knight, *Public Education in the South* (Boston, 1922), 276, found McGuffey's *Readers* to be one of the most popular books in the South as well.

38. Details of the Ohio years from Skrabec, *McGuffey*, ch. 9.

39. William H. McGuffey, *The Eclectic Fourth Reader*, 6th ed. (Cincinnati, 1838; repr., Milford, Mich., 1982), vii.

40. The phrase internal gyroscope is from David Riesman et al., *The Lonely Crowd: A Study of the Changing American Character* (New Haven, Conn., 1950).

41. William H. McGuffey, *The Eclectic Third Reader* (Cincinnati, 1837; repr., Milford, Mich., 1982), 226.

42. McGuffey, *Fourth Reader*, vii.

43. Ibid., 251–58. Byron was clearly a source of anxiety because the following selection also dealt with his life and art, concluding that despite his genius and talent, his life lacked purpose and meaning. Ibid., 259–61.

44. William H. McGuffey, *The Eclectic Second Reader* (Cincinnati, 1836; repr., Milford, Mich., 1982), 120–23.

45. Ibid., 188–90.

46. McGuffey, *Third Reader*, 17–21. See also McGuffey, "Love of Applause," in *Fourth Reader*, 178–81.

47. The classic discussion of this point is in Paul Boyer, *Urban Masses and Moral Order in America, 1820–1920* (Cambridge, Mass., 1978).

48. Quoted in Kathryn Pippin, "The Common School Movement in the South, 1840–1860" (PhD diss., University of North Carolina, Chapel Hill, 1977), 154.

49. Gorn, *The McGuffey Readers*, 12.

50. McGuffey, *Fourth Reader*, 238–39.

51. Examples include ibid., Lessons, 47, 48, 92, 110, 129. For the role of land and landscapes in generating national sentiment, see Andrew Burstein, *Sentimental Democracy: The Evolution of America's Romantic Self-Image* (New York 1999); Lloyd Kramer, *Nationalism in Europe and America: Politics, Cultures, and Identities since 1775* (Chapel Hill, N.C., 2011), ch. 3.

52. For example, see François Furstenberg, *In the Name of the Father: Washington's Legacy, Slavery, and the Making of a Nation* (New York, 2006); Mosier, *Making the American Mind*.

53. McGuffey, *Fourth Reader*, 201–4.

54. Ibid., 213–15.

55. A good overview of McGuffey's ideas in relation to Christianity can be found in Westerhoff, *McGuffey and His Readers*, ch. 3.

56. Preface to McGuffey, *Third Reader*; preface to McGuffey, *Fourth Reader*.

57. Skrabec, *McGuffey*, 191–94.

58. Discussions and examples from R. Laurence Moore, "Bible Reading and Non-sectarian Schooling: The Failure of Religious Instruction in 19th-Century Public Education," *Journal of American History* 68, no. 4 (Mar. 2000), 1581–99.

59. JoEllen McNergney Vinyard, *For Faith and Fortune: The Education of Catholic Immigrants in Detroit, 1805–1925* (Urbana, Ill., 1998), 19–20.

60. Raymond Culver, *Horace Mann and Religion in the Public Schools* (New Haven, Conn., 1929).

61. Liam Riordan, *Many Identities, One Nation* (Philadelphia, 2007); Robert Bellah, "Civil Religion in America," *Daedalus* 96, no. 1 (Winter 1967), 1–21; Timothy L. Smith, "Protestant Schooling and American Nationality, 1800–1850," *Journal of American History* 53, no. 4 (Mar. 1967), 679–95.

62. Eric Schlereth, *Age of Infidels* (Philadelphia, 2013); Philip Hamburger, *Separation of Church and State* (Cambridge, Mass., 2002).

63. On these questions, see Mark D. McGarvie, *Law and Religion in American History: Public Values and Private Conscience* (New York, 2016).

64. Bruce Kimball, *Orators and Philosophers: A History of the Idea of Liberal Education* (New York, 1986).

65. Carolyn Eastman, *A Nation of Speechifiers: Making an American Public after the Revolution* (Chicago, 2009), ch. 1.

66. Lindley Murray, *The English Reader* (1799; Concord, N.H., 1827), 4.

67. Sandra Gustafson, *Imagining Deliberative Democracy in the Early American Republic* (Chicago, 2011).

68. Charles Monaghan & E. Jennifer Monaghan, "Schoolbooks," in *A History of the Book in America*, vol. 2: *An Extensive Republic: Print, Culture, and Society in the New Nation, 1790–1840*, ed. Robert A. Gross & Mary Kelley (Chapel Hill, N.C., 2010), 305–12.

69. Chace quoted in Carr et al., *Archives of Instruction*, 8. On Chace's life, see Sephi Allen, "Abolitionist, Suffragist, Philanthropist: The Life and Work of Reformer Elizabeth Buffum Chace," *Journal of Women's History* 16, no. 4 (Winter 2004), 183–90.

70. E. E. White & T. W. Harvey, eds., *A History of Education in the State of Ohio: A Centennial Volume* (Columbus, Ohio, 1876), 103.

71. William Russell, *Suggestion on Education: Relating Particularly to the Method of Instruction Commonly Adopted in Geography, History, Grammar, Logic, and the Classics* (New Haven, Conn., 1823).

72. E. Jennifer Monaghan & E. Wendy Saul, "The Reader, the Scribe, the Thinker: A Critical Look at the History of American Reading and Writing Instruction," in *The Formation of School Subjects: The Struggle for Creating an American Institution*, ed. Thomas S. Popkewitz (New York, 1987), ch. 4; Gerald F. Moran & Maris A. Vinovskis, "Schools," in Gross & Kelley, *A History of the Book in America*, 2:286–303; Jonathan Rose, "Arriving at a History of Reading," *Historically Speaking* 5, no. 3 (Jan. 2004), 36–39.

73. Catherine O'Donnell Kaplan, *Men of Letters in the Early Republic: Cultivating Forums of Citizenship* (Chapel Hill, N.C., 2008); Eastman, *Nation of Speechifiers*.

74. Mary Kelley, *Learning to Stand and Speak: Women, Education, and Public Life in America's Republic* (Chapel Hill, N.C., 2006), ch. 5. See also Louise Stevenson, "Homes, Books, and Reading," in *A History of the Book in America*, vol. 3: *The Industrial Book, 1840–1880*, ed. Scott E. Casper et al. (Chapel Hill, N.C., 2007), 319–30; Andrew Cayton, "The Authority of the Imagination in an Age of Wonder," *Journal of the Early Republic* 33, no. 1 (Spring 2013), 1–27.

75. Molly McCarthy, *The Accidental Diarist: A History of the Daily Planner in America* (Chicago, 2013); Joyce O. Appleby, *Inheriting the Revolution: The First Generation of Americans* (Cambridge, Mass., 2000); Karen Sánchez-Eppler, *Dependent States: The Child's Part in 19th-Century American Culture* (Chicago, 2005), esp. ch. 1.

76. John Lyons, *The Invention of the Self: The Hinge of Consciousness in the Eighteenth Century* (Carbondale, Ill., 1978); Dror Wahrman, *The Making of the Modern Self: Identity and Culture in Eighteenth-Century England* (New Haven, Conn., 2004); Jerrold Seigel, *The Idea of the Self: Thought and Experience in Western Europe since the Seventeenth Century* (Cambridge, 2005). See also Barbara Finkelstein, "Reading, Writing, and the Acquisition of Identity in the United States: 1790–1860," in *Regulated Children / Liberated Children: Education in Psychohistorical Perspective*, ed. Finkelstein (New York, 1979), 114–40.

77. M. H. Abrams, *The Mirror and the Lamp* (New York, 1953); Judith Plotz, "The Perpetual Messiah: Romanticism, Childhood, and the Paradoxes of Human Development," in Finkelstein, *Regulated Children / Liberated Children*, 63–95; Lucille M. Schultz, *The Young Composers: Composition's Beginnings in 19th-Century Schools* (Carbondale, Ill., 1999).

78. William Ellery Channing, "Self-Culture" (1838), reprinted in *William Ellery Channing: Selected Writings*, ed. David Robinson (New York, 1985), 221–66.

79. Horace Mann, *Second Annual Report* (1838), in Mann & Mann, *Life and Works*, 2:524; Schultz, *Young Composers*; Ian Michael, *The Teaching of English: From the 16th Century to 1870* (Cambridge, 2005); Lee Soltow & Edward Stevens, *The Rise of Literacy and the Common School in the United States* (Chicago, 1981), 96–102; Nila Banton Smith, *American Reading Instruction* (Newark, Del., 1965), 1–114. On the relationship between language and the ability to realize the divinity of the world, see Kuklick, *Churchmen and Philosophers*, 123–26.

80. "Popular Education," *North American Review* 23, no. 52 (July 1826), 49–67.

81. William H. McGuffey, "Suggestions to Teachers," in *Second Reader*. See Geraldine E. Rodgers, *History of Beginning Reading: From Teaching by "Sound" to Teaching by "Meaning"* (N.p., 2001); John Nietz, *Old Text Books: Spelling, Grammar, Reading, Arithmetic, Geography, American History, Civil Government, Physiology, Penmanship, Art, Music, as Taught in the Common Schools from Colonial Days to 1900* (Pittsburgh, 1961), 70–80; Harvey Minnich, *William Holmes McGuffey and His Readers* (New York, 1936), 65; Monaghan & Monaghan, "Schoolbooks." For some context, see also Michael, *Teaching of English*, 250–61, 278–90, 320–71; Carr et al., *Archives of Instruction*, 81–147; Courtney Weikle-Mills, *Imaginary Citizens: Child Readers and the Limits of American Independence, 1640–1868* (Baltimore, 2013).

82. *Berkshire County Whig* 8, no. 380 (June 15, 1848), 3.

83. Mann, *Second Annual Report*, 2:524.

84. Ibid., 2:510–11, 517.

85. Horace Mann, "Lecture 6: On District School Libraries," in Mann & Mann, *Life and Works*, 2:307. See also William S. Cardell, *Essay on Language, associated with the Faculties of the Mind, and as applied to Things in Nature and Art* (New York, 1825).

86. Stanley Schultz, *The Culture Factory: Boston Public Schools, 1789–1860* (New York, 1973), 17–18.

87. Bingham quoted in Patricia Cline Cohen, *A Calculating People: The Spread of Numeracy in Early America* (Chicago, 1982), 120. More generally, see Robert Middlekauff, *Ancients and Axioms* (New Haven, Conn., 1963), 75–110 154–72.

88. "School-Room Experience—Teaching Arithmetic," *North Carolina Journal of Education* 2, no. 1 (Jan. 1859), 3–7.

89. On Colburn, see James K. Bidwell & Robert C. Glason, eds., *Readings in the History of Mathematics Education* (Washington, D.C., 1970), 13.

90. On the influence of Pestalozzi and Colburn on math education, see Charles Carpenter, *History of American Schoolbooks* (Philadelphia, 1963), 141–45; Cohen, *Calculating People*, 116–49, esp. 134–38. For the South, see Knight, *Public Education*, 276–77.

91. George Martin, *Evolution of the Massachusetts Public School System* (New York, 1894), 146.

92. Warren Colburn, preface to *First Lessons in Arithmetic, on the Plan of Pestalozzi*

(1825 ed.), in Bidwell & Glason, *Readings in the History of Mathematics Education*, 15–20.

93. Colburn, "Teaching of Arithmetic" (1830), in Bidwell & Glason, *Readings in the History of Mathematics*, 24–37.

94. Charles Davies, *The Logic and Teaching of Mathematics* (1850), in Bidwell & Glason, *Readings in the History of Mathematics*, 38–61.

95. Reese, *Origins*, 103–22; Maris A. Vinovskis, *The Origins of Public High Schools: A Reexamination of the Beverly High School Controversy* (Madison, Wis., 1985); John E. Stout, *Development of High School Curricula in the North Central States from 1860 to 1918* (Chicago, 1921); George F. Miller, *The Academy System of the State of New York* (New York, 1969), 107–11; Ellwood Cubberley, *Public Education in the United States: A Study and Interpretation of American Educational History* (Boston, 1934), ch. 9. See charts in Stout, *Development*, 13–14, 17–18.

96. See table in Stout, *Development*, 62, 71–74. See also Michael Katz, *Irony of Early School Reform: Educational Innovation in Mid-19th Century Massachusetts* (Cambridge, Mass., 1968), 230; Cubberley, *Public Education*, 257. For the South, see Knight, *Public Education in the South*, ch. 8.

97. George Callcott, *History in the United States, 1800–1860* (Baltimore 1970), 58–59; see also Chauncey Jacobs, "The Development of School Textbooks in United States History from 1795–1885" (PhD diss., University of Pittsburgh, 1956), 9–12; Stout, *Development*, 62, 71–74.

98. Mansfield, *American Education*, 100.

99. A. S. Welch, *An Address delivered before the State Teachers' Institute* (Detroit, 1853), New-York Historical Society collections, New York.

100. Mansfield, *American Education*, 101.

101. "On the Study of Geometry," *North Carolina Journal of Education* 1, no. 11 (Nov. 1858).

102. Mansfield, *American Education*, 123–34.

103. Ibid., 220–22, 230.

104. Ibid., 182–205.

105. Callcott, *History*, 62.

106. Emma Willard, *History of the United States, or Republic of America* (Philadelphia, 1843), iii–iv.

107. Calvin Henderson Wiley, *First Annual Report of the General Superintendent of Common Schools* (Raleigh, N.C., 1854), 26. See also Wiley, "Address to the People of North Carolina," in *Conference of Teachers and Friends of Education* (Raleigh, N.C., 1861). On nationalism in American textbooks, see Barry Joyce, *The First U.S. History Textbooks: Constructing and Disseminating the American Tale in the Nineteenth Century* (Lanham, Md., 2015); Johann N. Neem, "History Wars, Then and Now: The Politics of Unity in American History Textbooks before the Civil War," *Common-place* 15, no. 4 (Summer 2015); Ruth Elson, *Guardians of Tradition: American Schoolbooks of the 19th Century* (Lincoln, Neb., 1964), ch. 5; Reese, *Origins*, ch. 6. For a thoughtful appraisal, see Margaret Nash, "Contested Identities: Nationalism, Regionalism, and Patriotism

in Early American Textbooks," *History of Education Quarterly* 49, no. 4 (Nov. 2009), 417–41. See also Jean Baker, *Affairs of Party: The Political Culture of Northern Democrats in the mid-19th Century* (Ithaca, N.Y., 1983), 78–87.

108. Willard, *History of the United States*, v.

109. Marcius Willson, *History of the United States* (New York, 1854), 194.

110. Charles Eliot, "The New Education," *Atlantic Monthly* (Feb. 1869). More generally, see Andrew Jewett, *Science, Democracy, and the American University: From the Civil War to the Cold War* (New York, 2012).

111. Linda Kerber, *Federalists in Dissent: Imagery and Ideology in Jeffersonian America* (Ithaca, N.Y., 1970), ch. 3; Scott L. Montgomery, "Science, Education, and Republican Values: Trends of Faith in America: 1750–1850," *Journal of Science Education and Technology* 2, no. 4 (Dec. 1993), 521–40; Jon H. Roberts & James Turner, "Religion, Science, and Higher Education," in *The Sacred and the Secular University* (Princeton, N.J., 2000), ch. 1; Johann N. Neem, "Thomas Jefferson's Philosophy of History and the Future of American Christianity," in *Prophesies of Godlessness: Predictions of America's Imminent Secularization, from the Puritans to Postmodernity*, ed. Charles T. Mathewes & Christopher McKnight Nichols (New York, 2008), 35–52.

112. Asa Gray, *Botany for Young People and Common Schools* (New York, 1858). On Gray and Darwin, see David Dobbs, "How Charles Darwin Seduced Asa Gray," *Wired Magazine* online (Apr. 2011), http://www.wired.com/2011/04/how-charles-darwin-se duced-asa-gray/.

113. See George DeBoer, *A History of Ideas in Science Education: Implications for Practice* (New York, 1991). See also Carpenter, *American Schoolbooks*, ch. 16.

114. Hiram Orcutt, *Gleanings from School-Life Experience; or, Hints to Common School Teachers, Parents, and Pupils* (Boston, 1858), ch. 5.

115. Edward Everett, "The Importance of Education in a Republic" (1839), reprinted in *Turning Points in American Educational History*, ed. David B. Tyack (Lexington, Mass., 1967), 127–31.

116. Christopher Clark et al., *Who Built America: Working People and the Nation's History* (Boston, 2007), 1:A-23–A-24. See Irvin Wyllie, *The Self-Made Man in America: The Myth of Rags to Riches* (New York, 1954).

117. See chapter 1 for a discussion of the changing economy.

118. For a good discussion, see Skrabec, *McGuffey*, ch. 18.

119. William H. McGuffey, *Newly Revised Eclectic Second Reader* (Cincinnati, 1853), 45–48.

120. Joshua Yates, ed., *Thrift in America: Capitalism and Moral Order from the Puritans to the Present* (New York, 2011).

121. This section draws from Reese, *Origins*, 119–21; Elson, *Culture Factory*, ch. 8.

122. Francis Wayland, *The Elements of Political Economy* (New York, 1837), vi, 3, 109.

123. Beecher quoted in Elson, *Guardians*, 254.

124. Meyer, *Instructed Conscience*, ch. 11.

125. Brian Balogh, *A Government Out of Sight* (New York, 2009).

126. Christopher Tomlins, *Law, Labor, and Ideology in the Early American Republic* (New York, 1993).

127. Seth Rockman, "The Unfree Origins of American Capitalism," in *The Economy of Early America: Historical Perspectives and New Directions*, ed. Cathy Matson (University Park, Pa., 2006), ch. 12.

128. James Huston, *Securing the Fruits of Labor: The American Concept of Wealth Distribution, 1765–1900* (Baton Rouge, La., 1998).

129. John Larson, "An Inquiry into the Nature and Causes of the Wealth of Nations," *Journal of the Early Republic* 35, no. 1 (Spring 2015), 1–23; Alasdair Roberts, *America's First Great Depression: Economic Crisis and Political Disorder after the Panic of 1837* (Ithaca, N.Y., 2012); Jessica Lepler, *The Many Panics of 1837: People, Politics, and the Creation of a Transatlantic Financial Crisis* (New York, 2013).

130. Wayland, *Elements*, 440–63.

131. Gabriel Abend, *The Moral Background: An Inquiry into the History of Business Ethics* (Princeton, N.J., 2014), ch. 3; Stewart Davenport, *Friends of the Unrighteous Mammon: Northern Christians and Market Capitalism, 1815–1860* (Chicago, 2008); Mark Noll, "Protestant Reasoning about Money and the Market, 1790–1860: A Preliminary Probe," in *God and Mammon: Protestants, Money, and the Market, 1790–1860*, ed. Noll (New York, 2001), ch. 12. See also Deidre McCloskey, *The Bourgeois Virtues: Ethics for an Age of Commerce* (Chicago, 2006).

132. Walthall (1857) quoted in Robert Hunt, "Organizing a New South: Education Reformers in Antebellum Alabama, 1840–1860" (PhD diss., University of Missouri, 1988), 160–61.

133. "Common Schools and Their Relations to Higher Seminaries," *New Englander* 23 (July 1848), 313–30.

134. I. W. Andrews, "Report on the connection between Schools and Colleges, and their influence upon each other; read before the Ohio State Teachers' Association, at the Annual meeting, January 1, 1852, by I. W. Andrews, Professor of Mathematics and Natural Philosophy in Marietta College," *Ohio Journal of Education* 1 (1852), 98.

135. "The Object of an Educational System," *Alabama Educational Journal* (1857), quoted in Hunt, "Organizing a New South," 283. More generally, see ibid., chs. 3–4.

136. As Taylor, *Modern Social Imaginaries*, 65, writes, "on the first level, we are always socially embedded; we learn our identities in dialogue." But, he continues, "on the level of content, what we may learn is to be an individual, have our own opinions, attain our own relation to God, our own conversion experience."

CHAPTER THREE: Politics of Education

1. Horace Mann, *First Annual Report* (1837), in *Life and Works of Horace Mann*, ed. Mary Mann & George Mann (Boston, 1891), 2:384–415.

2. This chapter is indebted to the insights of Nancy Beadie, *Education and the Creation of Capital in the Early American Republic* (New York, 2010) and "Education, Social Capital, and State Formation in Comparative Historical Perspective," *Pedagogica Historica* 46, nos. 1–2 (Feb.–Apr. 2010), 15–32; David Mathews, *Why Public*

Schools? Whose Public Schools? What Early Communities Have to Tell Us (Montgomery, Ala., 2002); Claudia Goldin & Lawrence Katz, "Human Capital and Social Capital: The Rise of Secondary Schooling in America, 1910–1940," *Journal of Interdisciplinary History* 29, no. 4 (Spring 1999), 683–723. See also Johann N. Neem, "Creating Social Capital in the Early American Republic: The View from Connecticut," *Journal of Interdisciplinary History* 39, no. 4 (Spring 2009), 471–95. On social capital, see Robert D. Putnam, *Bowling Alone: The Collapse and Revival of American Community* (New York, 2000), quote at 19; Adam Seligman, *The Problem of Trust* (Princeton, N.J., 1997), esp. 75–100; Eric M. Uslaner, "Democracy and Social Capital," in *Democracy and Trust*, ed. Mark E. Warren (New York, 1999), 121–50; Francis Fukuyama, *Trust: The Social Virtues and the Creation of Prosperity* (New York, 1995), esp. 3–12. For discussions about the definition(s) of social capital, see John Farr, "Social Capital: A Conceptual History," *Political Theory* 33 (2004), 6–33; John Field, *Social Capital* (London, 2003).

3. Carl Kaestle, *Pillars of the Republic: Common Schools and American Society, 1780–1860* (New York 1983), 13; David Jaffee, "The Village Enlightenment in New England, 1760–1820," *William and Mary Quarterly* 47, no. 3 (July 1990), 327–46.

4. Carl Kaestle & Maris Vinovskis, *Education and Social Change in Nineteenth-Century Massachusetts* (Cambridge, 1980), 20–21.

5. Alexis de Tocqueville, *Democracy in America*, trans. Arthur Goldhammer (New York, 2004), 2, pt. 2:595.

6. Oscar Handlin & Mary Flug Handlin, *Commonwealth: A Study of the Role of Government in the American Economy: Massachusetts, 1774–1861* (Cambridge, Mass., 1969); Stanley Kutler, *Privilege and Creative Destruction: The Charles River Bridge Case* (Philadelphia, 1971); Andrew Schocket, *Founding Corporate Power in Early National Philadelphia* (DeKalb, Ill., 2007); Johann N. Neem, *Creating a Nation of Joiners: Democracy and Civil Society in Early National Massachusetts* (Cambridge, Mass., 2008), ch. 1; Robert Middlekauff, *Ancients and Axioms: Secondary Education in 18th-century New England* (New York, 1963), ch. 10.

7. My discussion of academies relies on Theodore R. Sizer, *The Age of the Academies* (New York, 1964); J. M. Opal, *Beyond the Farm: National Ambitions in Rural New England* (Philadelphia, 2008), 96–125; Nancy Beadie & Kimberley Tolley, eds., *Chartered Schools: Two Hundred Years of Independent Academies in the United States, 1727–1925* (New York, 2002), esp. "Mapping the Landscape of Higher Schooling," 19–43. Beadie and Tolley's volume has been invaluable to our understanding of the important contribution academies have made to American education.

8. On curriculum, see Sizer, *Age of the Academies*; Kim Tolley, "The Rise of the Academies: Continuity or Change?," *History of Education Quarterly* 41, no. 2 (2001), 225–39; Nancy Beadie, "Market-Based Policies of School Funding: Lessons from the History of the New York Academy System," *Educational Policy* 13, no. 2 (May 1999), 296–317, at 298–99; Mary Kelley, *Learning to Stand and Speak: Women, Education, and Public Life in America's Republic* (Chapel Hill, N.C., 2006); James Mulhern, *A History of Secondary Education in Pennsylvania* (1933; New York, 1969), 315–61; George Frederick Miller, *Academy System of the State of New York* (1922; New York, 1969), 58–63;

Harriet Marr, *The Old New England Academies Founded before 1826* (New York, 1959); Edgar W. Knight, *The Academy Movement in the South* (Chapel Hill, N.C., 1919).

9. Sizer, *Age of the Academies*, 12.

10. Numbers from Tolley, "Rise of the Academies," 229.

11. Kaestle, *Pillars*, 193.

12. Maris A. Vinovskis, *The Origins of Public High Schools: A Reexamination of the Beverly High School Controversy* (Madison, Wis., 1985), 63.

13. Marr, *Old New England Academies*, 11–33.

14. Opal, *Beyond the Farm*, 104.

15. Numbers in Kelley, *Learning*, 67. See ibid., ch. 3; Lucia McMahon, *Mere Equals: The Paradox of Educated Women in the Early American Republic* (Ithaca, N.Y., 2012); Nancy Cott, *Bonds of Womanhood: "Woman's Sphere" in New England, 1780–1835* (New Haven, Conn., 1977); Margaret Nash, "A Triumph of Reason: Female Education in Academies in the New Republic," in Beadie & Tolley, *Chartered Schools*, 64–86; Jonathan D. Wells, *Women Writers and Journalists in the 19th-Century South* (Cambridge, 2011), ch. 2.

16. Nancy Beadie, "Tuition Funding for Common Schools: Education Markets and Market Regulation in Rural New York, 1815–1850," *Social Science History* 32, no. 1 (2008), 107–33; Opal, *Beyond the Farm*, 106–8, Miller, *Academy System*, 75–78; Elsie G. Hobson, *Educational Legislation and Administration in the State of New York from 1777 to 1850* (Chicago, 1918), 193–98; Fletcher Swift, *A History of Permanent Common School Funds in the United States, 1795–1905* (New York, 1911), 23–106.

17. Albert Mock, "The Midwestern Academy Movement: A Composite Picture of 514 Indiana Academies" (self-published, 1949).

18. E. E. White & T. W. Harvey, eds., *A History of Education in the State of Ohio: A Centennial Volume* (Columbus, Ohio, 1876), 10.

19. Kim Tolley, "A Chartered School in a Free Market: The Case of Raleigh Academy, 1801–1823," *Teachers College Record* 107 (January 2005), 59–88; Beadie, "Market."

20. The one exception might be what is known as the "venture" school, but to call this a profit-generating enterprise is distorting. What defined a "venture" school was that it was entirely dependent on tuition, and thus on students able and willing to pay to attend. Many were run by single teachers, often women. They were not designed to enrich their proprietors, but instead to provide a service in return for a reasonable fee. Venture school teachers were closer to music teachers today, who earn a living from offering private music lessons, but rarely can be said to be getting rich from their students. See Tolley, "Rise of the Academies," 232.

21. Robert Middlekauff, *Ancients and Axioms* (New Haven, Conn., 1963), 141.

22. Tolley, "A Chartered School in a Free Market."

23. Nancy Beadie, "Internal Improvement: The Structure and Culture of Academy Expansion in New York State in the Antebellum Era, 1820–1860," in Beadie & Tolley, *Chartered Schools*, 89–116, at 92.

24. Opal, *Beyond the Farm*, 103–4.

25. Quoted in ibid., 104.

26. William Fischel, *Making the Grade: The Economic Evolution of American School Districts* (Chicago, 2009), 13–39.

27. Opal, *Beyond the Farm.*

28. As the number of public elementary schools expanded in the first three decades of the 1800s, there were more students who were prepared to receive and desired higher education, leading to high attendance rates both in academies and, over time, in public high schools. Beadie, "Internal Improvement," 98–99.

29. Ellwood P. Cubberley, *Public Education in the United States: A Study and Interpretation of American Educational History* (Boston, 1919, 1934), 249.

30. Data in the preceding three paragraphs from Hobson, *Legislation*, 38–46, 111, 115, 120–21, 138–44, 193–98; Miller, *Academy System*, 101; Beadie, "Market."

31. Beadie, "Market," 304–10.

32. Miller, *Academy System*, 65–100; Beadie, "Tuition Funding," 126. For a list of legislation providing special support to individual academies, see Hobson, *Legislation*, 193–98.

33. Edgar W. Knight, *Public Education in the South* (Boston, 1922), 89–93, 139–45, 164–67, 228–34; Robert H. White, *Development of the Tennessee State Educational Organization, 1796–1929* (Kingsport, Tenn., 1929), 6–77; Kathryn Pippin, "The Common School Movement in the South, 1840–1860" (PhD diss., University of North Carolina, 1977), 176–78.

34. Nancy Beadie, "Academy Students in the Mid-19th Century: Social Geography, Demography, and the Culture of Academy Attendance," *History of Education Quarterly* 41, no. 2 (Summer, 2001), 252–63, at 255–57; Beadie, "Internal Improvement," 100–101; Kelley, *Learning*, 81–83. See also Opal, *Beyond the Farm*, 106–7; Claudia Goldin & Lawrence Katz, "'Virtues' of the Past: Education in the First Hundred Years of the Republic," NBER Working Paper 9958 (Cambridge, Mass., 2003) 44, http://www.nber.org/papers/w9958.pdf.

35. Mark Boonshoft, "Creating a 'Civilized Nation': Religion, Social Capital, and the Cultural Foundations of Early American State Formation" (PhD diss., The Ohio State University, 2015).

36. Adams quoted in George Martin, *Evolution of the Massachusetts Public School System* (New York, 1894), 128–30; Neem, *Creating a Nation of Joiners*, 27–28.

37. Quoted in F. Rudolph, ed., *Essays on Education in the Early Republic* (Cambridge, Mass., 1965), 66.

38. Jonathan Messerli, *Horace Mann: A Biography* (New York, 1972), 224–25.

39. Regents and Clinton from Hobson, *Legislation*, 26.

40. James Henry, *An Address upon Education in the Common Schools* (1843), 24, quoted in Merle Curti, *The Social Ideas of American Educators* (New York, 1935), 27.

41. On Murphey, see Hugh Lefler & Albert Newsome, *North Carolina: The History of a Southern State* (Chapel Hill, N.C., 1954), ch. 21; John Larson, *Internal Improvement: National Public Works and the Promise of Popular Government in the Early United States* (Chapel Hill, N.C., 2001), 98–105. Report printed in Charles Coon, ed., *The*

Beginnings of Public Education in North Carolina: A Documentary History, 1790–1840 (Raleigh, N.C., 1908), 1:105–10.

42. Wolcott (1825) quoted in Orwin B. Griffin, *The Evolution of the Connecticut State School System* (New York, 1928), 23.

43. This section draws from Goldin & Katz, "Virtues."

44. Fischel, *Making the Grade*, 38–39.

45. Kaestle, *Pillars*, ch. 1.

46. James Herring, *Autobiography*, unpublished manuscript, 1863, New-York Historical Society collections, New York (NYHS).

47. Wayne Fuller, *The Old Country School: The Story of Rural Education in the Middle West* (Chicago, 1982), 26–27. See also Malcolm Rohrbough, *The Trans-Appalachian Frontier: People, Societies, and Institutions, 1775–1850* (New York, 1978), 152–56, 183–84, 215–16.

48. Example from Timothy L. Smith, "Protestant Schooling and American Nationality, 1800–1850," *Journal of American History* 53, no. 4 (Mar. 1967), 679–95, at 688.

49. Mathews, *Why Public Schools?*, 54–59.

50. Fuller, *The Old Country School*, 46–48; Paul Theobald, *Call School: Rural Education in the Middle West to 1918* (Carbondale, Ill., 1995), 54–59; Beadie, *Education*, ch. 9; David Tyack, *The One Best System: A History of American Urban Education* (Cambridge, Mass., 1974), 16–21.

51. Atwater quoted in David Tyack, *Seeking Common Ground: Public Schools in a Diverse Society* (Cambridge, Mass., 2003), 129.

52. *North East, New York, School District No. 8 Records*, NYHS.

53. Donald H. Parkerson & Jo Ann Parkerson, *The Emergence of the Common School in the U.S. Countryside* (Lewiston, N.Y., 1988), 39–56; Michael Katz, *The Irony of Early School Reform: Educational Innovation in Mid-19th Century Massachusetts* (Cambridge, Mass., 1968).

54. Beadie, *Education*, 139.

55. Mary Babson Fuhrer, *A Crisis of Community: The Trials and Transformation of a New England Town, 1815–1848* (Chapel Hill, N.C., 2014), 132–35; Robert A. Gross & John Esty, "The Spirit of Concord," *Education Week* (Oct. 5, 1994).

56. Kaestle & Vinovskis, *Education and Social Change*, 150–53.

57. Theobald, *Call School*, 54–55.

58. Kaestle & Vinovskis, *Education and Social Change*, 238–39 (Mass.), table A2.1, and 15 (N.Y.), table 2.2.

59. Kaestle, *Pillars*, 10–11.

60. Goldin & Katz, "Virtues," 22–24.

61. Sun Go & Peter Lindert, "The Uneven Rise of American Public Schools to 1850," *Journal of Economic History* 70, no. 1 (Mar. 2010), 1–26.

62. Here I build on the insights of scholars in American Political Development. See Richard R. John, "American Political Development and Political History," in *The Oxford Handbook of American Political Development*, ed. Richard Valelly, Suzanne

Mettler, & Robert Lieberman (New York, 2016), 185–206, and "Governmental Institutions as Agents of Change: Rethinking American Political Development in the Early Republic, 1787–1835," *Studies in American Political Development* 11, no. 2 (1997), 347–80. On the police power, see Gary Gerstle, *Liberty and Coercion: The Paradox of American Government* (Princeton, N.J., 2015), ch. 2; William J. Novak, *The People's Welfare: Law and Regulation in 19th-Century America* (Chapel Hill, N.C., 1996).

63. Robert Middlekauff, *Ancients and Axioms: Secondary Education in 18th-Century New England* (New Haven, Conn., 1963).

64. Hobson, *Legislation*, ch. 6.

65. Thomas Finegan, *Free Schools: A Documentary History of the Free School Movement in New York State* (Albany, N.Y., 1921), ch. 3. Act reprinted in ibid., 43–51. See also Lawrence Cremin, *The American Common School: An Historic Conception* (New York, 1951), 97–98; Hobson, *Legislation*, 30–34.

66. S. S. Randall, *The Common School System of New York* (1851), 15; John L. Brooke, *Columbia Rising: Civil Life on the Upper Hudson from the Revolution to the Age of Jackson* (Chapel Hill, N.C., 2010), 423.

67. James W. Taylor, *The Ohio School System and School Laws in Force* (Cincinnati, 1857), 142–46; Edward Miller, *History of Educational Legislation in Ohio from 1803 to 1850* (Chicago, 1920), 19–20.

68. Miller, *History*, 43.

69. Ibid., 21.

70. E. E. White & T. W. Harvey, eds., *A History of Education in the State of Ohio: A Centennial Volume* (Columbus, Ohio, 1876), 336.

71. Ibid., 445–49.

72. James Wickersham, *A History of Education in Pennsylvania* (New York, 1969), 270–71, 313–16.

73. For an overview, see John Hardin Best, "Education in the Forming of the American South," *History of Education Quarterly* 36, no. 1 (Spring 1996), 39–51; Kaestle, *Pillars*, ch. 8; Kathleen D. McCarthy, *American Creed: Philanthropy and the Rise of Civil Society, 1700–1865* (Chicago, 2003), pt. 2. When the South is compared with the North, it appears to be behind, but when placed in a global context, the South appears closer to the North than to other countries. See Peter Kolchin, *A Sphinx on the American Land: The Nineteenth-Century South in Comparative Perspective* (Baton Rouge, La., 2003); Ed Ayers, "What We Talk about When We Talk about the South," in Ayers et al., *All Over the Map* (Baltimore, 1996).

74. Donald Ratcliffe, "The Right to Vote and the Rise of Democracy, 1787–1828," *Journal of the Early Republic* 33, no. 2 (Summer 2013), 219–54; Andrew W. Robertson, "Did the Election of Andrew Jackson Usher in the Age of the Common Man?," *Common-place* 9, no. 1 (Oct. 2008); Fletcher M. Green, "Democracy in the Old South," *Journal of Southern History* 12, no. 1 (Feb. 1946), 3–23.

75. Sally Hadden, *Slave Patrols: Law and Violence in Virginia and the Carolinas* (Cambridge, Mass., 2001); Peter Wallenstein, *From Slave South to New South: Public Policy in 19th-Century Georgia* (Chapel Hill, N.C., 1987), 43–44; Harry S. Laver,

"Rethinking the Social Role of the Militia: Community-Building in Antebellum Kentucky," *Journal of Southern History* 68, no. 4 (Nov. 2002), 777–816. On evangelicals, see John Kuykendall, *Southern Enterprize: The Work of National Evangelical Societies in the Antebellum South* (Westport, Conn., 1982); Anne C. Loveland, *Southern Evangelicals and the Social Order, 1800–1860* (Baton Rouge, La., 1980).

76. American Bible Society statistic in John L. Brooke, "Cultures of Nationalism, Movements of Reform and the Composite-Federal Polity: From Revolutionary Settlement to Antebellum Crisis," *Journal of the Early Republic* 29, no. 1 (2009), 1–33. Recent work includes Jonathan D. Wells, *The Origins of the Southern Middle Class, 1800–1861* (Chapel Hill, N.C., 2004), ch. 4; John G. Deal, "Middle-Class Benevolent Societies in Antebellum Norfolk, Virginia," in *The Southern Middle Class in the Long Nineteenth Century*, ed. Jonathan Daniel Wells & Jennifer R. Green (Baton Rouge, La., 2011), 84–104; Johann N. Neem, "Civil Society and American Nationalism, 1776–1865," in *Politics and Partnerships: The Role of Voluntary Associations in America's Political Past and Present*, ed. Elisabeth Clemens & Doug Guthrie (Chicago, 2011), 29–53; Timothy Lockley, *Welfare and Charity in the Antebellum South* (Gainesville, Fla., 2007); John W. Quist, *Restless Visionaries: The Social Roots of Antebellum Reform in Alabama and Michigan* (Baton Rouge, La., 1998); Elizabeth Varon, *We Mean to Be Counted: White Women and Politics in Antebellum Virginia* (Chapel Hill, N.C., 1998); Suzanne Lebsock, *The Free Women of Petersburg: Status and Culture in a Southern Town, 1784–1860* (New York, 1984).

77. Wells, *Origins*; Lockley, *Welfare and Charity*, ch. 5; Bruce Eelman, *Entrepreneurs in the Southern Upcountry: Commercial Culture in Spartanburg, South Carolina, 1845–1880* (Athens, Ga., 2008), ch. 3.

78. John G. Richardson, "Settlement Patterns and Governing Structures of Nineteenth-Century School Systems," *American Journal of Education* 92, no. 2 (Feb. 1984), 178–206; Albert Ogden Porter, *County Government in Virginia: A Legislative History, 1607–1904* (New York, 1947), 155–226; Charles Sydnor, *Gentlemen Freeholders: Political Practices in Washington's Virginia* (Chapel Hill, N.C., 1952), esp. ch. 6; Robert M. Ireland, *The County Courts in Antebellum Kentucky* (Lexington, Ky., 1972).

79. Erik Mathisen, "State Formation in Mississippi between Slavery and Redemption" (PhD diss., University of Pennsylvania, 2009); Charles C. Bolton, *Poor Whites of the Antebellum South: Tenants and Laborers in Central North Carolina and Northeast Mississippi* (Durham, N.C., 1994), 114–16; J. Mills Thornton III, *Politics and Power in a Slave Society: Alabama, 1800–1860* (Baton Rouge, La., 1978), 59–60.

80. Lacy K. Ford, "Ideology of the Old South's Plain Folk," in *Plain Folk of the Old South Revisited*, ed. Samuel C. Hyde Jr. (Baton Rouge, La., 1997), 205–27; Fletcher M. Green, "Democracy in the Old South," *Journal of Southern History* 12, no. 1 (1946), 3–23.

81. Knight, *Public Education in the South*, 129–33, 169–70, 215–29 (Middleton quote, p. 130); Eelman, *Entrepreneurs*, ch. 3; Henry Thompson, *The Establishment of the Public School System of South Carolina* (Columbia, S.C., 1927), 5–9; Pippin, "Common School Movement," 160–63.

82. Knight, *Public Education in the South*, 143–45, 232–33.

83. Ibid., 255–58; Stephen B. Weeks, *History of Public School Education in Arkansas*, United States Bureau of Education Bulletin 500 (Washington, D.C., 1912), esp. ch. 3; Josiah Shinn, *History of Education in Arkansas* (Washington, D.C., 1900), ch. 1.

84. Mathews, *Why Public Schools?*, 134.

85. Ibid., chs. 6, 8, statistic at 107–13; Thornton, *Politics and Power*, 293–95, 300–302.

86. Both Knight, *Public Education in the South*, 246–50, and Pippin, "Common School Movement," 181–85, argue that enrollments grew despite decentralization rather than because of it, as do many other scholars. Yet, perhaps it was the opposite: when responsibility was placed at the local levels, and citizens were spurred to action, legislators could draw on existing social capital. See, for example, Nita K. Pyburn, "Public Schools in Mississippi before 1860," *Journal of Mississippi History* 21 (1959), 113–30. See also William Weathersby, *A History of Educational Legislation in Mississippi from 1798 to 1860* (Chicago, 1921), chs. 2–5.

87. Pippin, "Common School Movement," 156, from Avery Craven, *Growth of Southern Nationalism* (Baton Rouge, La., 1953), 170. See also Herman G. Richey, "Reappraisal of the State School Systems of the Pre-Civil-War Period," *Elementary School Journal* 41, no. 2 (Oct. 1940), 118–29.

88. Lockley, *Welfare and Charity*, 191.

89. William Ellis, *A History of Education in Kentucky* (Lexington, Ky., 2011), 22.

90. Milton S. Heath, *Constructive Liberalism: The Role of the State in Economic Development in Georgia to 1860* (Cambridge, Mass., 1954).

91. The report is reprinted in Coon, *Beginnings of Public Education*, 2:826–49.

92. Summary of the 1841 law in *Annual Reports for the Department of the Interior for the fiscal year ended June 30, 1897: Report of the Commissioner of Education* (Washington, D.C., 1898), 2:1422.

93. Edgar W. Knight, *Public School Education in North Carolina* (New York, 1916 [1969]), 145; Pippin, "Common School Movement," 192.

94. Lockley, *Welfare and Charity*, 183–84.

95. Mann quoted in Fischel, *Making the Grade*, 49. See also "School Supervisors," *Massachusetts Teacher* 3, no. 5 (May 1850), 129–37.

96. This is the classic Madisonian dilemma. See James Madison, "Vices of the Political System of the United States" (April 1787), in *James Madison: Writings*, ed. Jack Rakove (New York, 1999), 69–80.

97. Thomas L. Haskell, ed., *The Authority of Experts: Studies in History and Theory* (Bloomington, Ind., 1984).

98. Handlin & Handlin, *Commonwealth*; L. Ray Gunn, *The Decline of Authority: Public Economic Policy and Political Development in New York, 1800–1860* (Ithaca, N.Y., 1988); Thomas Bender, *Community and Social Change in America* (New Brunswick, N.J., 1975); Richard R. Lingeman, *Small Town America: A Narrative History, 1620–the Present* (New York, 1980); Neem, *Creating a Nation of Joiners*, ch. 5.

99. Jon C. Teaford, *The Municipal Revolution in America: Origins of Modern Ur-*

ban Government, 1650–1825 (Chicago, 1975); Martin Schiesl, *The Politics of Efficiency: Municipal Administration and Reform in America, 1800–1920* (Berkeley, Calif., 1977); Bender, *Community and Social Change*; John Higham, *From Boundlessness to Consolidation: The Transformation of American Culture, 1848–1860* (Ann Arbor, Mich., 1969).

100. Diane Ravitch, *The Great School Wars, 1805–1973: A History of the Public Schools as a Battlefield of Social Change* (New York, 1974).

101. Stanley Schultz, *The Culture Factory: Boston Public Schools, 1789–1860* (New York, 1973), 7–72, 79–81, 132–53.

102. Ellis, *Education in Kentucky*, 9–10; Nancy Jean Rosenbloom, "Cincinnati's Common Schools: The Politics of Reform, 1829–1853 (Ph.D. diss., University of Rochester, 1981), 130–32.

103. Cubberley, *Public Education*, 159; Cubberley, *Public School Administration* (Boston, 1916), 58. For professionalization and its challengers, see Tyack, *One Best System*; Charles L. Glenn Jr., *The Myth of the Common School* (Amherst, Mass., 1987), chs. 6–8.

104. Orestes Brownson, "Education of the People," *Boston Quarterly Review* 2 (Oct. 1839), 393–434.

105. Tyler quoted in Lockley, *Welfare and Charity*, 176.

106. Douglas R. Egerton, *Charles Fenton Mercer and the Trial of National Conservatism* (Jackson, Miss., 1989), ch. 8; Cameron Addis, *Jefferson's Vision for Education, 1760–1845* (New York, 2003); Johann N. Neem, "'To diffuse knowledge more generally through the mass of the people': Thomas Jefferson on Individual Freedom and the Distribution of Knowledge," in *Light and Liberty: Thomas Jefferson and the Power of Knowledge*, ed. Robert M. S. McDonald (Charlottesville, Va., 2012), 47–74.

107. Thomas Jefferson, "A Bill for the More General Diffusion of Knowledge" in *Thomas Jefferson: Writings*, ed. Merrill Peterson (New York, 1984), 365–73.

108. Jefferson to Joseph Cabell (Feb. 2, 1816), in Peterson, *Writings*, 1377–81.

109. For other perspectives, see Addis, *Jefferson's Vision*, ch. 2; Maurizio Valsania, *Nature's Man: Thomas Jefferson's Philosophical Anthropology* (Charlottesville, Va., 2013), 100–101.

110. Jefferson to Joseph Cabell (Feb. 2, 1816), in Peterson, *Writings*, 1377–81. See also Jefferson to John Cartwright (June 5, 1824), in ibid., 1492–93.

111. George Faber Clark, *A History of the Town of Norton, Bristol County, from 1669–1859* (Boston, 1859), 276–77.

112. Henry Suzzallo, *The Rise of Local School Supervision in Massachusetts* (New York, 1906), 123; Cremin, *American Common School*, 91–95.

113. Jonathan Earle, "Marcus Morton and the Dilemma of Jacksonian Antislavery in Massachusetts, 1817–1849," *Massachusetts Historical Review* 4 (2002), 60–87.

114. See Stanley Kutler, *Privilege and Creative Destruction: The Charles River Bridge Case* (Philadelphia, 1971).

115. Neem, *Creating a Nation of Joiners*, 131–33.

116. Details of Barnard's life and quotes in above three paragraphs from Robert B. Downs, *Henry Barnard* (Boston, 1977), ch. 1; Edith Nye MacMullen, *In the Cause of*

True Education; Henry Barnard & 19th-century School Reform (New Haven, Conn., 1991), chs. 1–2.

117. Griffin, *Evolution*, 23–24.

118. Christopher Collier, *Connecticut's Public Schools: A History, 1650–2000* (Orange, Conn., 2009), ch. 4.

119. Downs, *Barnard*, ch. 2; MacMullen, *In the Cause of True Education*, 94–99.

120. Barnard to Mann, June 11, 1842, in *Henry Barnard, American Educator*, ed. Vincent Lannie (New York, 1974), 72–73.

121. Mann to Barnard, March 2, 1842, quoted in MacMullen, *In the Cause of True Education*, 97.

122. Johann N. Neem, "Path Dependence and the Emergence of Common Schools: Ohio to 1853," *Journal of Policy History* 28, no. 1 (Jan. 2016), 48–80.

123. Kaestle, *Pillars*, 155; Gunn, *Decline*, 86–87.

124. Senate Committee on Literature report (1854), quoted in Gunn, *Decline*, 209. See ibid., 204–16. The railroad commission was abolished in 1857 when the commissioners recommended it. It was later discovered that the commissioners had been bribed by the railroads.

125. Kaestle, *Pillars*, 112–13.

126. Donald Scott McPherson, "The Fight against Free Schools in Pennsylvania: Popular Opposition to the Common School System, 1834–1875" (PhD diss., University of Pittsburgh, 1977), 140.

127. Calvin Henderson Wiley, *First Annual Report of the General Superintendent of Common Schools* (Raleigh, N.C., 1854).

128. Perry quoted in Robert Eno Hunt, "Organizing a New South: Education Reformers in Antebellum Alabama, 1840–1860" (PhD diss., University of Missouri, 1988), 55–56.

129. Martin, *Evolution*, 204–5; Kaestle & Vinovskis, *Education and Social Change*, 160–61.

130. Elsie G. Hobson, *Educational Legislation and Administration in the State of New York from 1777 to 1850* (Chicago, 1918), ch. 4, quote on 66.

131. Wickersham, *Pennsylvania*, 315–16.

132. McPherson, "Fight," ch. 2.

133. Ibid., 109–44; Wickersham, *Pennsylvania*, 505–8, 520, 522–26.

134. Wickersham, *Pennsylvania*, 527–35.

135. Cubberley, *Public Education in the United States*, 158.

136. Knight, *Public Education in the South*, 89–93, 139–45, 164–67, 228–34; Robert H. White, *Development of the Tennessee State Educational Organization, 1796–1929* (Kingsport, Tenn., 1929), 6–77; Pippin, "Common School Movement," 176–78.

137. Marc Kruman, *Parties and Politics in North Carolina, 1836–1865* (Baton Rouge, La., 1983), 83; Knight, *North Carolina*, 162.

138. Barbara Finkelstein, "In Fear of Childhood: Relationships between Parents and Teachers in Popular Primary Schools in the Nineteenth Century," *History of Child-

hood Quarterly 3 (Winter 1976), 321–35; David Tyack, "The Tribe and the Common School: Community Control in Rural Education," *American Quarterly* 24, no. 1 (Mar. 1972), 3–19.

139. Both quotes from Kaestle, *Pillars*, 150.

140. Beadie, "Education, Social Capital, and State Formation"; Mathews, *Why Public Schools?*; Michael Katz, *Reconstructing American Education* (Cambridge, Mass., 1987), 32–37, 41–53; Katz, *The Irony of Early School Reform: Educational Innovation in Mid-19th Century Massachusetts* (Cambridge, Mass., 1968); Kaestle, *Pillars*, 150–54.

141. Henry Barnard to Horace Mann, May 29, 1842, in Lannie, *Henry Barnard: American Educator*, 12–13.

142. Fuller, *Old Country School*, 32–38; Theobald, *Call School*, 50–54; McPherson, "Fight," ch. 10; Kaestle & Vinovskis, *Education and Social Change*, ch. 8. On the tension between evangelical and moderate understandings of self-formation, see Philip Greven, *The Protestant Temperament: Patterns of Child-Rearing, Religious Experience, and the Self in Early America* (New York, 1977).

143. *Lebanon County Republican* (Feb. 1834), quoted in McPherson, "Fight," 286.

144. *Pottsville Miner's Journal* (Nov. 15, 1834), quoted in McPherson, "Fight," 287.

145. *Raleigh Register* (1829), in Coon, *Beginnings of Public Education*, 1:431–33. See also Alan Taylor, "The Virtue of an Educated Voter," *American Scholar* 85, no. 4 (Autumn 2016), 18–27.

146. Discussion from Parkerson & Parkerson, *Emergence of the Common Schools in the U.S. Countryside* (Hackley discussed in pp. 51–52); Fuller, *Old Country School*, ch. 3.

147. The amount spent per student increased about 130 percent as voters invested more money per child; see Kaestle & Vinovskis, *Education and Social Change*, 186–91. In New York, 75 percent of school revenue came from tuition in 1825, but only 22.4 percent in 1850 and 7.9 percent in 1870; see Go & Lindert, "Uneven Rise," 1–26, 5–6; Sun Go, "The Rise and Centralization of America's Public Schools in the 19th Century" (PhD diss., University of California, Davis, 2009), 63. In Massachusetts in 1850, about 75 percent of school income came from public funds while Ohio schools derived 67 percent from public sources. Nationally by 1870, American schools had an income of $95,402,726, of which two-thirds came from the public sector. Of this amount, in 1850 about 12 percent came from endowed funds, a number which dwindled to 6 percent in 1870. Numbers are from Lawrence Cremin, *American Education: The National Experience, 1783–1876* (New York, 1980), 182–85.

148. In 1850 the fifteen northern states spent on average $2.45 per pupil, of which $1.50 came from mostly local taxes, $.66 from state funds, and $.24 from tuition. That same year the fifteen southern states spent $4.67 per pupil, of which $.84 was from mostly local taxes, $1.23 from state funds, and $2.52 from tuition. Nationally by 1873 the bulk of school revenue came from taxes, of which about 17.3 percent was levied at the state level and the rest collected locally. Sun Go & Peter Lindert, "The Curious Dawn of American Public Schools," NBER Working Paper 13335 (2007), 32, http://papers.ssrn.com/sol3/papers.cfm?abstract_id=1008827.; Go, "Rise," 64.

149. Go & Lindert, "Uneven Rise"; Go, "Rise," ch. 2; Peter Lindert, *Growing Public: Social Spending and Economic Growth since the 18th Century* (Cambridge, 2004), 1:104–7, 122–27.

150. Fischel, *Making the Grade*, 14–15.

151. Hobson, *Legislation*, 108–10.

152. Go, "Rise."

153. Beadie, "Tuition Funding," 118, table 3.

154. Kaestle & Vinovskis, *Education and Social Change*, 16.

155. Fischel, *Making the Grade*, 63–64; Kaestle & Vinovskis, *Education and Social Change*, table A7.5.

156. Quotes and discussion from Theobald, *Call School*, ch. 2.

157. Neem, "Path Dependence"; Ira Katznelson & Margaret Weir, *Schooling for All: Class, Race, and the Decline of the Democratic Ideal* (New York, 1985).

158. McPherson, "Fight," 132.

159. William Russell, *An Address, delivered at a Meeting Held in Dorchester . . . for the Purpose of Forming an Association of Teachers, for Norfolk County* (Boston, 1830).

160. C. H. Wiley, "Directions for the Formation of County and District Educational Associations," *North Carolina Journal of Education* 1, no. 1 (Jan. 1858); "Educational Associations," *North Carolina Journal of Education* 1, no. 1 (Jan 1858).

161. Henry Barnard, *First Annual Report of the Board of Commissioners of Common Schools in Connecticut, together with the First Annual Report of the Secretary of the Board* (Hartford, Conn., 1839), 9. The power of organization was something Americans were learning in all kinds of places. See Neem, *Creating a Nation of Joiners*, ch. 4.

162. *First Annual Report of the Wisconsin Teachers' Association, with the Constitution and Proceedings, and the Addresses delivered at the Annual Meeting, August 9th and 10th, 1854* (Madison, Wis., 1854), NYHS.

163. Cremin, *Common School*, 50–51. For Pennsylvania, see Wickersham, *Pennsylvania*, 494–511, 642–51.

164. Cremin, *Common School*, 101; Kaestle, *Pillars*, 150; Finegan, *Free Schools*, chs. 6–7.

165. Go, "Rise," 75–77; Ellwood Cubberley, *Public Education in the United States* (Boston, 1919), 148–51.

166. Cremin, *Common School*, 100–102; Finegan, *Free Schools*, chs. 7–8.

167. Cremin, *Common School*, 101–3; Finegan, *Free Schools*, ch. 10; Fischel, *Making the Grade*, 60.

168. Quote in Wickersham, *Pennsylvania*, 321.

169. Thaddeus Stevens, "On the School Law" (speech delivered to the Pennsylvania House of Representatives, Apr. 11, 1835), in *The Selected Papers of Thaddeus Stevens*, vol. 1: *January 1814–March 1865*, ed. Beverly Wilson Palmer & Holly Byers Ochoa (Pittsburgh, 1997), 19–29.

170. Shunk, *Annual Report* (1838), quoted in McPherson, "Fight," 68.

171. Quoted in McPherson, "Fight," 76.

172. Cremin, *Common School*, 107–9; McPherson, "Fight," chs. 15–18.

173. Robin Einhorn, *American Taxation, American Slavery* (Chicago, 2008), 219–30, 314 n. 37.

174. J. Mills Thornton III, "Fiscal Policy and the Failure of Radical Reconstruction in the Lower South," in *Region, Race, and Reconstruction: Essays in Honor of C. Vann Woodward,* ed. J. Morgan Kousser & James M. McPherson (New York, 1982), 349–94, at 351–54.

175. Einhorn, *American Taxation, American Slavery.* See also Pippin, "Common School Movement," 111–19, 153–56; John J. Wallis, Richard E. Sylla, & Arthur Grinath III, "Sovereign Debt and Repudiation: The Emerging-Market Debt Crisis in the U.S. States, 1839–1843," NBER Working paper 10753 (2004).

176. John Joseph Caldwell, *Letters on Popular Education, Addressed to the People of North Carolina* (1832), Letter 2, in Coon, *Beginnings of Public Education,* 2:554.

177. Quoted in Pippin, "Common School Movement," 154.

178. Harry Watson, "The Man with the Dirty Black Beard: Race, Class, and Schools in the Antebellum South," *Journal of the Early Republic* 32, no. 1 (Spring 2012), 1–26.

179. Thornton, "Fiscal Policy," 356–57.

180. Pippin, "Common School Movement," 196–97; Thornton, "Fiscal Policy," 378–82; Richey, "Reappraisal," esp. 120–21.

181. As David Tyack, *One Best System,* 27, put it, too often communities were "oblivious of possible local tyranny and parochialism," while reformers did not understand "how fragile, finally, is a sense of voluntary community in a mass society." See also Jürgen Herbst, "Nineteenth-Century Schools between Community and State: The Cases of Prussia and the United States," *History of Education Quarterly* 42, no. 3 (Fall 2002), 317–41.

CHAPTER FOUR: Teachers and Students

1. John W. Chadwick, "The World's Teachers. A Poem, delivered at the Semi-Annual Examination of the Bridgewater State Normal School, Tuesday, Feb. 15, 1859," Massachusetts Historical Society Collections, Boston (MHS).

2. Rev. R. C. Waterston, *Address at the Third Triennial Convention of the West Newton State Normal School, July 26, 1848* (Boston, 1848).

3. Henry Barnard, *School Architecture; or, Contributions to the Improvement of School-Houses in the United States* (New York, 1848), 41.

4. Electa Lincoln diary, Feb. and Apr. 12, 1849, MHS.

5. Jürgen Herbst, *And Sadly Teach: Teacher Education and Professionalization in American Culture* (Madison, Wis., 1989), 22–23. California statistic from Barry Joyce, *The First U.S. History Textbooks: Constructing and Disseminating the American Tale in the 19th Century* (Lanham, Md., 2015), 29. See also Carl Kaestle & Maris Vinovskis, *Education and Social Change in 19th-Century Massachusetts* (New York, 1980), 153–55.

6. *An Ohio Schoolmistress: The Memoirs of Irene Hardy,* ed. Louis Filler (Kent, Ohio, 1980), vii–ix.

7. All quotes from ibid.

8. David B. Tyack & Elisabeth Hansot, *Learning Together: A History of Coeducation in American Schools* (New Haven, Conn., 1990), 60–69.

9. Caroline Cowles Richards, *Village Life in America, 1852–1872* (New York, 1913), 21–22.

10. Calvin Henderson Wiley, *First Annual Report of the General Superintendent of Common Schools* (Raleigh, N.C., 1854), 23–24. Another example from North Carolina is Archibald Murphey's "Report on Education" (1817), in *The Beginnings of Public Education in North Carolina: A Documentary History, 1790–1840*, ed. Charles Coon (Raleigh, N.C., 1908), 1:140–41.

11. William Holmes McGuffey, "Suggestions to Teachers," in *The Eclectic Second Reader* (Cincinnati, 1836; repr., Milford, Mich., 1982).

12. "Abraham Lincoln to Jesse W. Fell, Enclosing Autobiography," in *American Lives: An Anthology of Autobiographical Writing*, ed. Robert F. Sayre (Madison, Wis., 1994), 351.

13. American Normal School Association, *American Normal Schools: Their Theory, their Workings, and their Results, as Embodied in the Proceedings of the First Annual Convention of the American Normal School Association, held at Trenton, New Jersey, August 19 and 2, 1859* (New York, 1860), 17.

14. George B. Emerson, *The Schoolmaster* (New York, 1842), in *The School and the Schoolmaster: A Manual for the Use of Teachers*, by Alonzo Potter & George B. Emerson (New York, 1842), 273.

15. Orcutt, *Reminiscences of School Life* (1898), excerpted in Barbara Finkelstein, *Governing the Young: Teacher Behavior in Popular Primary Schools in 19th-Century America* (New York, 1989), 159–67.

16. John Greenleaf Whittier, "A Winter Idyl" (1866).

17. John Greenleaf Whittier, "To My Old Schoolmaster" (1851).

18. Richard Penn Smith, "The Village School," *Atlantic Souvenir* (1830).

19. Bye-Laws of Groton, Relative to Schools; and Instructions of the School Committee. 1805 (Cambridge, Mass., 1806), in Groton, Massachusetts, School Records 1806–69, MS. N-1332, MHS.

20. Lewis quoted in Edward Adams Richardson, *Moors School at Old District No. 2: The Story of a District School* (Ayer, Mass.), 21–22, MHS.

21. See William J. Reese, *Testing Wars in the Public Schools: A Forgotten History* (Cambridge, Mass., 2013), for a good discussion. See also David Hogan, "Modes of Discipline: Affective Individualism and Pedagogical Reform in New England, 1820–1850," *American Journal of Education* 99, no. 1 (Winter 1990), 1–56.

22. Thomas Palmer, *The Teacher's Manual: Being an Exposition of an Efficient and Economical System of Education, Suited to the Wants of a Free People* (Boston, 1840), 28–29, 51.

23. E. D. Mansfield, *American Education: Its Principles and Elements: Dedicated to the Teachers of the United States* (New York, 1851), 77–82.

24. Emerson, *The Schoolmaster*, 311, 314.

25. Palmer, *Teacher's Manual*, 87–89, 94–98.

26. John Ogden, "To What Extent Can the Art of Teaching Be Taught in Our Normal Schools? What Are the Best Methods of Doing This?," in American Normal School Association, *American Normal Schools*, 70.

27. Richardson, *Moors School*, 22.

28. Frank C. Morse diary, Jan. 2, 1855, in Frank C. Morse Papers, MHS.

29. Leavitt Thaxter Norton diary, 1858–60, Oct. 5 and 18, Nov. 11, Nov. 22, and Nov. 29, 1858, MHS.

30. Morse diary, Jan. 8 and 9, 1855, MHS.

31. Ibid., Jan. 26, 1855.

32. Ibid., Feb. 1, 1855.

33. Finkelstein, *Governing the Young*; Ohio Teachers Association, *A History of Education in the State of Ohio* (Columbus, Ohio, 1876), ch. 2.

34. Recited by William H. Clarke, *Mid Century Memories* (n.d.), cited in Frank Smith, *A History of Dedham* (Dedham, Mass., 1936), 140.

35. James Baldwin, *In My Youth* (1915), quoted in Finkelstein, *Governing the Young*, 97.

36. Michael Katz, *Irony of Early School Reform: Educational Innovation in Mid-Nineteenth Century Massachusetts* (Cambridge, Mass., 1968), 115–60; Myra Glenn, "School Discipline and Punishment in Antebellum America," *Journal of the Early Republic* 1, no. 4 (Winter 1981), 395–408.

37. A. S. Welch, *An Address delivered before the State Teachers' Institute* (Detroit, 1853), New-York Historical Society collections, New York (NYHS).

38. Journal of Electa Lincoln (Wallton), 1848, MHS. Lincoln's biography available in Mary Elvira Elliott et al., *Representative Women of New England*, ed. Julia Ward Howe (Boston, 1904), 246–49.

39. For context see Herbst, *And Sadly Teach*, ch. 2.

40. Edgar Knight, ed., *Reports on European Education* (New York, 1930), 3–13, introduction.

41. J. A. Green, ed., *Pestalozzi's Educational Writings* (New York, 1912); Sarah Anne Carter, "Object Lessons in American Culture" (PhD diss., Harvard University, 2010), chs. 1–2; Gerald Lee Gutek, *Joseph Neef and the Americanization of Pestalozzianism* (University, Ala., 1978); Maria Laubach & Joan Smith, "Educating with Heart, Head, and Hands," *American Educational History Journal* 38, nos. 1–2 (Spring 2011), 341–56.

42. Calvin Stowe, "Report on Elementary Public Instruction in Europe," in Knight, *Reports on European Education*, 243–316.

43. Jonathan Messerli, *Horace Mann: A Biography* (New York, 1982), 381–424.

44. All quotes here and below from Horace Mann, *Seventh Annual Report* (1843), in *Life and Works of Horace Mann*, ed. Mary Mann & George Mann (Boston, 1891), 3:230–418.

45. This section relies on Carl Kaestle, *Joseph Lancaster and the Monitorial School Movement: A Documentary History* (New York, 1973).

46. DeWitt Clinton, "Address" (1809), in Kaestle, *Lancaster*, 157.

47. "Reminiscence of the Lancasterian School in Detroit (ca. 1818)," in Kaestle, *Lancaster*, 167–80.

48. "My School-Boy Days in New York City Forty Years Ago," *New York Teacher, and American Educational Monthly* (March 1869), 89–100.

49. Horace Mann, *Ninth Annual Report* (1845), in Mann & Mann, *Life and Works*, 4:29.

50. Mann, *Seventh Annual Report* (1843), 3:279; Kaestle, *Lancaster*, 184.

51. Association of Boston School Masters, *Remarks on the 7th Annual Report of the Hon. Horace Mann* (Boston, 1844), 3.

52. Ibid., 37.

53. On moral discipline, see ibid., 103–45.

54. This section draws from Reese, *Testing Wars*.

55. On this second point, see ibid.; Dana Goldstein, *Teacher Wars: A History of America's Most Embattled Profession* (New York, 2014).

56. American Normal School Association, *American Normal Schools*, 20–28.

57. The best overviews of the normal school movement are Christine Ogren, *The American State Normal School: An Instrument of Great Good* (New York, 2005), 9–52; James W. Fraser, *Preparing America's Teachers: A History* (New York, 2007); and Herbst, *And Sadly Teach*.

58. Craven (1850) quoted in Edgar W. Knight, *Public School Education in North Carolina* (New York, 1916 [1969]), 172.

59. "Normal Schools," *North Carolina Journal of Education* 1, no. 3 (1858), 67–70.

60. Henry Barnard, *Normal Schools and other Institutions, Agencies, and Means for the Professional Education of Teachers* (Hartford, Conn., 1851), 3.

61. On the foundation of normal schools in Massachusetts, see Herbst, *And Sadly Teach*, ch. 3.

62. Ogren, *American State Normal School*, 24–29; Herbst, *And Sadly Teach*, chs. 3–4.

63. Fraser, *Preparing*, 79–86.

64. Ogren, *American State Normal School*, 16–17.

65. Elsie G. Hobson, *Educational Legislation and Administration in the State of New York from 1777 to 1850* (Chicago, 1918), 71–77.

66. Ogren, *American State Normal School*, 17–20.

67. The preceding two paragraphs rely heavily on ibid., 20–22; Fraser, *Preparing*, 61–70.

68. Crosby in American Normal School Association, *American Normal Schools*, 26–27. This is similar to what educators today call "pedagogical content knowledge." For a good critical assessment, see David Labaree, *The Trouble with Ed Schools* (New Haven, Conn., 2004).

69. Hovey in American Normal School Association, *American Normal Schools*, 49.

70. Sawyer in ibid., 50.

71. Labaree, *The Trouble with Ed Schools*; E. D. Hirsch Jr., *The Schools We Need and Why We Don't Have Them* (New York, 1999), esp. 54–60, 115–25.

72. Herbst, *And Sadly Teach*, 69, 83–89.

73. *Catalogue of the Normal School, at Bridgewater, Mass., 1840–44* (Boston, 1844).

74. Kelly Ann Kolodny, *Normalites: The First Professionally Prepared Teachers in the United States* (Charlotte, N.C., 2014), ch. 2.

75. Henry L. Pierce to Edward L. Pierce, Apr. 18, 1845, in Pierce Family Letters, 1818–51, MHS.

76. Caroline Goodale diary, Feb. 11, 1845, MHS.

77. Ibid., Nov. 21, 1844, MHS.

78. Electa Lincoln diary, Apr. 12, 1849, MHS.

79. Ibid., Sept. 20, 1848, MHS.

80. Ibid., Apr. 13, 1849, MHS.

81. Ibid., Apr. 19, 1849, MHS.

82. Goodale, diary, Feb. 25, 1845, MHS; Stow, Nov. 15, 1841, quoted in Kolodny, *Normalites*, 61.

83. *Records of the First Class of the First State Normal School in America, Established at Lexington, Massachusetts, 1839* (Boston, 1903).

84. On Beecher, see Kathryn Kish Sklar, *Catharine Beecher: A Study in American Domesticity* (New Haven, Conn., 1973).

85. Litchfield Historical Society, *To Ornament Their Minds: Sarah Pierce's Litchfield Academy, 1792–1833*, ed. Catherine Fields & Lisa Kightlinger (Litchfield, Conn., 1993); Mark Boonshoft, "The Litchfield Network: Education, Social Capital, and the Rise and Fall of a Political Dynasty, 1784–1833," *Journal of the Early Republic* 34, no. 4 (Winter 2014), 561–96.

86. Mary Kelley, *Learning to Stand and Speak: Women, Education, and Public Life in America's Republic* (Chapel Hill, N.C., 2006).

87. Alma Lutz, *Emma Willard: Daughter of Democracy* (Washington, D.C., 1975).

88. Emma Willard, *An Address to the Public; Particularly to the Members of the Legislature of New York, Proposing a Plan for Improving Female Education* (Middlebury, Vt. 1819).

89. See, for example, Lucia McMahon, *Mere Equals: The Paradox of Educated Women in the Early American Republic* (Ithaca, N.Y., 2012).

90. [Catharine Beecher], "Female Education," *American Journal of Education* 2, nos. 4 and 5 (1827), 219–23, 264–69.

91. Sklar, *Beecher*, xiv, 82–83, 134–35, lists those virtues as "devotion and service to others, selflessness, sacrifice."

92. Catharine Beecher, *Suggestions Respecting Improvements in Education, presented to the Trustees of the Hartford Female Seminary* (Hartford, Conn., 1829), 4, 9, 54.

93. Catharine Beecher, *An Essay on the Education of Female Teachers* (New York, 1835).

94. Catharine Beecher, *The Duty of American Women to Their Country* (New York, 1845), 27–29, 66–69.

95. Horace Mann, "Lecture 2: Special Preparation a Prerequisite to Teaching," in Mann & Mann, *Life and Works*, 2:99–100.

96. Tyack & Hansot, *Learning Together*, 65–69.

97. Herbst, *And Sadly Teach*, 61.

98. M. W. Rury, "Who Became Teachers? The Social Characteristics of Teachers in American History," in *American Teachers: Histories of a Profession at Work*, ed. D. Warren (New York, 1989), 17. See also Kaestle & Vinovskis, *Education and Social Change*, 284–85; Vinovskis & Richard Bernard, "The Female School Teacher in Ante-Bellum Massachusetts," *Journal of Social History* 10, no. 3 (Apr. 1977), 332–45; Herbst, *And Sadly Teach*, 24–30.

99. Redding Sugg, *Motherteacher: The Feminization of American Education* (Charlottesville, Va., 1978); Goldstein, *Teacher Wars*.

100. Mark D. Hall, "Beyond Self-Interest: The Political Theory of and Practice of Evangelical Women in Antebellum America," *Journal of Church and State* 44, no. 3 (2002), 477–79; Lucia McMahon, "'Of the Utmost Importance to Our Country': Women, Education, and Society, 1780–1820," *Journal of the Early Republic* 29, no. 3 (Fall 2009), 475–506.

101. *Annual Report of the School Committee of the Town of Concord* (1855), quoted in Kaufman, *Women Teachers*, xxi. For discussion, see Geraldine Clifford, *Those Good Gertrudes: A Social History of Women Teachers in America* (Baltimore, 2014), ch. 3.

102. *Eleventh Annual Report of the Condition of the Common Schools, to the City Council of Cincinnati. Rendered June 30, 1840, by the Board of Trustees and Visitors . . .* (Cincinnati, 1840), 4.

103. Kaestle & Vinovskis, *Education and Social Change*, 155–56. By 1880, Boxford female teachers on average made 86 percent what male teachers made.

104. Herbst, *And Sadly Teach*, 24–30; Kim Tolley & Nancy Beadie, "Transformations in Teaching: Toward a More Complex Model of Teacher Labor Markets in the United States, 1800–1850," in *Transformations in Schooling: Historical and Comparative Perspectives*, ed. Tolley (New York, 2007), ch. 8.

105. *North Carolina Journal of Education* 1 (1858), 175, 283.

106. For example, see Stanley Schultz, *The Culture Factory: Boston Public Schools, 1789–1860* (New York, 1973).

107. Mann, *Seventh Annual Report* (1843), 3:302–3.

108. Maris Vinovskis, David L. Angus, & Jeffrey E. Mirel, "Historical Development of Age Stratification in Schooling," reprinted in Vinovskis, *Education, Society, and Economic Opportunity* (New Haven, Conn., 1995), 171–93; Howard Chudacoff, *How Old Are You? Age Consciousness in American Culture* (Princeton, N.J., 1989), esp. 29–40.

109. Joseph F. Kett, *Rites of Passage: Adolescence in America, 1790 to the Present* (New York, 1977), 18–22.

110. H. H. Barney, *Report on the American System of Graded Free Schools* (Cincinnati, 1851), 4, 13, 15–16, 71–72.

111. William H. Wells, *The Graded School: A Graded Course of Instruction for Public Schools: With Copious Practical Directions to Teachers* (New York 1862), 15–16.

112. Ohio Teachers Association, *A History of Education in the State of Ohio*, ch. 3.

113. Joseph Kett, *Merit: The History of a Founding Ideal from the American Revolution to the 21st Century* (Ithaca, N.Y., 2013), ch. 4.

114. William Fischel, *Making the Grade: The Economic Evolution of American School Districts* (Chicago, 2009), ch. 3, argues that the decline of the one-room school, and the emergence of consolidated districts with age-graded schools, in the twentieth century had three factors. First, mobility meant that students had to be able to be placed into new schools around the nation as their families moved, which required a standardized curriculum. Second, cars allowed for school districts to cover larger territories and for students to live farther away from their schools. And, third, as state funding replaced local funding during the twentieth century, the local district became less relevant. Graded schools led to unexpected problems, some of them the reformers' own making. Graded schools established rules and structures designed to elevate, step by step, the human spirit. As it was implemented and, in the early twentieth century, used to sort rather than elevate, it became bureaucratic and systematic, undermining the very life it was designed to cultivate. To condemn the results a century later might make sense, but we must not lose sight of educators' aspiration in implementing grades: to allow teachers to devote more time to students and to design coherent curricula that would form each child's intellectual and moral character. See David B. Tyack, *The One Best System: A History of American Urban Education* (Cambridge, Mass., 1974). On the one-room schoolhouse in American thought, see Jonathan Zimmerman, *Small Wonder: The Little Red Schoolhouse in History and Memory* (New Haven, Conn., 2009).

115. Donald Scott McPherson, "The Fight against Free Schools in Pennsylvania: Popular Opposition to the Common School System, 1834–1874" (PhD diss., University of Pittsburgh, 1977), 89, table 3.

116. Francis P. Weisenburger, *Passing of the Frontier, 1825–1850* (Columbus, Ohio, 1941), 172.

117. Kaestle & Vinovskis, *Education and Social Change*, 25, 118–19.

118. Nancy Beadie, "Tuition Funding for Common Schools: Education, Markets, and Market Regulation in Rural New York, 1815–1850," *Social Science History* 32, no. 1 (Spring 2008), 117.

119. Kaestle & Vinovskis, *Education and Social Change*, 6.

120. My discussion herein relies on Reese, *Testing Wars*.

121. Elizabeth Clapp diary, 1852–54, David Clapp diaries and account book, 1827–86, MHS.

122. Henry Lunt diary, Nov. 12, 18, 19, 20, and 21, 1856, NYHS.

123. Morse diary, Feb. 28 and 29, 1856, MHS.

124. Ibid., Mar. 6, 1856.

125. Ohio Teachers Association, *A History of Education in the State of Ohio*, 126.

126. John Swett (1911) quoted in Reese, *Testing Wars*, 161.

127. Discussion of Stow and Harris from Kolodny, *Normalites*, chs. 5–6.

128. Ibid., 57.

129. This episode taken from ibid., 75–79.

130. From diary of Arozina Perkins, in Kaufman, *Women Teachers*, 55–152.

131. Augusta E. Hubbell to Miss Swift, Nov. 19, 1853, in Kaufman, *Women Teachers*, 156–61.

132. Mary Roper letters to Miss Swift, Oct. 1852, June 1853, and July 1853, in Kaufman, *Women Teachers*, 160–65.

133. Mary Chase to Miss Swift, Aug. 27, 1853, in Kaufman, *Women Teachers*, 165–68.

134. Rogers to Swift, Sept. 18, 1850, in Kaufman, *Women Teachers*, 184–90.

135. Fraser, *Preparing*, 131.

136. Morse diary, Jan. 5, 1855, MHS.

137. Ibid., Jan. 2, 1856.

138. Barbara Finkelstein, "In Fear of Childhood: Relationships between Parents and Teachers in Popular Primary Schools in the Nineteenth Century," *History of Childhood Quarterly* 3 (Winter 1976), 321–35; David B. Tyack, "The Tribe and the Common School: Community Control in Rural Education," *American Quarterly* 24, no. 1 (Mar. 1972), 3–19.

139. My discussion is indebted to Finkelstein, *Governing the Young*, 41–139. See also Geraldine Clifford, *Those Good Gertrudes: A Social History of Women Teachers in America* (Baltimore, 2014) and "Home and School in 19th Century America: Some Personal-History Reports from the United States," *History of Education Quarterly* 18, no. 1 (Spring 1978), 3–34; Clifton Johnson, *The Country School in New England* (New York, 1893); Andrew Guilford, *America's Country Schools*, 3rd ed. (Niwot, Colo., 1996), 46–61; William Reese, *The Origins of the American High School* (New Haven, Conn., 1995), 123–41; Paul Theobald, *Call School: Rural Education in the Middle West to 1918* (Carbondale, Ill., 1995), ch. 4.

140. Caton, "Teaching in a New York District School, c. 1820," reprinted in Finkelstein, *Governing the Young*, 155–58.

141. Orcutt in Finkelstein, *Governing the Young*, 163.

142. Daniel Thompson, *Locke Amsden; or, The Schoolmaster, a Tale* (Boston, 1848). For a discussion of the novel, see Richard Allen Foster, *The School in American Literature* (Baltimore, 1930), 109–16.

143. For a good discussion of what it was like to be in a district school, see Mark J. Sammons, "'Without a Word of Explanation': District Schools of Early Nineteenth-Century New England," in *Families and Children*, ed. Peter Benes (Boston, 1987), 78–90. This section is inspired by the recent effort to recover children's perspectives in history, and with it the recognition that children experience the world in their own ways and that historians need to understand their perspectives. Representative texts include Peter Benes, ed., *The Worlds of Children, 1620–1920* (Boston, 2004); Karen Sánchez-Eppler, *Dependent States: The Child's Part in 19th-Century American Culture* (Chicago, 2005); Wilma King, ed., *African American Childhoods* (New York, 2005); Howard Chudacoff, *Children at Play: An American History* (New York, 2007); James Marten, ed., *Children and Youth during the Civil War Era* (New York, 2012).

144. Quotes from Warren Burton, *The District School As It Was*, rev. ed. (Boston, 1850).

145. Recollections of Julia Anne Hieronymus Tevis, reprinted in *Recollections of the Early Republic: Selected Autobiographies*, ed. Joyce Appleby (Boston, 1997), 68–102.

146. John Ball diary, reprinted in Appleby, *Recollections*, 1–38.

147. Clapp diary, MHS.

148. Quotation and discussion from Tyack & Hansot, *Learning Together*, 101–3, 114–45.

149. Alexander J. Field, "Educational Expansion in Mid-19th Century Massachusetts: Human Capital Formation or Structural Reinforcement?," *Harvard Educational Review* 46, no. 4 (Nov. 1976), 521–52, at 538.

150. Kaestle & Vinovskis, *Education and Social Change*, ch. 4.

151. Samuel A. Bigelow diary, in Bigelow Family Papers, 1830–1917, MHS.

152. For an interesting discussion, see Rebecca R. Noel, "Cultures of Boys' Play in Mid-19th-Century New England: The Case of James Edward Wright," in Benes, *Worlds of Children*, 9–23.

153. Recollection of Chauncey Jerome, in Appleby, *Recollections*, 162.

154. Levi Beardsley, *Reminiscences* (1852), in *Growing Up in the Cooper Country: Boyhood Recollections of the New York Frontier*, ed. Louis C. Jones (Syracuse, N.Y., 1965), 59–62.

155. Quoted in Edgar W. Knight, *Public Education in the South* (Boston, 1922), 296–97.

156. Ibid., 300–301.

157. Quoted in Finkelstein, *Governing the Young*, 121.

158. Burton, *District School*, ch. 18. See also "The Schoolmaster in Georgia," *National Magazine* (July 1852), 61–64.

159. Joseph Caldwell, "On Popular Education" (1832), in *A Documentary History of Education in the South before 1860*, ed. Edgar W. Knight (Chapel Hill, N.C., 1950), 2:397–99 (Letter 9).

160. Chudacoff, *Children at Play*, 1–18.

161. Goodale diary, June 21, 1844, MHS.

162. See appendix, table 3.

163. Havens quoted in Chudacoff, *Children at Play*, 49.

CHAPTER FIVE: Containing Multitudes

1. Hodges's speech in *First Annual Report of the Wisconsin Teachers' Association, with the Constitution and Proceedings, and the Addresses delivered at the Annual Meeting, August 9th and 10th, 1854* (Madison, Wis., 1854), New-York Historical Society collections, New York (NYHS).

2. Stowe quoted in David B. Tyack, *Seeking Common Ground: Public Schools in a Diverse Society* (Cambridge, Mass., 2003), 20.

3. Among many sources, see Bob Pepperman Taylor, *Horace Mann's Troubling Leg-*

acy: *The Education of Democratic Citizens* (Lanham, Md., 2006), ch. 3; E. D. Hirsch Jr., *The Making of Americans: Democracy and Our Schools* (New Haven, Conn., 2009); Tyack, *Seeking Common Ground*; Jean Baker, *Affairs of Party: The Political Culture of Northern Democrats in the Mid-19th Century* (New York, 1998), ch. 2. My understanding is influenced by Danielle S. Allen, *Talking to Strangers: Anxieties of Citizenship since Brown v. Board of Education* (Chicago, 2004); Stephen Macedo, *Diversity and Distrust: Civic Education in a Multicultural Democracy* (Cambridge, Mass., 2000).

4. *Proceedings of a Convention for the Promotion of Common School Education* (Newburgh, N.Y., 1837), NYHS.

5. John Pierce, "Report of the Superintendent of Public Instruction" (1837), quoted in JoEllen McNergney Vinyard, *For Faith and Fortune: The Education of Catholic Immigrants in Detroit, 1805–1925* (Urbana, Ill., 1998), 18.

6. Free School Society, 1825 annual report, quoted in Steven Green, *The Bible, the School, and the Constitution: The Clash That Shaped Modern Church-State Doctrine* (New York, 2012), 20.

7. Horace Mann, *First Annual Report* (1837), in *Life and Works of Horace Mann*, ed. Mary Mann & George Mann (Boston, 1891), 2:410.

8. Ibid., 2:417.

9. "The Barry Report" quoted in William E. Ellis, *A History of Education in Kentucky* (Lexington, Ky., 2011), 16–17. See Edgar Knight, *Public Education in the South* (Boston, 1922); Timothy Lockley, *Welfare and Charity in the Antebellum South* (Gainesville, Fla., 2007), 177–79.

10. Ray Allen Billington, *The Protestant Crusade, 1800–1860: A Study of the Origins of American Nativism* (New York, 1938) 69–75; Jenny Franchot, *Roads to Rome: The Antebellum Protestant Encounter with Catholicism* (Berkeley, Calif., 1994), 137–38.

11. *Report of the Committee, Relating to the Destruction of the Ursuline Convent, August 11, 1834* (Boston, 1834); Jonathan Messerli, *Horace Mann: A Biography* (New York, 1982), 192–93.

12. Mann, *First Annual Report* (1837), 2:417.

13. Horace Mann, *Ninth Annual Report* (1845), in Mann & Mann, *Life and Works*, 4:37. See also Horace Mann, *Twelfth Annual Report* (1848), in ibid., 4:277–78, on the need for laws, not violence and rebellion.

14. Paul Gilje, *Rioting in America* (Bloomington, Ind., 1996), 60–63; Seth Rockman, "Mobtown, USA: Baltimore," *Common-place* 3, no. 4 (July 2003).

15. Michael Feldberg, *The Philadelphia Riots of 1844: A Study of Ethnic Conflict* (Westport, Conn., 1975), 4–5.

16. Billington, *Protestant Crusade*, 71–75.

17. Tyack, *Seeking Common Ground*, 168–69; Green, *Bible*, 36–40.

18. Both St. Louis and Baltimore from Gilje, *Rioting*, 67.

19. Billington, *Protestant Crusade*, 60.

20. Hilary J. Moss, *Schooling Citizens: The Struggle for African American Education in Antebellum America* (Chicago, 2009), 18.

21. Ibid., 1–3.

22. Ibid., 62. For a discussion of the extent of antiabolition violence, see Manisha Sinha, *The Slave's Cause: A History of Abolition* (New Haven, Conn., 2016), 228–39.

23. Tyler Anbinder, "Isiah Rynders and the Ironies of Popular Democracy in Antebellum New York," in *Contested Democracy: Freedom, Race, and Power in American History*, ed. Manisha Sinha & Penny von Eschen (New York, 2007), ch. 2.

24. Reeve Huston, *Land and Freedom: Rural Society, Popular Protest, and Party Politics in Antebellum New York* (New York, 2000); Charles W. McCurdy, *The Anti-Rent Era in New York Law and Politics, 1839–1865* (Chapel Hill, N.C., 2001).

25. Gilje, *Rioting*, 77–79. On frontier justice, see Randolph Roth, *American Homicide* (Cambridge, Mass., 2009), ch. 5.

26. Meyer Weinberg, *A Chance to Learn: The History of Race and Education in the United States* (Cambridge, 1977), 24.

27. Moss, *Schooling Citizens*, 164–65; Gilje, *Rioting*, ch. 4.

28. Moss, *Schooling Citizens*, 93.

29. Rachel Hope Cleves, *The Reign of Terror in America: Visions of Violence from Anti-Jacobinism to Antislavery* (New York, 2009).

30. Gilje, *Rioting*, 10; Cleves, *Reign of Terror*; Johann N. Neem, "Taking Modernity's Wager: Tocqueville, Social Capital, and the American Civil War," *Journal of Interdisciplinary History* 41, no. 4 (Spring 2011), 591–618. Roth, *American Homicide*, 21–23, concludes that "a sense of patriotism or kinship with countrymen, plays a decisive role in determining whether men will subject other members of their society to violence. Nothing suppresses homicide within a social group more powerfully than a sense of connectedness that extends beyond the bounds of family and neighborhood and forges a strong bond among people who share race, ethnicity, religion, or nationality." Roth recognizes that solidarity can also spur violence as one group opposes another, but continues, "when fellow feeling expands to encompass a large portion of the population, it can deter homicide significantly." Roth, *American Homicide*, ch. 7, indicates that homicide rates "exploded across the nation" in the 1840s and 1850s in response to "immigration, economic hardship, and the conquest of areas populated by Hispanic and Native peoples."

31. John L. Murrin, "A Roof without Walls: The Dilemma of American National Identity," in *Beyond Confederation: Origins of the Constitution and American Identity*, ed. Richard Beeman et al. (Chapel Hill, N.C., 1987), 333–48.

32. Neem, "Taking Modernity's Wager."

33. Liam Riordan, *Many Identities, One Nation* (Philadelphia, 2007); William R. Hutchison, *Religious Pluralism in America: The Contentious History of a Founding Ideal* (New Haven, Conn., 2003), ch. 3; Nicholas Guyatt, *Providence and the Invention of the United States, 1607–1876* (New York, 2007).

34. Mann, *Twelfth Annual Report* (1848), 4:306.

35. Christopher Beneke, *Beyond Toleration: The Religious Origins of American Pluralism* (New York, 2006). See also Steven D. Smith, *The Rise and Decline of American Religious Freedom* (Cambridge, Mass., 2014).

36. Nathan Hatch, "Second Great Awakening and the Market Revolution," in

Devising Liberty: Preserving and Creating Freedom in the New American Republic, ed. David Thomas Konig (Stanford, Calif., 1995), ch. 8; Jon Butler, *Awash in a Sea of Faith: Christianizing the American People* (Cambridge, Mass., 1990).

37. Green, *Bible*, 13. Discussion from ibid., ch. 1. See also Carl F. Kaestle, "Moral Education and Common Schools in America: A Historian's View," *Journal of Moral Education* 13, no. 2 (May 1984), 101–11.

38. William Dunn, *What Happened to Religious Education? The Decline of Religious Teaching in the Public Elementary School, 1776–1861* (Baltimore, 1958), ch. 4.

39. On Barnard, see "Barnard, Daniel Dewey," in *Biographical Directory of the United States Congress, 1774–Present*, http://bioguide.congress.gov/scripts/biodisplay .pl?index=b000152.

40. [Daniel Barnard], *Barnard's Report on the Use of the Bible in Common Schools* (Providence, R.I., 1838).

41. Charles Leslie Glenn Jr., *The Myth of the Common School* (Amherst, Mass., 1988), 151. See also ibid., ch. 7; Raymond Culver, *Horace Mann and Religion in the Massachusetts Public Schools* (London, 1929).

42. Fenwick (1828) quoted in Dunn, *What Happened*, 207.

43. Ruth Elson, *Guardians of Tradition: American Schoolbooks of the 19th Century* (Lincoln, Neb., 1964), esp. ch. 3; Dunn, *What Happened*, 204–20.

44. Mann, *Twelfth Annual Report* (1848), 4:292.

45. Ibid., 4:280, 296–97. More generally, see ibid., 4:292–340.

46. James W. Fraser, *Pedagogue for God's Kingdom: Lyman Beecher and the Second Great Awakening* (Lanham, Md., 1985).

47. Lyman Beecher, *Autobiography of Lyman Beecher*, ed. Barbara Cross (Cambridge, Mass., 1961), 253; Johann N. Neem, "Creating Social Capital in the Early American Republic: The View from Connecticut," *Journal of Interdisciplinary History* 39, no. 4 (Spring 2009), 471–95.

48. All quotes from Lyman Beecher, *A Plea for the West* (Cincinnati, 1835), 13, 49, 52, 54, 60, 68, 83, 91, 105, 118.

49. Nathan Hatch, *The Sacred Cause of Liberty: Republican Thought and the Millennium in Revolutionary New England* (New Haven, Conn., 1977); J. C. D. Clark, *The Language of Liberty, 1660–1832: Political Discourse and Social Dynamics in the Anglo-American World* (Cambridge, Mass., 1994); Harry Stout, *The New England Soul* (New York, 1986); Linda Colley, *Britons: Forging the Nation, 1707–1837* (New Haven, Conn., 2009); Allison Malcolm, "Anti-Catholicism and the Rise of Protestant Nationhood in North America, 1830–1871" (PhD diss., University of Illinois, Chicago, 2011), esp. ch. 2; Franchot, *Roads to Rome*; Beneke, *Beyond Toleration*, 180–201, 208–14.

50. John T. McGreevy, *Catholicism and American Freedom* (New York, 2003).

51. W. P. Strickland, *The History of the American Bible Society, from Its Organization to the Present Time* (New York, 1849), xxvii, quoted in Malcolm, "Anti-Catholicism," 38–39.

52. Billington, *Protestant Crusade*, 34–36; Dale Knobel, *Paddy and the Republic:*

Ethnicity and Nationality in Antebellum America (Middletown, Conn., 1986); Thomas Archdeacon, *Becoming American: An Ethnic History* (New York, 1983), ch. 3.

53. Quoted in Billington, *Protestant Crusade*, 58.

54. Ibid., 122–25.

55. Ronald Formisano, *For the People: American Populist Movements from the Revolution to the 1850s* (Chapel Hill, N.C., 2008), ch. 9; Billington, *Protestant Crusade*, ch. 8.

56. Tyler Anbinder, *Nativism and Slavery: The Northern Know-Nothings and the Politics of the 1850s* (New York, 1992), 11–13.

57. This is the central argument of Anbinder, *Nativism and Slavery*. See also Dale Knobel, *"America for the Americans": The Nativist Movement in the United States* (New York, 1996).

58. On the Know-Nothings' electoral success, see Michael F. Holt, "The Antimasonic and Know Nothing Parties," in *History of U.S. Political Parties*, ed. Arthur M. Schlesinger Jr. (New York, 1973), 1:575–620, at 594; Philip Gleason, "American Identity and Americanization," in *Harvard Encyclopedia of American Ethnic Groups*, ed. Stephan Thernstrom (Cambridge, Mass., 1980), at 35.

59. Kevin Kenny, *The American Irish: A History* (New York, 2000), 104.

60. Jay Dolan, *The American Catholic Experience: A History from Colonial Times to the Present* (Notre Dame, Ind., 1992), 128.

61. James Olson, *Catholic Immigrants in America* (Chicago, 1987), 20–21.

62. Kenny, *American Irish*, 104.

63. Dolan, *American Catholic Experience*, 130.

64. Ibid., 160–61, 168.

65. Philip Hamburger, *Separation of Church and State* (Cambridge, Mass., 2002), 230–31; Raymond Grew, "Liberty and the Catholic Church in 19th-Century Europe," in *Freedom and Religion in the 19th Century*, ed. Richard Helmstadter (Stanford, Calif., 1997), ch. 7.

66. Quoted in Timothy Walch, *Parish School: American Catholic Parochial Education from Colonial Times to the Present* (New York, 1996), 31.

67. Jon Gjerde, *Catholicism and the Shaping of Nineteenth-Century America*, ed. S. Deborah Kang (New York, 2012), 158.

68. As Jay Dolan, *In Search of an American Catholicism: A History of Religion and Culture in Tension* (New York, 2002), 45, writes, in the 1830s, Catholic "church leaders rejected the democratic impulse and enlightened piety" and "chose to stand against the [American] culture." See also McGreevy, *Catholicism and American Freedom*, ch. 2.

69. Lawrence Kehoe, ed., *Complete Works of the Most Reverend John Hughes D.D.* (New York, 1866), 2: 22.

70. For the connection between American and European nationalism, see Don H. Doyle, *Nations Divided: America, Italy, and the Southern Question* (Athens, Ga., 2002).

71. Glenn, *Myth*, xi. See also Michael Sandel, "The Procedural Republic and the Unencumbered Self," *Political Theory* 12, no. 1 (Feb. 1984), 81–96.

72. The phrase is from Diane Ravitch, *The Great School Wars: A History of the New York City Public Schools* (Baltimore, 2000), which informs my discussion.

73. In addition to Ravitch, *Great School Wars*, see Carl F. Kaestle, *Evolution of an Urban School System: New York City, 1750–1850* (Cambridge, Mass. 1973); Vincent Lannie, *Public Money and Parochial Education: Bishop Hughes, Governor Seward, and the New York School Controversy* (Cleveland, Ohio, 1968). See also Jason Stacy, "Becoming Illuminated: New York City's Public School Society and Its Religious Discontents, 1805–1840," *American Educational History Journal* 37, no. 2 (2010), 455–71.

74. "John DuBois," in *Dictionary of American Biography*, ed. Allen Johnson & Dumas Malone (New York, 1928), 5:470–72.

75. Ravitch, *Great School Wars*, 35; Timothy L. Smith, "Protestant Schooling and American Nationality, 1800–1850," *Journal of American History* 53, no. 4 (Mar. 1967), 679–95.

76. Gjerde, *Catholicism*, ch. 2; Green, *Bible*, 55; John Hassard, *Life of the Most Reverend John Hughes, D.D.* (New York, 1866).

77. Lannie, *Public Money and Parochial Education*, 13–28.

78. Seward's message extracted in William O. Bourne, *History of the Public School Society of the City of New York* (New York, 1870), 179. See also discussion in Glyndon Van Deusen, *William Henry Seward* (New York, 1967), ch. 5.

79. "Petition of the Catholics of New York for a Portion of the Common-School Fund" (1840), in *Catholic Education in America*, ed. Neil G. McCluskey (New York, 1964), 65–77.

80. Kaestle, *Evolution*, 179–84; Lannie, *Public Money and Parochial Education*, chs. 6–10.

81. Hughes quoted in a discussion from Thomas J. Shelley, "Empire City Catholicism: Catholic Education in New York," in *Urban Catholic Education: Tales of 12 American Cities*, ed. Thomas Hunt & Timothy Walch (Notre Dame, Ind., 2010), 63–88.

82. Hughes, in Bourne, *History of the Public School Society*, 203–24.

83. McGreevy, *Catholicism and American Freedom*, ch. 1; Jon Gjerde, *Minds of the West: Ethnocultural Evolution in the Rural Middle West, 1830–1917* (Chapel Hill, N.C., 1997), 66–73.

84. John Hughes, "The Decline of Protestantism and Its Causes" (1850), in Kehoe, *Works*, 2: 87–102.

85. John Hughes, "The Church and the World" (1850), in Kehoe, *Works*, 2:69–87. See also Hughes, "A Lecture on the Importance of a Christian Basis for the Science of Political Economy, and Its Application to the Affairs of Life" (1844), in ibid., 1:513–34. Philip Gleason, "American Catholics and Liberalism, 1789–1960," in *Catholicism and Liberalism: Contributions to American Public Philosophy*, ed. R. Bruce Douglass & David Hollenbach (Cambridge, 1994), ch. 2.

86. Oscar Handlin, *The Uprooted: The Epic Story of the Great Migrations that Made the American People* (Boston, 1951), 131–34; Olson, *Catholic Immigrants*, 29; Kenny, *American Irish*, ch. 3.

87. McGreevy, *Catholicism and American Freedom*; Olson, *Catholic Immigrants*, ch. 3.

88. Lawrence Fuchs, *The American Kaleidoscope: Race, Ethnicity, and the Civic Culture* (Middletown, Conn., 1990), ch. 2; Dolan, *American Catholic Experience*, ch. 11; David Noel Doyle, "The Remaking of Irish America, 1845–1880," in *Making the Irish American: History and Heritage of the Irish in the United States*, ed. Joseph Lee & Marion Casey (New York, 2006), ch. 5; Jay Dolan, "Religion in the Immigrant Community: 1820–1920," in *American Catholics*, ed. Joseph Kelly (Wilmington, Del., 1989), 27–50. For a later period, see James R. Barrett, *The Irish Way: Becoming American in the Multiethnic City* (New York, 2012).

89. For overviews and interpretations of how assimilation happens, or not, see Gary Gerstle, "Liberty, Coercion, and the Making of Americans," *Journal of American History* 84, no. 2 (Sept. 1997), 524–58; Peter D. Salins, *Assimilation, American Style* (New York, 1997); Russell Kazal, "Revisiting Assimilation: The Rise, Fall, and Reappraisal of a Concept in American Ethnic History," *American Historical Review* 100, no. 2 (Apr. 1995), 437–41; Olivier Zunz, with comments by John Bodnar & Stephan Thernstrom, "American History and the Changing Meaning of Assimilation," *Journal of American Ethnic History* 4, no. 2 (Spring 1985), 53–84; Harold J. Abramson, "Assimilation and Pluralism," in Thernstrom, *Harvard Encyclopedia*, 150–60.

90. On Philadelphia, see Dale B. Light Jr., "The Role of Irish-American Organisations in Assimilation and Community Formation," in *The Irish in America: Emigration, Assimilation, and Impact*, ed. P. J. Drudy (Cambridge, 1985), 113–42; on Buffalo, see David A. Gerber, *The Making of an American Pluralism: Buffalo, New York, 1825–1860* (Urbana, Ill., 1989); for the Midwest, see Gjerde, *Minds of the West*, esp. 229–48.

91. Fuchs, *American Kaleidoscope*, 42–48; Barrett, *The Irish Way*, ch. 5; Gerber, *Making of an American Pluralism*, 113–410; Kerby Miller, *Emigrants and Exiles: Ireland and the Irish Exodus to North America* (New York, 1985), 328–35.

92. Tyler Anbinder, "Moving Beyond 'Rags to Riches': New York's Irish Famine Immigrants and Their Surprising Savings Accounts," *Journal of American History* 99, no. 3 (Dec. 2012), 741–70.

93. Quote and discussion from Noel Ignatiev, *How the Irish Became White* (New York, 1995), 102–6. See also Kenny, *The American Irish*, 66, 109–12. Dolan, *American Catholic Experience*, 329–41, focuses on the post–Civil War era.

94. Numbers in Kenny, *American Irish*, 123–24.

95. Ignatiev, *How the Irish Became White*; Barrett, *The Irish Way*; Sinha, *The Slave's Cause*, 359–63. The Catholic Church, including Father John Hughes, opposed the antislavery movement, reinforcing the Catholic alliance with proslavery Democrats, and also alienating the church from the Whig and Republican parties. See Kenny, *American Irish*, 119.

96. Dolan, *American Catholic Experience*, 323–39.

97. Dolan, "Religion in the Immigrant Community: 1820–1920," at 38–39; Dolan, *Catholic Revivalism: The American Experience, 1830–1900* (Notre Dame, Ind., 1978).

98. On discussions within the church, see Dolan, *American Catholic Experience*, 267–75.

99. Olson, *Catholic Immigrants*, 37–38.

100. Ibid., 38.

101. Vinyard, *Faith or Fortune*, 23.

102. John T. James, "Gateway City Catholicism: Catholic Education in St. Louis," in Hunt & Walch, *Urban Catholic Education*, 160.

103. Walch, *Parish School*, 19.

104. Dolan, *American Catholic Experience*, 263.

105. Discussion from Walch, *Parish School*, ch. 3; Dolan, *American Catholic Experience*, 278–83.

106. Discussion and quote from Vinyard, *Faith or Fortune*, ch. 2.

107. Jeffrey M. Burns, "Bay City Catholicism: Catholic Education in San Francisco," in Hunt & Walch, *Urban Catholic Education*, ch. 12.

108. Dolan, *American Catholic Experience*, 263–64.

109. Jay Dolan, *The Immigrant Church: New York's Irish and German Catholics, 1815–1865* (Baltimore, 1975), 105–6. According to Martin Marty, *A Short History of American Catholicism* (Allen, Tex., 1995), 134–35, in 1884, the year of the Third Plenary Council, 40 percent of American parishes had started schools, and by 1880 there were 2,246 schools enrolling more than 400,000 students.

110. Dolan, *American Catholic Experience*, 278.

111. Walch, *Parish School*, 1.

112. *Niles National Register* (1832), quoted in Gjerde, *Minds of the West*, 143.

113. This is the primary argument of Gjerde, *Minds of the West*, esp. 54–66. For the evolution of the idea of pluralism, and its importance in confronting a mass commercial society, see Olivier Zunz, "From Voluntarism to Pluralism," in *Why the American Century?* (Chicago, 1998), ch. 6. On the development of the idea of minority rights, see Kyle Volk, *Moral Minorities and the Making of American Democracy* (New York, 2014). For a discussion of how one community negotiated these tensions, see Carl Bowman, *Brethren Society: The Cultural Transformation of a "Peculiar People"* (Baltimore, 1995).

114. Gjerde, *Minds*, 88–96.

115. Paul Theobald, "Country School Curriculum and Governance: The One-Room School and Experience in the 19th-Century Midwest," *American Journal of Education* 101, no. 2 (Feb. 1993), 116–39, at 125–26; Theobald, *Call School: Rural Education in the Midwest to 1918* (Carbondale, Ill., 1995), ch. 1.

116. Burrowes quoted in Donald Scott McPherson, "The Fight against Free Schools in Pennsylvania: Popular Opposition to the Common School System, 1834–1874" (PhD diss., University of Pittsburgh, 1977), 123. For discussions of Pennsylvania Germans, see Steven Nolt, *Foreigners in Their Own Land: Pennsylvania Germans in the Early Republic* (University Park, Pa., 2002); Kathleen Neils Conzen, "Germans," in Thernstrom, *Harvard Encyclopedia*, 405–25.

117. McPherson, "Fight," 356.

118. See ibid., chs. 7–8. This is an example of what Robert Putnam, *Bowling Alone: The Collapse and Revival of American Community* (New York, 2000), calls "bonding" versus "bridging" social capital.

119. McPherson, "Fight," 266.

120. Ibid., 356–64.

121. Bernard Sheehan, *Seeds of Extinction: Jeffersonian Philanthropy and the American Indian* (Chapel Hill, N.C., 1973); Joseph S. Lucas, "Civilization or Extinction: Citizens and Indians in the Early United States," *Journal of the Historical Society* 6, no. 2 (June 2006), 235–50. Some Native Americans sought to develop their own public schools. On this point, see Julie L. Reed, *Serving the Nation: Cherokee Sovereignty and Social Welfare, 1800–1907* (Norman, Okla., 2016).

122. Jon Reyhner & Jeanne Eder, *American Indian Education: A History* (Norman, Okla., 2004), 43–47; Henry Warner Bowden, *American Indians and Christian Missions: Studies in Cultural Conflict* (Chicago, 1981).

123. Quoted in Reyhner & Eder, *American Indian Education*, 46.

124. Ibid., chs. 3–6; David Wallace Adams, *Education for Extinction: American Indians and the Boarding School Experience, 1875–1928* (Lawrence, Kans., 1995).

125. Quotes and discussion from Anne M. Boylan, *Sunday School: The Formation of an American Institution, 1790–1880* (New Haven, 1988), esp. 52–59. See also Glenn, *Myth*, ch. 8; Michael Irwin Katz, "The Origins and Early Development of the American Sunday School Movement, 1815–1840" (MA thesis, University of Virginia, 1975).

126. Moss, *Schooling Citizens*, 9–11; Volk, *Moral Minorities*, 116–31; Robert L. McCaul, *The Black Struggle for Public Schooling in Nineteenth-Century Illinois* (Carbondale, Ill., 1987), esp. ch. 1.

127. Among many good sources, see Barbara Young Welke, *Law and the Borders of Belonging in the Long Nineteenth Century United States* (New York 2010); Rogers M. Smith, *Civic Ideals: Conflicting Visions of Citizenship in U.S. History* (New Haven, Conn., 1997).

128. On colonization, see Christa Dierksheide, *Amelioration and Empire: Progress and Slavery in the Plantation Americas* (Charlottesville, Va., 2014).

129. Andrew Robertson, "Democracy: America's Other 'Peculiar Institution,'" *Democracy, Participation, and Contestation: Civil Society, Governance, and the Future of Liberal Democracy*, ed. Emmanuelle Avril & Johann N. Neem (New York, 2015), ch. 5; Paul Finkelman, "Laws and Legislation," in *Encyclopedia of African American History, 1619–1895: From the Colonial Period to the Age of Frederick Douglass*, ed. Finkelman (New York, 2006), 2:263–65.

130. The preceding two paragraphs rely on Finkelman, "Laws and Legislation"; Moss, *Schooling Citizens*, 17–18; Carl Kaestle, *Pillars of the Republic: Common Schools and American Society, 1780–1860* (New York, 1983), 179; Carter G. Woodson, *The Education of the Negro Prior to 1861* (Washington, D.C., 1919; repr., Salem, N.H., 1986), ch. 13; Carleton Mabee, *Black Education in New York State: From Colonial to Modern Times* (Syracuse, N.Y., 1979), ch. 5; Meyer Weinberg, *A Chance to Learn: A History of Race and Education in the United States* (New York, 1977), ch. 1. For an overview of changing

approaches to African Americans in the history of education, see Ronald E. Butchart, "'Outthinking and Outflanking the Owners of the World': A Historiography of the African American Struggle for Education," *History of Education Quarterly* 28, no. 3 (Autumn 1988), 333–66.

131. Moss, *Schooling Citizens*, 102–6, 136–37; Mabee, *Black Education* ch. 4. African Americans thus developed a kind of counterpublic. See Joanna Brooks, "The Early American Public Sphere and the Emergence of a Black Print Counterpublic," *William and Mary Quarterly* 62, no. 1 (Jan. 2005), 67–92.

132. Moss, *Schooling Citizens*, 27, 96; Kaestle, *Pillars*, 174. See also Stanley Schultz, *The Culture Factory: Boston Public Schools, 1789–1860* (New York, 1973), ch. 7.

133. The preceding paragraphs from Kaestle, *Pillars*, 173, 175–79; Schultz, *Culture Factory*, chs. 7–8; Stephen Kantrowitz, *More than Freedom: Fighting for Black Citizenship in a White Republic, 1829–1889* (New York, 2012), ch. 4; Stephen Kendrick & Paul Kendrick, *Sarah's Long Walk: The Free Blacks of Boston and How Their Struggle for Equality Changed America* (Boston, 2004); Woodson, *Education*, 320–25. Roberts quoted in Kendrick & Kendrick, *Sarah's Long Walk*, 97.

134. *New York Herald* (1855), quoted in Kaestle, *Pillars*, 179.

135. Assessment and discussion in Moss, *Schooling Citizens*, 150–63.

136. Heather Williams, *Self-Taught: African American Education in Slavery and Freedom* (Chapel Hill, N.C., 2005), 12–16, 216.

137. Thomas Webber, *Deep like the Rivers: Education in the Slave Quarter Community, 1831–1865* (New York, 1978), 29.

138. Discussion and quote from Webber, *Deep like the Rivers*, ch. 1.

139. Quotes in Williams, *Self-Taught*, 18, 20. For discussion, see Webber, *Deep like the Rivers*; Williams, *Self-Taught*, ch. 1; Janet Duitsman Cornelius, *"When I Can Read My Title Clear": Literacy, Slavery, and Religion in the Antebellum South* (Columbia, S.C., 1991); Woodson, *Education*, ch. 9.

140. King quoted in Weinberg, *A Chance to Learn*, 13–14.

141. Williams, *Self-Taught*, esp. chs. 4–5; Ronald E. Butchart, *Schooling the Freed People: Teaching, Learning, and the Struggle for Black Freedom, 1861–1876* (Chapel Hill, N.C., 2010); Christopher M. Span, *From Cotton Field to Schoolhouse: African American Education in Mississippi, 1862–1875* (Chapel Hill, N.C., 2009); James D. Anderson, *The Education of Blacks in the South, 1860–1935* (Chapel Hill, N.C., 1988), ch. 1.

142. Williams, *Self-Taught*, ch. 9; Anderson, *Education of Blacks*, ch. 1. On violence, see especially Douglas R. Egerton, *Wars of Reconstruction: The Brief, Violent History of America's Most Progressive Era* (New York, 2014).

143. Frederick Douglass, *Narrative of the Life of Frederick Douglass, an American Slave* (1845), in *Frederick Douglass: Autobiographies*, ed. Henry Louis Gates (New York, 1994), 15. On Douglass's life, see L. Diane Barnes, *Frederick Douglass: Reformer and Statesman* (New York, 2013).

144. Frederick Douglass, "The Meaning of July Fourth for the Negro," in *Frederick Douglass: Selected Speeches and Writings*, ed. Philip S. Foner, abridged and adapted by

Yuval Taylor (Chicago, 1999), 188–206; Jason Frank, *Constituent Moments: Enacting the People in Postrevolutionary America* (Durham, N.C., 2010), ch. 7.

145. Douglass, *Narrative*, 18.

146. Ibid., 37.

147. Ibid., 39–42. On the *Columbian Orator*, see Caleb Bingham, *The Columbian Orator*, ed. David Blight (New York, 1998).

148. Douglass, *Narrative*, 64–65.

149. Neem, "Taking Modernity's Wager."

150. McGreevy, *Catholicism and American Freedom*, ch. 3.

151. Ibid., ch. 4.

152. Discussion and quotes for the remainder of this section from Green, *Bible*, chs. 3–5.

153. Mayo, *Religion in the Common Schools: Three Lectures Delivered in the City of Cincinnati* (1869), quoted in Green, *Bible*, 99.

154. Quotes and discussion from Green, *Bible*, ch. 3; *The Board of Education of Cincinnati v. John D. Minor et al.*, 23 Ohio St. 211 (1872).

155. Quoted in Green, *Bible*, 159.

156. Ibid., ch. 5.

157. Abraham Lincoln, "Address to the Young Men's Lyceum of Springfield, Illinois" (Jan. 1838) and "First Inaugural Address" (Mar. 4, 1861), in *The Portable Abraham Lincoln*, ed. Andrew Delbanco (New York, 1992), 17–26, 226–35; James A. Rawley, "The Nationalism of Abraham Lincoln," *Civil War History* 9, no. 3 (Sept. 1963), 283–98; Rawley, "The Nationalism of Abraham Lincoln Revisited," *Journal of the Abraham Lincoln Society* 22, no. 1 (Winter 2001), 33–48.

158. Abraham Lincoln, "Second Inaugural Address" (Mar. 4, 1865), in Delbanco, *Portable Abraham Lincoln*, 348–49.

159. Walt Whitman, 1855 preface to *Leaves of Grass*, in Justin Kaplan, ed., *Walt Whitman: Poetry and Prose* (New York, 1996), 5. See Samuel H. Beer, "Liberty and Union: Walt Whitman's Idea of the Nation," *Political Theory* 12, no. 3 (Aug. 1984), 361–86.

Conclusion

1. Jürgen Herbst, *The Once and Future School: 350 Years of American Secondary Education* (New York, 1996), 163–64; Larry Cuban *How Teachers Taught: Constancy and Change in American Classrooms, 1890–1980* (New York, 1984); Theodore R. Sizer, *Horace's Compromise: The Dilemma of the American High School* (Boston, 1984).

2. Robert D. Putnam, *Our Kids: The American Dream in Crisis* (New York, 2015); Ira Katznelson, *When Affirmative Action Was White: An Untold History of Racial Inequality in Twentieth-Century America* (New York, 2005).

3. William A. Fischel, *Making the Grade: The Economic Evolution of American School Districts* (Chicago, 2009); David E. Campbell, *Why We Vote: How Schools and Communities Shape Our Civic Life* (Princeton, N.J., 2006).

4. For a discussion of the historiography, see Johann N. Neem, "State of the Field: What Is the Legacy of the Common Schools Movement? Revisiting Carl Kaestle's 1983 *Pillars of the Republic*," *Reviews in American History* 44, no. 2 (June 2016), 342–55. Examples include Michael Katz, *Irony of Early School Reform: Educational Innovation in Mid-Nineteenth Century Massachusetts* (Cambridge, Mass., 1968); Samuel Bowles & Herbert Gintis, *Schooling in Capitalist America: Educational Reform and the Contradictions of Economic Life* (New York, 1976); William J. Reese, *The Origins of the American High School* (New Haven, Conn., 1995); Reese, *America's Public Schools: From the Common Schools to "No Child Left Behind"* (Baltimore, 2005); Joel H. Spring, *The American School, 1624–2004* (Boston, 2005). This has become the common sense of the common schools movement.

5. Michael Katz, *Class, Bureaucracy, and Schools* (New York, 1971), 3.

6. Carl Kaestle, *Pillars of the Republic: Common Schools and American Society, 1780–1860* (New York, 1983), 222–23.

7. For a good discussion of the conservative historiography, see Milton Gaither, "The Revisionists Revised: The Libertarian Historiography of Education," *History of Education Quarterly* 52, no. 4 (Nov. 2012), 488–505. Examples include Philip Hamburger, *Separation of Church and State* (Cambridge, Mass., 2002); Charles L. Glenn Jr., *The Myth of the Common School* (Amherst, 1988); Samuel Blumenfeld, *Is Public Education Necessary?* (Old Greenwich, Conn., 1981).

8. Abraham Lincoln, "To the People of Sangamo County" (1832), in *The Portable Abraham Lincoln*, ed. Andrew Delbanco (New York, 1992), 5–9.

9. Abraham Lincoln, "Address to the Wisconsin State Agricultural Society" (1859), in Delbanco, *The Portable Abraham Lincoln*, 181–92.

INDEX